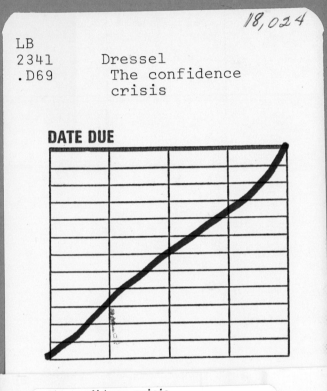

The Confidence Crisis

*An Analysis of
University Departments*

Paul L. Dressel
F. Craig Johnson
Philip M. Marcus

THE CONFIDENCE CRISIS

Jossey-Bass Inc., Publishers
San Francisco · Washington · London · 1971

THE CONFIDENCE CRISIS
An Analysis of University Departments
        by Paul L. Dressel, F. Craig Johnson, Philip M. Marcus

Copyright © 1969 by Jossey-Bass, Inc., Publishers

Published in Great Britain by
Jossey-Bass, Inc., Publishers
St. George's House
44 Hatton Garden, London E.C. 1

Library of Congress Catalogue Card Number LC 70–110642

International Standard Book Number ISBN 0–87589–063–6

Manufactured in the United States of America

JACKET DESIGN BY WILLI BAUM, SAN FRANCISCO

FIRST PRINTING: *April 1970*

SECOND PRINTING: *October 1971*

Code 7014

THE JOSSEY-BASS SERIES IN HIGHER EDUCATION

Editors

JOSEPH AXELROD
*San Francisco State College
and University of California, Berkeley*

MERVIN B. FREEDMAN
*San Francisco State College
and Wright Institute, Berkeley*

Preface

The *Confidence Crisis* originated in the long experience of the senior author in studying the problems and operations of departments on his own campus and in consulting with faculties and administrators at other institutions, ranging from small liberal arts colleges to large universities. Regardless of their size, institutions are concerned about departmental organization and operation. Even institutions without departments show concern over an appropriate organization, and the relative advantages of departmental versus some other structure are regularly debated. Departments, because they approximate the disciplinary emphases of graduate education, are generally favored by faculty. They provide a commonality of interests, and they relate more directly to curricular development than do other units. However, departments do have a specialized orientation, and they tend to develop an independent life and goals which are not always consonant with those of the institution, especially in regard to undergraduate education. Thus, conflict—arising out of differences in goals, competition among departments for students and resources, and poor communication—is common. Administrators complain about departments individually and collectively, and departments complain about administrators, also individually and collectively.

The Confidence Crisis represents a combination and, in places, even a synthesis of several different ventures. The first seven chapters are based primarily on a research project, supported by the esso Education Foundation, and involving fifteen universities. Chapters Eight, Nine, and Ten draw somewhat upon observations in these same fifteen universities, as well as upon consultation and accreditation review experienced with many others. Perhaps most significantly, however, these chapters reflect efforts made at Michigan State University to study, understand, and contribute to the solution of departmental problems. Chapter Eleven is based upon everything preceding and presents some tentative conclusions, hypotheses, and possibly biases of the researchers.

In our initial thinking, we considered a study viewing departments in all types and sizes of institutions and embracing all disciplines. After discussions with many persons, we concluded that this task would be unreasonable. The department in the large university is our critical problem today, because the university affects so many students and because the university department, with its involvement in graduate education and research and its professional dedication to the discipline, is a complex entity, oriented almost as much to the national scene as to the university of which it is a part. We concluded, too, that it would be impossible to cover all of the disciplines embraced by departments and, believing that the discipline might be an important factor in departmental operation, we agreed that we should study departments representing the same group of disciplines in a number of universities. Finally, we were led to believe by our prior experiences that the major concerns with departments and the most difficult problems are found in the larger departments, which tend to be those serving many students other than their own majors. Indeed, it is often this service role which causes the concerns and problems. Our prior experiences also indicated that departments in professional schools are sufficiently different from the departments of arts and sciences to deserve inclusion in even a limited study. With an eye to sampling the various areas of knowledge, we chose from the arts and sciences departments of mathematics, psychology, history, English, and chemistry. We selected business and engineering as representative professional schools, and chose management (or its equivalent) and electrical engineering as representative departments.

Our choice of universities for our main study took into account geographical spread, ratings in the Cartter report,[1] private-public status, and, of necessity, the willingness of the administrators and of the departments to cooperate in the project. (The list of cooperating institutions is provided following this preface.)

Although we reviewed much of the literature on departments, we were unable to find definite hypotheses which were acceptable for guiding our investigation. We became convinced that we should look at the communication and decision-making patterns in departments, rather than focusing on the chairmen. We also felt that departmental priorities might be an important consideration, and were sure that interrelations with higher echelons of administration were significant in the study.

We offer our sincere thanks to the many administrators, department chairmen, and faculty members who gave freely of their time to this project. The efforts of Donald J. Reichard, who assisted in the review of literature, and contributed significantly to several chapters, and Ruth Frye and Marion M. Jennette, who contributed immensely to the book, deserve special acknowledgment. We also acknowledge with deep appreciation the work of our five consultants who visited the various campuses, conducted the interviews, and presented us with uniformly excellent reports: William P. Albrecht, dean of The Graduate School, University of Kansas; G. Lester An-

---

[1] Allan M. Cartter, *An Assessment of Quality in Graduate Education* (Washington, D.C.: American Council on Education, 1966).

derson, professor of higher education, State University of New York
at Buffalo; Richard H. Davis, dean of the Milwaukee Campus,
University of Wisconsin; Donald C. Lelong, director of the Office
of Institutional Research, The University of Michigan; and Lewis
N. Pino, assistant to the chancellor at Oakland University; John E.
Dietrich, assistant provost, Michigan State University, contributed
much to the development of the ideas and the materials presented
in Chapter Eight. Finally, we are indebted to the ESSO Education
Foundation; its executive director, George M. Buckingham; and its
associate director, Frederick deW. Bolman, for the grant which
made this study possible. Frederick Bolman was especially helpful
in the early planning, and gave helpful advice at later stages.

East Lansing, Michigan   PAUL L. DRESSEL
March, 1970

Contents

Cooperating Universities

INSTITUTION *and* CHIEF CONTACT

University of Arizona, Tucson, Arizona
FRANCIS A. ROY, Dean, College of Liberal Arts

Boston College, Chestnut Hill, Massachusetts
CHARLES F. DONOVAN, S.J., Academic Vice-President

University of Cincinnati, Cincinnati, Ohio
THOMAS N. BONNER, Provost

University of Denver, Denver, Colorado
WILBUR C. MILLER, Vice-Chancellor

University of Florida, Gainesville, Florida
FREDERICK W. CONNER, Vice-President

The University of Georgia, Athens, Georgia
FRED C. DAVISON, President

Louisiana State University, Baton Rouge, Louisiana
BERNARD SLIGER, Dean of Academic Affairs

University of North Carolina at Chapel Hill
C. HUGH HOLMAN, Provost

Northwestern University, Evanston, Illinois
PAYSON S. WILD, Vice-President and Dean of Faculties

University of Notre Dame, Notre Dame, Indiana
JOHN E. WALSH, C.S.C., Vice-President, Academic Affairs

Pennsylvania State University, University Park, Pennsylvania
LESLIE P. GREENHILL, Assistant Vice-President, Research

University of Southern California, Los Angeles, California
MILTON S. KLOETZEL, Vice-President, Academic Affairs

Syracuse University, Syracuse, New York
WILLIAM P. TOLLEY, Chancellor

Temple University, Philadelphia, Pennsylvania
R. ROBB TAYLOR, Director, Institutional Research and Studies

The University of Tennessee, Knoxville, Tennessee
HERMAN E. SPIVEY, Academic Vice-President

The
Confidence
Crisis

An Analysis of
University Departments

1

Beginnings and Development

The historical development of the modern university department is not entirely clear. This lack of clarity is not surprising in view of the many forces that have helped to shape the modern university and that have resulted in individual departments which, in number, in size, in resources, and in range of functions, far exceed the departments of most colleges and universities existing prior to 1900. Nevertheless, a brief look at the historical origins of the department is both interesting and instructive.

1

Specialization, the first factor leading to the modern departmental structure, was a gradual result of the increasing amount and organization of knowledge. The great medieval universities were generally composed of four separate faculties: Law, Theology, Medicine, and Arts. Although this level of organization corresponds more nearly to the college and professional school pattern of the modern university than to departmental organization, it does represent an early stage of specialization. Within the arts, specialization was a gradual development. As long as emphasis was on the classics and books were in short supply, the master of arts not only possessed the *Ius Ubique Docendi* (the license to teach anywhere), but he was also expected to be able to lecture on any subject. Rashdall recorded an early reference to "departments" at the University of Paris:[1]

> The agreement of 1213 recognizes the right of each faculty—including the medical doctors (who are here for the first time mentioned in connection with the university)—to testify to the qualifications of candidates to the license in its own *department*, and this right practically involved the regulation of the studies and the discipline of the students [emphasis added].

In this usage, department seems clearly to relate directly back to the faculty organization and associated field of study.

The early American college was not departmentalized, but the development was foreshadowed by the early appearance at Harvard of endowed chairs and professorships after the pattern of its Cambridge prototype: Professorship of Divinity in 1720; Professorship of Mathematics and Natural Philosophy in 1727; Hancock Professor of Hebrew in 1764. In 1767, the four tutors at Harvard were specialists: one in Latin; one in Greek; one in logic, metaphysics and ethics; and one in natural philosophy, mathematics, geography, and astronomy. All four taught rhetoric, elocution, and English composition.[2] Prior to this, there were examples of specialized assignments for tutors (Hebrew, science), but the usual pattern

---

[1] Hastings Rashdall, in F. M. Powicke and A. B. Emden (eds.), *The Universities of Europe in the Middle Ages*, Vol. I (London: Oxford University Press, 1958), p. 324.

[2] Samuel Eliot Morison, *Three Centuries of Harvard, 1636–1936* (Cambridge: Harvard University Press, 1936), p. 90.

was for the tutor to work with a class in all studies and for the entire period of three or four years of study (if the tutor remained that long).[3]

Andersen quotes Josiah Quincy's *History of Harvard University*, which refers to something called a department at Harvard College in 1739:[4]

> The zeal and anxiety of the Board of Overseers at this period extended not only to the religious principles held by the Professors and Tutors at the time of the election, but also to the spirit and mode in which they afterwards conducted their respective *departments* [emphasis added].

A more formal recognition of departments came nearly a century later. In 1823, a student rebellion at Harvard resulted in the expulsion of forty-three of a class of seventy, and prompted the Board of Overseers to a thorough examination of the college. Among the resulting changes effected in 1825 was the reorganization of the university (so recognized in 1780 by the Massachusetts State Constitution) into six departments.[5]

The University of Virginia, which began instruction in 1825, was organized into schools headed by professors. The schools included Ancient Languages, Modern Languages, Mathematics, Natural Philosophy, Natural History, Moral Philosophy, as well as Anatomy, Medicine, and Law.[6] These schools were essentially the equivalents of departments.

The initial departmental structure bore limited resemblance to the modern university department. Usually there was but one professor or chair to a department, and a varying number of lesser lights whose activities and careers were dominated by the professor. The number of professors in the early colonial colleges during the second half of the eighteenth century was estimated by Carrell at not

    [3] *Ibid.*, p. 32.
    [4] Kay J. Andersen, "The Ambivalent Department," *Educational Record*, Spring 1968, quoting Josiah Quiney, *The History of Harvard University* (Cambridge: Harvard University Press, 1840), p. 207.
    [5] Richard J. Storr, *The Beginnings of Graduate Education in America* (Chicago: University of Chicago Press, 1953), p. 21.
    [6] John S. Brubacher and Willis Rudy, *Higher Education in Transition* (New York: Harper and Row, 1968), p. 99.

more than 210.[7] College faculties gradually increased in size so that, in 1839, Harvard's faculty numbered twenty-one professors and two tutors. Yale had sixteen professors and seven tutors, and Dartmouth had an aggregate faculty of fifteen, whereas Transylvania, Sydney, Union, and Columbia each had ten to thirteen faculty members.[8]

Gradually, with the increased number of professors, differentiation among ranks evolved. In 1876, instruction began at Johns Hopkins University, with a faculty consisting of six full professors and several associates (not associate professors) equivalent in rank to assistant professors elsewhere. In 1879, the rank of instructor was introduced below that of associate and, in 1883, the rank of associate professor was created between the ranks of associate and professor. The rank of associate professor not only provided a convenient means for maintaining an academic hierarchy, but also was useful in diverting younger faculty from representation in academic councils.[9] The department was but an extension of the professor, until further specialization into disciplinary subdivisions, the requirement of a graduate degree for all faculty members, and increasing departmental size forced some democratization.

By the 1880's Cornell and Johns Hopkins had succeeded in establishing autonomous departments, but the real solidification of departmental structure and the academic rank system came in the 1890's. Harvard moved decidedly toward departmentalization around 1891–1892. Columbia was thoroughly departmentalized by the late nineties, with Yale and Princeton only somewhat slower in adopting this organizational style.[10] However, no institution could match the University of Chicago in complex organizational arrangements, which, in 1892–1893, at the end of the first year of instruction, listed twenty-six departments organized into three faculties:

[7] William D. Carrell, "American College Professors: 1750–1800," *History of Education Quarterly*, 1968, 8 (3), 289.

[8] Richard Hofstadter and Walter P. Metzger, *The Development of Academic Freedom in the United States* (New York: Columbia University Press, 1955), p. 223.

[9] Hugh Hawkins, *Pioneer: A History of the Johns Hopkins University 1874–1889* (Ithaca: Cornell University Press, 1960), p. 127.

[10] Laurence R. Veysey, *The Emergence of the American University* (Chicago: University of Chicago Press, 1965), pp. 320–321.

Divinity; University Extension; and Arts, Literature, and Science. Thirteen head professors presided as virtually absolute monarchs of departments which included staff members holding twelve distinct ranks.[11] The professor not only ran his department; he was its sole representative in the Academic Senate. There were no divisions or colleges, so that each department became an autonomous unit, free to do anything which it could find the resources to support. By including in the table of ranks associate professors and professors with permanent appointments, as well as the head professor, the seed for rotating chairmen (the temporarily first among equals) was planted, but not until 1911 was an attempt made to improve the morale of younger faculty by reducing the power of the departmental chairmen and allowing them to be elected by the department rather than to be selected by the higher-echelon administrators.

With the development of new specializations and increasing size, departmentalization has continued. Appointment versus election of the chairmen continues to be an issue. Graduate education, federal support of research, and large undergraduate enrollments have forced expansion of departments—especially in state universities—to the point where, in facilities, personnel, and budget, many departments have available resources exceeding those of many liberal arts colleges. Departmental interests and departmental autonomy are major forces in every modern American university.

PERSPECTIVES AND PROBLEMS

The identification of an academic in the university involves name, rank, social security number, and department; but rank, tenure, discipline, and department are so closely bound that the rank designation usually includes the discipline, which also reveals the name of the department, and, despite the AAUP's predilection for separation of rank and tenure, it reveals the individual's tenure status. In many institutions, the man without a department, no matter the source and quality of his degrees, is a man without tenure.

The department is both the refuge and support of the pro-

[11] Richard J. Storr, *Harper's University: The Beginnings* (Chicago: University of Chicago Press, 1966), pp. 75–76.

fessor. The department provides his working space: an office, an adjacent classroom or seminar, and (for the scientist) a well-equipped laboratory. The department also sanctions his course or seminar, and may provide the financial support for his research and his doctoral candidates. The professor looks to the university for his research and his doctoral candidates. The professor looks to the university for a parking place, although he believes that if universities were well run, each department would have its own facilities surrounded by parking places restricted to the departmental staff. The department exists to nurture the professor, and the university exists primarily to nurture the departments. Colleges and their deans screen the departments, in the name of academic freedom, from the interference of central administration, and may even be helpful in acquiring more resources and greater autonomy for the department.

The preceding paragraph reflects the views of too many university professors who focus almost exclusively on their own instruction and research and show little interest and considerable contempt for the activities of the deans and of central administration. The department is the key unit for the academic, as is reflected in its many missions, which include the following: instruction and advising of undergraduate majors; instruction of undergraduate non-majors; instruction of graduate students; postdoctoral fellowships; advising or consulting with professors from other disciplines; basic research; applied research (practical, problem-oriented); promoting discipline within the university (course requirements, resources, acquiring majors); promoting departmental views and interests in the college and the university; promoting the discipline and profession nationally; exploring interfaces of the disciplines; promoting career development of junior staff; attaining national recognition for the department; consultation services to business and industry; consultation services to governmental units; provision of scholarly and congenial environment in which to work; and provision of a social and recreational network for those affiliated with the department. Some of these missions are of much greater concern to the departmental faculties than are others, and there is some variation among departments. Basic research, instruction of graduate students, and national reputation tend to rank highest in the "best" departments; whereas applied research, instruction of undergraduates, and service to government, business, and industry are at the low end. Some of the missions are only facilitative. Thus, promotion of departmental views and interests is essential to attaining adequate support, and a scholarly and congenial environment is essential to effective work. If the department as a whole does not serve a social and recreational role, it is likely that there are several cliques or social subgroups within it which do.

Many factors affect and modify the departmental organization: the size of the institution, the number of departments, the size of departments, balance between graduate and undergraduate instruction, and the extent and nature of faculty and student participation in governance. The resources available and the method of allocation used affect both departments and interdepartmental relations. The effect of size is most apparent in comparing the small, single-purpose liberal arts college with the university. The smallest colleges require no formal structure, for the faculty works with the dean as a committee of the whole. A larger college may adopt a divisional structure (social science, natural science, humanities, fine arts, and so on) to provide for some of the departmental missions, although the major concern is with curriculum and instruction. Despite the predilection of faculty for the departmental structure, rising out of their experiences in specialized study in the graduate school, and despite, too, the apparently greater relevance of the disciplinary-based department for curriculum development, the size of the faculty in a small college is not sufficient to support a departmental structure. Larger liberal arts colleges may use it, although the departmental-disciplinary organization is better adapted to faculty aspirations for more courses and more majors than for an integrated liberal undergraduate education.

Large departments in the university generate several possibly crucial situations. First, these departments are often ones which teach many nonmajors, either in special courses or in introductory offerings, which serve both majors and nonmajors. Mathematics and chemistry are illustrative. These departments use many junior faculty outside the tenure track, often doctoral candidates, to meet their obligations, but, despite this boon to the graduate program, they may resent the monotony of the service burden and the inferior —so they often complain—students. The instruction is often poor, and grades unrealistically severe. These departments reasonably demand and obtain support for their large undergraduate enrollments, but often divert much of it to support graduate education and research. Recurrent repercussions are to be expected.

If a department offers the doctorate, the demand is made for expansion of staff to cover all significant subdivisions of the discipline. Cliques may arise out of mutual interests in research and instruction, and competition develops among the cliques for new positions. Both load and balance of power within the department are involved. Ultimately, a section of the department with strong leadership, buttressed possibly by outside support, breaks loose to establish a new department. Departments of biophysics, biochemistry, anthropology, American history, European history, German, or French are evidence of this type of fragmentation. Meanwhile, the university also begets new schools and colleges which may replicate the departmental structure and course offerings. Genetics, statistics, and psychology exemplify fields of study and even departments which may appear in more than one place in a university. Alternately, basic disciplines may be captured by a specialized school or college and fail to serve the broader needs of the university. Economics in colleges of business and psychology in colleges of education are examples.

As a university becomes overcompartmentalized and categories harden, departments and the professors in them become isolated and ever more narrow. Exploration and development of promising new fields such as behavioral sciences, area studies, or public health are thereby retarded or denied. Administrators and faculty members who chafe under these restraints to innovation are driven to formation of institutes, centers, and other units which, initially at least, accommodate new ideas and programs and develop combinations of instruction, research, and service not admissible under the departmental structure. Thus the inadequacies of the department spawn a competitor more flexible and usually more dynamic, which takes its place at the budget trough with a voracity only occasionally restrained by the fact that tenure appointments must, in many universities, still be made in the departments, and that the disciplinary affiliations still constitute the passport for maximal motility. Departments are well standardized units in higher education, but institutes tend to be idiosyncratic to institutions and personalities in them. There are exceptions, of course. Competency in African studies is highly salable at the moment.

Faculty and student participation in governance highlights another deficiency of the department. Faculty representation on university committees, academic councils, and senate is not usually on a departmental basis. Student representation in student government or on joint faculty-student committees has, in the past, often been by class or place of residence, but is now often determined by college or school. Thus the department's isolation and preoccupation with its own concerns are reinforced. Furthermore, though many of the current student concerns relate to curriculum and instruction, departments have not generally established any systematic way in which the student voice can be effectively heard. The same communications gap exists with graduate students whose future— both educationally and economically—is so closely interwoven with the department that their complaints are more subdued and even more ignored than those of the undergraduate who can and does communicate with deans and other university officers who wield some influence on the department. One recurring difficulty with the discipline-based department is that the uncooperative, indifferent, or recalcitrant unit can refuse to make changes on the plea that these changes would destroy both standards and the integrity of the discipline. And what dean dare reprimand a department when the discipline itself justifies that department.

However, the department is not equivalent to a discipline. Unless the qualifying adjective *academic* is added, such units as Maintenance Department and Custodial Services Department qualify. An Engineering Services Department is not clearly identifiable by name as part of a College of Engineering or as a campus service unit. As a matter of fact, this designation in one institution applies to two units, one of each type. What is a department on one campus may be a school including several departments on another; for example, journalism or music. A department is by no means synonymous with a discipline, as is indicated by the existence of departments of theater, human development, humanities, linguistics, Oriental and African languages, metallurgy, mechanics and materials science, and biological science. Schools may be professional units ranking with the College of Arts and Sciences and be subdivided into departments which emphasize one facet of the profession, such as management or electrical engineering. Schools may be administratively equated to departments, but with somewhat more autonomy in curricular matters. Our study revealed one school which operated as a subdivision of a department. Divisions may be groupings of departments within a college or units within a school. Large departments are sometimes divided into sections corresponding to major subdivisions of the discipline or field represented by the department. Section heads (bureaucracy is apparent) may be informally provided with a title of chairman, via a committee, or simply recognized by common consent, possibly because of research stature, as the leader of the section.

Certain departments involving disciplines basic to several fields may be concurrently listed in several colleges. In such circumstances, individual staff members may be appointed in one of the colleges or jointly appointed in two or three. When the departmental budget comes from several sources, the department may be more successful in wangling generous support than a department supported by one college and accountable to one dean. In a few universities, certain departments, such as psychology, statistics, or mathematics, have been designated as university-wide departments, with status in all relevant colleges and reporting to a committee of deans or to a vice-president. This organization avoids duplication in several colleges or departments covering the same discipline, but it generates an administrative gap which makes the department almost the equivalent of a college.

Departments in the same field differ markedly in what they include. Mathematics may include pure and applied mathematics, or the two may appear as two departments in separate colleges. It may include statistics and probability, or the latter two may appear as one or two additional departments.

The terminology and designation of academic units is confusing and misleading. There is enough common usage to cause one to forget that actual usage is idiosyncratic to institutions and to influential personalities on campuses.

Departments develop their own priorities and modes of operation to pursue them; but the curricular and instructional problems of a Department of Linguistics and Oriental and African Languages are not identical with those of a Department of Linguistics or of a Department of Foreign Languages. The problems of management, research, or selection of personnel are quite different. A chairman of a department including two foreign languages reported that the two sections never meet together. A department of physics in a state university, which operated as a teachers college only a few years ago, was revealed to be very different in staff, in facilities, and in operation from a physics department renowned for its research and graduate program. A range in quality, outlook, and mode of operation almost as great as this can be observed among the departments of a single university. Comparisons and generalizations involving departments must be made with great caution.

The factors productive of disagreement, conflict, and tension are evident in the preceding comments. Departments expect the resources and the autonomy to develop their own programs; but the resources are never adequate to satisfy all departments. The choice is almost inevitably mediocrity, or worse, for all departments, or the denial of some to cultivate excellence in others. Either decision generates suspicion and dissatisfaction. Autonomy is another source of difficulty. Departments would like to determine salaries, rank, and tenure; add and schedule courses as suits the staff; and use funds as the staff wishes with minimal accountability. Indeed, any outside attempt to analyze departmental operations tends to be regarded as inappropriate to the professional character of the task and the personnel. Deans and vice-presidents who have a supradepartmental view are concerned that such autonomy can lead to expensive operation, ineffectiveness, and inequity. The administrator tends to view the department as an arm of the university to accomplish purposes agreed upon by faculty, administration, and board, whereas the department naturally prefers to go its own way. The range of programs is a key element in the conflict. More courses, reduced teaching load for research, introduction of graduate education all add to costs and introduce issues of priority for the university as well as the department. Often the university must look to its supporting clientele and coordinating board and consider needs and programs in the region. A department wanting to offer the doctorate is not concerned with duplication of effort, even if six other universities within a few miles offer the same degree in the field. Rather, it may find this one of the major reasons for adding the degree, since otherwise the department is doomed to inferior status. Unfortunately for taxpayers and benefactors of higher education, deans and presidents may condone and abet these aspirations.

In some rapidly developing institutions, conflict arises in the opposite direction. A new administration, seeking to revitalize an institution, may find that departments, comfortable and unconcerned about their mediocrity, require violent shake-ups, such as early retirements, change in chairman, and importation of new faculty at markedly higher salaries.

Much of the preceding comment may be read as critical of departments and their staff because of the eagerness with which they pursue advancement of individuals and of the department. Yet most administrators prefer to have such dynamism rather than placidity, provided only that aspirations are accompanied by an awareness of university-wide priorities and budgetary problems.

NEED FOR STUDY

Something can also be said for the department in these disagreements and conflicts. A university department, to attain stature nationally or even in the institution, must foster research and graduate study, which, in turn, calls for apparently light teaching loads (measured in terms of credit hours). Graduate courses and dissertation direction are more time-consuming and challenging, so that high priority must be assigned to them. In costs and ultimate contribution, the Ph.D. is worth several B.A.'s. The department may be excused for diverting resources allotted for undergraduate education when the university encourages new graduate programs without having the fiscal resources to provide departments with the additional support needed.

Departments also have problems with their executives. Tradition and faculty demand require the chairman to be a scholar, but the demands placed upon the chairman include many functions: Chairmen initiate action on budget formulation; selection, promotion, and retention of academic staff; faculty salaries; sabbatical leaves; interdepartmental relationships; research grants; educational development and innovation; university committee membership; discipline representation; professional growth; advice to dean on departmental matters; administration to faculty relationship; new faculty orientation; departmental meetings; adequate nonacademic help; student administration; student advising; class scheduling; student personnel records; faculty load; graduate student application approval; grading standards and practices; and curriculum changes. Also, they have knowledge of the administrative routine of the college; institutional legislative organization; government grants procedures; policies relating to graduate students; and scholarly productivity of department faculty.

Most new chairmen lack familiarity with many of these activities, and there is usually no ready way to acquire familarity. They attain the familiarity at the expense of their scholarly effort. If, in the understandable wish to meet departmental desires in the face of seemingly unreasonable university rules and policies, the chairman develops ways of circumventing these, he may find his irritations and possible pangs of conscience promoting a state of tension which is by no means conducive to instruction or research. Thus, if he lingers as chairman for more than a few years, he may be beyond the point of no return. Despite complaints about the department's apparent indifference to university priorities and fiscal problems, it is usually true that the department is provided with limited information. Even information collected from the departments is not fed back unless some administrator is complaining about small courses, low teaching loads, high costs, or the like. A fuller sharing of university data with departments and adaptation of those data to departmental concerns and needs might materially improve the total situation. Deans tend to object to wide sharing in the fear that budgetary, and particularly salary, differentials will result in difficult confrontations. The answer seems obvious. If inequities exist among departments, they should be brought to light and remedied. If differences exist for a reason, the reasons should be stated and defended. Open communication will generate problems, but it will also allay suspicion, and assist in clarifying what the real issues are. Obviously, there is need for study of the problems and role of the department in the university.

Impressions and
Appraisals

The consultants who conducted the campus visits in this study were experienced university administrators who had served in departments and had viewed departments from various vantage points. Their experiences included departmental evaluation responsibilities as members of central administration in major institutions of higher education, of regional academic accrediting teams, and of national scholarship and fellowship review committees. Drawing on this rich background, they were able to make observations and contribute insights to our study which went beyond the basic data or the information gathered from faculty questionnaires. In this chapter their subjective impressions and appraisals of departments are examined.

Each consultant visited two universities, staying four or five days at each. Prior to the visit, he reviewed the catalog from that university, including its course offerings, and read whatever material was available on the constitution and other basic documents of the institution. A copy of the basic background data was also provided. At the beginning of the visit he met with the representative of the institution designated by the president as the coordinator for this study. Meetings were scheduled with the vice-president of academic affairs and/or the president, deans of the colleges whose departments were involved in this study, department chairmen, and selected faculty members from each department. From this study of basic institutional data and the personal interviews, each consultant wrote an extensive report giving his suggestions, impressions, and appraisals of the department. The consultants' reports were organized around general topics of: departmental organization, communication and the decision-making process, departmental records, concern for students, the department and the university, and departmental priorities. Chapters Four and Five deal in detail with these categories. In addition to this specific information, consultants were asked to give their general impressions on three aspects of departments. The first was the quality of the department. The consultant was asked to determine whether this was a good department or a poor one, as judged by several different people possibly using quite different sets of criteria. Second, they were asked to comment on the department chairman and/or his style of operations. Finally, the consultant was asked to characterize the relationships between this department and the rest of the university, as seen not only by other administrators, deans, and academic vice-presidents, but also by other department chairmen. The consultants' reports collectively reflected the variations in departments and universities, but some interesting factors that these consultants considered important recurred as they made their judgments of quality, style, and relationship with the rest of the university. A summary of these impressions follows; wherever possible, the exact language of the consultant is used, so that the reader might gain an appreciation of how consultants viewed departments.

QUALITY OF THE DEPARTMENT

An absolute judgment of quality was difficult to make for any single department. A distinguished department in an undistinguished institution and a mediocre department at a nationally recognized institution are not easily compared. A department may be well known for retired or departed research scholars whose names continue to provide an antique patina, while another department may have very active and promising young researchers who have not yet achieved national recognition. Some departments in our study had rather limited graduate programs, so that publications, research contracts, and grants were not of much concern. Other departments had given such great emphasis to research that any concern for the undergraduate student or for the quality of instruction had been lost. Recognizing all these complications, the consultants still undertook to judge whether, all things considered, a given department was or was not good. Consultants' reports provide some interesting insights that support their judgments.

Activity. In describing a department of high quality, one consultant wrote:

> The esprit de corps in this department appears to be good. While the former chairman is given credit for building a good faculty, with little deadwood, there is *enthusiasm*[1] for the new chairman, who is regarded as an outstanding scholar and a more aggressive and effective chairman. The department has attempted to staff at the assistant professor level because (1) that will continue to *revitalize* the department, and (2) it is felt that more talent can be secured for the money at that level.

Or again, another active department was described thus:

> This department is everywhere on the campus considered to be a quality department—one of the best on campus. It is an *active* and *activist* department. It is *striving* for excellence. It is *busy*. It is not without *tension*. Several of the divisional chairmen are

---

[1] Italics have been added for emphasis and are not a part of the consultants' reports.

aggressive and *dissatisfied* with the status quo. But one must conclude that this is only a concomitant of the *dynamic* nature of the department—a department that is sure that it is good and aims to do better.

When consultants described a department that was not very good, they tended to describe it in more passive terms. For example, one consultant offered the following evaluation of a department:

> This department is large. The chief executive is called the head and has occupied the post since 1940. He is considered a competent scholar and respected as a person. The department is, however, viewed as "weak." It appears that it has been *"drifting"* for some time and is *pedestrian* and *unexciting,* without any special distinctions. It is not in turmoil, deep trouble, or anything of the sort—"just not very good." The dean has let it be known that this is the perception that is commonly held of the department.

If great works are accomplished in quiet contemplation, this truism was lost on our consultants. Reports from the deans and from other departments rated "good" those departments that were stirring and active and were involved in a broad spectrum of university activities. The phrase was often heard, "we have been able to keep most of our scholars *active* throughout their academic careers." Sometimes departments and their individual faculty members responded to too many demands. They had teaching commitments, and many times they had more work cut out for themselves than they had the manpower to accomplish. Yet part of the conventional wisdom seems to say that, for professors to be regarded as "good" or departments to be regarded as "good," they must be *active* and *busy.* Is it better for a department or a faculty member to be overcommitted and furiously busy than to limit commitments to those that can be accomplished at an even pace? So it would seem. Note in the following excerpt our consultants' view of one department that was not considered to be very good:

> All in all this department gives the feeling of respectability, classical in outlook and operation, but it has sunk into *quiet mediocrity.* It could be raised to levels of distinction without great effort. The dean is nudging it to improve itself. Nothing was said about a new "head" or chairman. It would seem apparent that, while the present chairman is a scholar and a gentleman and perfectly adequate, his retirement and the appointment of a *"vigor-*

ous" chairman would be about all that would be required to bring this department to the general quality of the university as a whole.

To the consultants used for this study, at least one clear characteristic of quality is that of *dynamism* and *activity,* which may be partly accounted for by the fact that activity is much easier to sense by an outsider or by a dean or by other department chairmen. Perhaps it is as simple as the old adage about the squeaky wheel; or perhaps it is related to Irving J. Lee's observation that teaching is giving energy to truth. However, it may also explain why so many students complain that the faculty are too busy to see them.

Balance.   Our consultants seemed to feel that for a department to be good it should be balanced in its attention to its instruction of undergraduates and graduates, its research program, and its service activities. If a department either defined its scope too narrowly or did not balance its efforts with its objectives, it was rated poor. When the department chairman reported the broad interests of his faculty in instruction, research, and service *and* was able also to lead his faculty to the accomplishment of this broad range of objectives, the department rated very good. One department which was rated by our consultants and by persons in the university as a very good department was described as follows:

> In summary, we may say that we have here a well-organized department. Its structure has been developed in *harmony* with its objectives. It accepts goals of comprehensiveness, and it aims for real distinction. It is making progress toward this end. The chairman would appear to support the values of the department not only in his behavior but in his own person. He is a highly competent engineer. He is also an effective manager. There is a broad delegation to persons or groups who have appropriately designated roles in the management scheme.

Another department that seemed to be in balance or was striving to get itself into balance was described thus:

> This department has the reputation for good undergraduate instruction, probably in part because of the careful and painstaking way it goes about appointing new faculty members. While it is also regarded as a better than average instructional department on the graduate level, it evidently did not assume the same re-

sponsibility for supervising the progress of graduate students as other departments do. Nevertheless, the chairman implied a conscientious and deliberate effort to perform well in all three areas of graduate instruction, undergraduate instruction, and research.

As long as a department was aware that it had a broad responsibility for its instructional research and service programs, it seems to have been well regarded by deans and by our outside consultants. However, when this focus was narrowed to one aspect, then our consultants believed there were symptoms of trouble or weakness within the department:

> The department is regarded as a fairly good department by other units of the university. There is some question about the leadership that the head gives to the department and some question about his ability to reconcile the demands of teaching and the demands for research. For example, the head holds *research as the number one priority,* but it seems that some of the faculty believe that research and teaching are of equal priority in the department. And, in fact, the university has not made its position clear with respect to what the role of the department might play within the university. The faculty members were given encouragement to do research through the purchasing of necessary equipment, being kept off committees, receiving reduced teaching loads, and not being involved in the advising of students.

Such confusion in priorities appeared to throw a department off balance, created frictions internally, and questions and doubts externally. When these tensions continued for a long enough time, the following could occur, as reported by one consultant who visited a department that had been a very good department, but had gone downhill. He characterized the development as follows:

> . . . the result was a narrow orientation within the discipline. By 1965 the department's national standing had deteriorated. Despite the growth of the university, the faculty had scarcely increased in twenty years. The department had only one federal grant, which is now phased out, for this department was not interested in grants. The administration brought in an evaluation team of three distinguished scholars, who issued a rather negative report. For instance, only one of the department's Ph.D.'s was teaching at an AAU university.

Output. Another factor in judging quality was the output or production of a department. This tended to be a more objective measure, but it is interesting to note what our consultants selected from the many kinds of production measures available. One example of the output of a highly regarded department follows:

> Certainly one of the strongest departments in the university—and perhaps the strongest. The department has had a long tradition of excellence. The department is recognized, inside and outside the university, as an excellent one. Within the university it has received the *largest number of NDEA fellowships* (85 at present) and the *highest percentage of Woodrow Wilson designees*. It ranks very high, locally and nationally, in *Woodrow Wilson dissertation-year fellowships*. Until the spring of 1967 the department had always had its recommendations for promotion approved.

The publication list of the faculty in this department was also impressive, and the department was rated very high on the Cartter report[2] on graduate schools.

On the other hand, departments may be in trouble when they are expected to be very productive because of an increase in university aspirations for national stature and, for some reason or another, simply do not make it. The following was reported by one of our consultants and reflected this condition:

> This department is a weak one. The dean indicated that difficulties confronting the department reflect those which were "typical of what happens when it gets too wrapped up in its own affairs." The department was the last department to get the Ph.D. program off the ground, and it has an insider who is appointed to the headship. The department did not take the "quantum" jump ahead it should have. Moreover, the department has had a long history of ingrowth with many graduates on the faculty. At the present time it has no external research program of any significance and no research or publication. Some young faculty members have been added who have this potential, but it is as yet unrealized. The dean also felt the department is engaging too much in outside consulting as an alternative to research and publication.

Although such values as "publish or perish" may be thought of by some as not appropriate for judging departments or faculty, it is clear from our reports that deans at least considered publication

---

[2] Allan M. Cartter, *An Assessment of Quality in Graduate Education* (Washington, D.C.: American Council on Education, 1966).

records as one clear measure of the production, and therefore the quality, of departments.

The departments which received ratings of good quality tended to be those that were active in their university community and were led by a dynamic and aggressive chairman. The department attended, at least minimally, to the needs of undergraduates as well as the demands of graduates and research programs. But the departments regarded as really good were invariably those that were able to demonstrate an active and current output of research publications, graduate students, receipt of federal monies, and receipt of fellowships from national organizations. The paragon who leads this active, productive, balanced team of scholars does it—according to our consultants—with an individual style that is built on his direct experience with colleagues and the subject matter of his discipline.

STYLE OF THE DEPARTMENT

The consultants found difficulty in separating the quality of the department chairman from the overall quality of the department. Many of the departmental activities centered around the department chairman and the departmental office. In some departments, four or five senior faculty members held most of the power. In these cases, a chairman was selected who would determine and execute wishes of faculty leaders. In other departments, the head was appointed by the central administration and expected to execute the orders of central administration. But the most typical case was the one in which the chairman was appointed by the dean, who followed recommendations from the department. The chairman would try to learn and reflect the values of his faculty and represent these as accurately and honestly as he could to the dean. The dean, in turn, would use the chairman as a sounding board for new ideas relating to the department and discuss with him how the department might be improved. An administrative solution for a problem department has often been to remove the chairman, put another man in, and see if the problem would go away. This "fire the coach" approach to administration has worked well in some cases and proven a disaster in others. Often what was not recognized was the difference between the substance and the style of department administration. In the typical university organization, the chairman becomes the certifying agent for all actions of the department: new courses, assignment of teachers to courses, salary recommendations, and promotion and tenure actions. Although other officers of the university can stop actions, the chairman is the one who initiates action. How he goes about doing so and what procedures he uses to try to ascertain what his faculty would like to have him do are largely matters of personal style and faculty preferences or pressures. Some chairmen believe that the least administration is the best administration. These chairmen would like to be free to continue to teach their classes, counsel their graduate students, and then devote an afternoon or two per week to routine matters of the department. On the other hand, there are department chairmen who spend most of their time on the detail and minutiae of running the department, have not been in classrooms for years, and have given up research activity long ago. Sometimes the size of the department or the multiplicity of programs may require such detailed attention; however, the consultants found that most often the style of the department chairman and his involvement in detail were a very personal thing, and something which had no fixed pattern within disciplines, within universities, or with departmental size.

In studying the consultants' reports, we found that the style of the department chairman could be associated with three levels of activity. The first is those things the chairman did; the second, those things the chairman delegated; and finally, those things the chairman left undone. The effectiveness of a chairman is not solely determined by what he himself does. It has been said that a man can be an excellent chairman if he signs only one piece of paper a day, providing it is the right piece of paper.

The Doers. Perhaps the most extreme example of a department chairman who felt that he needed to do everything himself was found in the following comment by one consultant:

> It may be inferred that his is a collection of individuals bound together as an academic department for the common purpose of teaching and productive scholarship. It seems scarcely to be an organization. Its chairman reflects the purposes (values)

of the department. He also does its chores. The department seems to present no problems to its college or the university. It is adequate to the purposes but otherwise has no distinctiveness and apparently no distinction except perhaps in one area. The dean comments: "Perhaps the job is too much for the chairman. That is why he does the department's work." The implication is that the chairman serves as doer of the chores because he is inadequate as a leader. There seems to be no plan to broaden the scope of the department, to take in new areas of scholarship. The organization is a static one.

Other departments in the study were found to have chairmen who were strong and did a great deal of the work themselves but were very careful to distinguish what they themselves should decide from the decisions they should let others make:

> The reputation of this department within the university appears to be based primarily on the general caliber of its faculty and the ability of the chairman. However, the quality appears to be the result of a long period of building, particularly with respect to faculty members. The present chairman is given a great deal of credit for refining to the point of perfection the entrepreneurship and managerial control which he exercises. Many feel that he could not possibly control the department to the degree that he does if he did not distinguish carefully beween policy matters and administrative matters, following a completely democratic process with respect to policy. Even his administrative control would probably not be tolerated if he were not exceptionally fair and exceptionally efficient.

It was rather consistently reported that, where the department chairman was fair, consistent, and impartial, he was given a great deal of latitude by his faculty to make decisions on a wide variety of topics. When, on the other hand, he became so involved in the detail that he could not present real leadership, or he began to develop ideas and values not related to the department's thinking, he fell out of favor with his colleagues and very quickly out of favor with central administration. Much of the chore of the department chairman is knowing what kinds of things need to be delegated and what kinds of things are most efficiently done by one person.

The Delegators. The clearest case of a department chairman who has learned how to delegate was presented in the following report:

The department chairman has held the position for twelve years. He is dean-elect of the college. He may be described as a strong leader, dedicated to his responsibilities, proud of his department and of its achievements. He knows what is happening everywhere in his department, but in his own words is a "committed delegator." The department is considered among the "best," if not *the* best in the college of arts and science. It serves the normal and broad spectrum of responsibilities of a department in a complex university. It has marked success in meeting its research objectives in educating Ph.D.'s. It will be in the "top twenty" departments nationally in the production of doctors. It is respected nationally. Its faculty publishes one hundred research papers per year.

Department chairmen in general seemed to feel that they could accomplish more if they involved their faculty in decision-making procedures. Although the committee structure was cumbersome and involved much extra time on the part of the faculty, if the decisions were truly made by the committees, high morale seemed to result. An example of high morale was reported in the following description:

Department meetings of the entire membership are held once each month, and policy matters are fully discussed and votes taken. Members of the department have an equal voice in these meetings and in departmental affairs, except those on matters of promotion and tenure. These are handled by the Executive Committee, but members of that Committee do not vote on decisions concerning departmental members whose rank is above their own. Salary increases are left completely to the department head and dean. However, all members of the department vote on the selection of new members of the department. This department, like many others, has control over its own budget within the amount allocated by the dean, although it cannot shift monies from salary and wages to other nonsalary items and vice versa. It also has control over faculty teaching loads and class sizes, provided the decision on these matters does not result in changes in the budget. The chairman states that, as a result of departmental decision-making process, morale in the department is very high, and he is able to speak with certainty about the position of the department on major issues.

However, the committee system had pitfalls. One important factor seemed to be the quality of the faculty elected to the various committees. One consultant observed the following:

The most important committee is said to be the Personnel Committee because it recommends to the department head persons to be promoted, persons to be given tenure, and persons to be appointed. The Executive Committee is said to be weak and ineffective because the department elects it.

If a chairman had the confidence of his faculty, he was able to do things in an informal manner which might otherwise need to be delegated in some formal manner:

The department is a democratic one in a sense that all members are involved in major policy matters. Personnel action matters involve four members of the department. The fact that it is democratically run is based in large part upon the head. As one member of the department put it, "If the department chairman left, we would, if we did not know who the replacement was going to be, quickly get many things formalized that are now informal." It is true that the department is run a little loosely and the head recognizes it. Nevertheless, he makes many efforts to involve the faculty in most of the important decisions.

The consultants reported that many departments were good because they were closely knit. Through the committee structure and the opportunity to interact with each other on administrative or policy matters, faculty members developed a mutual trust which yielded a cohesiveness in the group. If the department chairman made all of the decisions himself, this opportunity for faculty to work together did not exist, and the result was that each faculty member pursued his activities without communicating to his colleagues. In such a situation, many things were left undone.

The Dalliers. In some cases the organization of the department was so loose and the chairman's style so laissez-faire that many important matters were left undone. Lack of a department chairman who was willing or able to play a creative role in the leadership of a department was evidenced in the following report:

Both formal and informal communication appeared to be moderate and adequate but neither highly organized nor extensive. Decisions are typically made by consensus with full professors having more than a proportionate voice because of the committee structure. A relatively large number of instructors who are on three-year nonrenewable-term appointments participate very little in department affairs and are not regarded as what I would call full members of the department. One staff member described decision making in the department as "indulgent," particularly in respect to the wishes of about half a dozen senior full professors. Although they no longer hold much power, their preferences are honored for the sake of keeping the department running smoothly. The chairman has the respect of all the members of the department and fulfills well the role of fair and impartial administrator, for which he was apparently appointed. However, there is evidence that decision making by consensus in this particular case has resulted in maintenance of the status quo at best, and deterioration of a first-rate faculty at worst. Because most of the recruiting effort has fallen upon the chairman, and because it is evidently extremely difficult to satisfy everyone in the appointment of new faculty members of professorial rank, few have been appointed in recent years. Both the chairman and the dean agree that the department could have easily added four or five professorial-rank persons immediately without overstaffing.

The lack of active and imaginative administration in the department, over time, created serious strains and tensions within the department.

The long-term consequences of a poor chairman were summed up by our consultants in the following commentary, which discussed the relative strength of the rotating versus the permanent chairman:

> A generalization that seems pretty evident is that the chairman, under any system of permanency or rotation, is a key man in the department's success. The effect of a poor chairman is less immediately felt in a good department. In fact, a good department may not suffer appreciably from an occasional weak chairman, but it will suffer from a succession of weak chairmen. A department is not likely to improve greatly under any kind of chairman but a strong one. A strong chairman brings the department as fully as possible into the decision-making process. He is responsive to departmental needs and pressures and exercises leadership in attaining and meeting them. He must also have the strength to think independently and, on many occasions, win the department over to his way of thinking.

Another consultant concluded:

> The five-year term for the chairman, with the full professors as an advisory group, makes it more difficult for chairmen to exercise effective leadership. It is possible, since professors are only advisory, for a strong chairman to work for changes such as appointment at a higher rank and higher salary for new people; but under this system he is less likely to do so. The system in-

curred discourages initiative. The weak chairman will be over-whelmed. If the department is already excellent, this system will not affect it much. If the department is weak, its chances for improvement are lessened. The possibility of bringing in a chairman from the outside is definitely decreased. The present dean of the graduate school believes that the rotating chairmanship works well, but also pointed out that the new chairman is rarely selected from outside the university.

Although our consultants may have disagreed on the merits of the five-year rotating chairmanship, they did agree that, over time, a department would suffer from a chairman who exercised little leadership. The chairman forms the vital link with the rest of the university administration.

RELATIONS WITH THE UNIVERSITY

Each consultant was asked to judge how well a department fitted into the administrative scheme of the university. In rendering their judgments, the consultants tended to rely on three aspects. The first was *what the department gave to the university* in the way of service to university committees and how well the department was represented on various councils. The second was *what the university gave to the department* in terms of budget, facilities, equipment, and special privileges. Third, the *procedures in reaching basic decisions* were explored.

What the Department Gives. There was a wide range of opinion as to the proper role of the faculty as members of a department and a university community. To many faculty members, service on university committees was an onerous chore, since their primary allegiance was to the discipline and to research. Since university committees had nothing to offer in advancing their specialization, these faculty members saw no value in wasting time on faculty committees; however, they recognized that they needed the university to support programs of research and were concerned with committees that determined research policies or distributed research funds.

A contrasting opinion was held by others who felt it was important to participate and to be involved in the decision-making process of the university, but not necessarily through the formal structure for faculty participation. One consultant's report brings this division into clear focus.

> I get the impression that some faculty members, particularly in the assistant and associate professor ranks, do participate in the university affairs but largely outside the formal decision-making channels. As one faculty member in the department put it, "If there's movement on the campus for a worthy cause, you can be sure that at least one or two members of our department will be involved." In contrast, the same consultant reported another faculty member as saying, "Our faculty members are little involved in campus affairs. We leave that to those who are not doing anything in their own field."

From another report comes the comment:

> . . . as one faculty [member] put it, "Most of us could care less about the Senate." There are no scientists on the Graduate Council; that is, no chemists, no mathematicians, no physicists, and no astronomers.

Our consultants did not say so, but some of these faculty reactions savor slightly of sour grapes. Although many professors definitely would resent the time demands of major committees, the recognition by appointment or election to such committees would not be altogether unwelcome. University involvement and departmental prestige are seldom identical. The interests of the department and of the departmental staff are, in most instances, represented by the chairman in his negotiations with the dean. Faculty representation on college or university committees is more personal than departmental in nature. The factors involved in selection are more likely to include visibility, verbal fluency, advocacy of faculty governance, and overt commitment on controversial matters) especially in opposition to administrators) rather than excellence in performing departmental functions. The expressed concern of some chairmen that departmental faculty members participating in major college and university committees or holding positions of importance in the faculty senate constituted something of a threat to them and to the orderly functioning of the department provides some basis for believing that faculty participation in university affairs is less a departmental contribution than a means of personal gratification for individuals variously motivated by aspirations for power, by strong commitment to the improvement of the university, by search for an alternate road to recognition other than research productivity, or by acquiescence to the necessity of such service when tapped by peers or administrators.

What the Department Gets. Consultants found no clear relationship between what a department contributed to the university and what it got from the university. Many times departments were able to remain aloof from university problems and pursued federal agencies and foundations for the support necessary for facilities and equipment. A well-recognized department within the institution was not necessarily one with a distinguished faculty, a consistent research output, and a national reputation. The converse, however, was true: if the department was nationally recognized, it was generally regarded as a good department within the university. Oftentimes a significant national reputation was enough for the department to receive support from the university approximating but never quite equaling that which it felt it deserved.

One disagreement between the university and the departments was in the spending of overhead monies. At one institution, a department head had made a survey of what happens to overhead monies in other departments at other universities. Once he had collected the data, however, he was advised not to make an issue of it, for, at the moment, all overhead went to the administration and became a special fund for the president's use. The consultant then went on to report the results of the survey:

> The results of his survey are very interesting. In ten universities that he surveyed, a third of the overhead went to the department, a third went to the graduate school, and a third went to the administration. In thirty-five of the schools surveyed, the department got nothing of the overhead. In ten other schools, the department could get access to some of the overhead through special petition in terms of special needs of the department which then would be considered one at a time by the administration. Here again the interests of the department and the interests of the university are clearly in conflict.

Some departments do very well in their relations with the university:

> It is evident that this department has been fairly well treated by

the university. A modern, new building is currently under construction for the department, and the fact that there are four full professorial positions which are held open for the department is some indication. Moreover, the dean has indicated that he has met many special requests of the department in terms of staff and other needs as it underwent development. Whether or not the department feels it has been well treated is another matter, since it feels that it has been discriminated against compared to some other departments.

Who Decides. The consultants' reports of the deans' views of the departments presented some useful insights into the decision-making process between the university as represented by the dean, and the department as represented by the chairman. One consultant reported:

> When discussing his departments, the dean indicated there is relatively little autonomy for any of them. He frequently used the term, "responsible department." He said that a responsible department is one which studies curriculum, [makes] changes, and spends a good deal of time on these matters, as well as emphasizing teaching and watching their majors while training them for university life. He admitted that many professors are tied to a discipline and not to the university, therefore giving little attention to overall university problems. On the other end of the continuum he said there were departments which were closely knit and involved in university problems. Laughingly, he suggested that democracy may be a factor affecting the interest in university affairs. The least democratic department gave the most attention to university matters. The less democratic departments, he said, tend to have few strong men in them, and as a result there are few factions which rival each other. The main problem with the nondemocratic departments is their inability to work on committees and to get any work done. On the other hand, a number of departments tended to be democratic in excess and insisted on voting on everything; generally these departments get little done.

Much of the discussion relating to who gets to decide was centered around the question of budget. There were probably as many different systems for receiving budget requests and allocating funds as there were universities and colleges. Within a given institution, there was not always a consistent procedure used from college to college, or even from department to department, as illustrated in the following example, which describes a discussion that took place among several department chairmen in the presence of our consultant:

> The major concern was in the lack of knowledge of just how much authority a department chairman had or how much he had in the way of funds on which to operate. One chairman said that he had no funds for travel, whereas another one said that he traveled a great deal and charged everything to his American Express card and sent the bill to the business office when it came in. Thus far, he had had everything paid without any question. He also said that he had told several of his staff to charge their bills to a credit card and handle them in the same way. Thus it appeared that this department had very extensive traveling, even to three persons going to San Francisco for a number of days, and had been funded without any questions being raised. Other chairmen expressed some admiration at the operation but obviously felt that they were not in the same position as far as getting away with it. Matters of salary seemed to be pretty well decided beyond the department chairmen, and they never did receive a definite salary budget. In other words, if a position is left unfilled, they do not have access to the money unless they make a special request for hiring temporary help. Several chairmen expressed the feeling that they could usually go to the vice-president to get the money for actual needs on equipment, supplies, and services, but that there was the difficult situation of really not knowing whether one was getting special attention or whether this was within some budget that the college had already set up.

In contrast to this procedure, the following was reported occurring at another university:

> At this university each department is given a lump sum which it may spend on any item, either personnel, supplies and services, or equipment at the chairman's discretion. The dean, department chairman, president and vice-president sit down to discuss every item in the proposed budget, but once the money is given to the department chairman, he may do with it as he sees fit.

These budgetary procedures often opened up for the consultants some interesting questions which they were then able to pursue at various levels in order to get some general understanding of how the university operated. Although these relationships are interesting, they form the basis for a separate study. What we learned from the consultants in this study was that procedures at various institutions were markedly different. Starting with the attempt to assess the general quality of the department, the consultants examined how actively or aggressively the department pursued its goals, whether or not the chairman used a style in line with these goals, and whether or not this resulted in an effective operation and a quality product. The department chairman was seen as the center and focus of the department, and it was generally his personality and previous experience that dictated the style and operation of the department. As the consultants looked at the external and internal expectations for departments, at the reward system, and specifically at the decision-making process, they found great variety across institutions and within institutions. Although departments would like to think that they make the university, it is equally true that university policies and expectations mold the departments.

External Pressures

Departments are not autonomous units existing in a vacuum; rather, the university in which they operate exerts pressures upon them, and the disciplines to which they affiliate guide their goals and programs. The pressures placed upon departments by universities stem from the overall priorities and goals which boards of regents or trustees feel as a mandate. In many schools, for example, this mandate may be the education of large numbers of state or city residents, in others it is the education of an elite who are expected to guide the nation in science, politics, or business. Other schools readily adapt themselves to the service of the community and provide staff and expertise in the solution of problems that beset the state or the region. (Many state universities were traditionally oriented along these lines.) The departments which fail to recognize these mandates and adjust their performance accordingly, seldom find sympathetic ears in the upper echelons to support demands for staff, facilities, and other resources. Unfortunately for some types of departments, they cannot adjust their subject matter easily and have difficulty finding favor except under special conditions. (Archeology may be an example of this type of department.)

The other type of pressure exerted upon the department stems from a source located entirely external to the university and in many ways relatively amorphous and psychological in nature. Disciplines seldom exist in the same concrete way that universities do, and yet they exert a powerful influence over the behavior of persons who identify with them. The training of graduates enforces certain mental sets upon the novices and continually emphasizes the standards of performance which are to be met when one enters the job world. Graduate education does not stress loyalty to any particular university; indeed, it encourages an identification with a discipline by emphasizing that the proper procedures learned as a student can be practiced anywhere. Ties to professors or other students are quickly broken upon graduation and the termination of training; the first job one holds requires the tyro to perform without the benefit of personal guidance and as an independent practitioner. His only guidelines for proper performance are what he has learned and what he believes others in his specialty throughout the world are doing. These guidelines stemming from the discipline become powerful pressures upon faculty within each department and may actually conflict with the pressures exerted by the university in pursuit of its own goals.

UNIVERSITY VERSUS DISCIPLINE

A discipline is not a department. Disciplines transcend universities; departments exist within them. The department is often caught between two sets of pressures that affect its operations: priorities and reputation. These pressures are not entirely consonant and, in fact, may generate a dissonance reflected in differences between university expectations and impacts and departmental emphases and aspirations. Several aspects of our study which bear primarily on the impact of the external world on the department shed light on the following question: Is the character and the operation of a department influenced more by the university in which the department is located or by the discipline which it represents?)

Our prior experience and initial impressions from this study led to two hypotheses: First, departments with high national standing based on productivity in research and doctoral degrees are characterized by more informal administrative organization and practices than departments of less stature. Second, departments of high national standing are less involved in local institutional matters and tend to ignore or evidence disdain for institutional practices, as contrasted with departments of lesser stature. Interview and questionnaire data appeared to support these two hypotheses, but for additional insights, consultants' reports covering seven identical disciplines in ten universities were examined in detail.

Some of our staff read the consultants' reports across disciplines (for example, chemistry, mathematics, history, and so on at all ten universities)', whereas others read across each university (for example, chemistry, mathematics, history, and so on within a given university)'. Our initial discussion indicated that on many points the overriding influence was the university. Our judgments were almost always colored by comments like "But, you must remember that department X is at a university with strong central administration and you must expect . . ."

To clarify variables further, we established, after much discussion and several trials, a set of scales for rating departments based on the consultants' reports. Comments pertinent to each variable were placed on an index card with no identification of either department or university. Six members of the research staff placed each card on the five-point scale for each variable. Ratings were then summarized for the universities and seven departments, yielding a matrix of departments by universities with cells representing a rating of each department on a five-point scale. The variables and scales were as follows:

A. *Authority Operation*

| 1 | | 5 |

Tight .... *Loose*

Autocratic-paternalistic-   democratic-   laissez-faire
  oligarchic   bureaucratic

B. *Relations with the University*

| 1 | | 5 |

Isolated .... *Deeply Involved*

Has taken steps to   Involved in   Involved and respected
  isolate itself   some areas   by others

C. *Organization*

| 1 | | 5 |

Simple .... *Complex*

Chairman and no   Chairman and associate
  formal committees;   chairman; an elaborate
  no faculty meetings   committee structure;
                                     meetings with all
                                     faculty

D. *Communication*

| 1 | | 5 |

Two-Way .... *One-Way*

Face-to-face; small   Written announcements
  groups

E. *Concern for Students*

| 1 | | 5 |

Lacking .... *Apparent*

Little nonmajor   Much nonmajor teaching;
  teaching; minimal   close personal advising
  advising

The first analysis of these data was directed at the independence of each function. Table 1 presents the results.

With the possible exception of the relationship of concern for students with organizational patterns and university relations, there was negligible correlation among these measures. Consultants were apparently able to provide distinctive comments on five departmental functions.

Table 1.

PEARSON PRODUCT-MOMENT CORRELATIONS OF DEPARTMENTAL
FUNCTION MEASURES WITH MEANS AND STANDARD DEVIATIONS

	Mean	Standard Deviation	Product-Moment Correlations			
Authority Operation	3.19	1.67	Authority Operation			
University Relations	2.99	1.45	.13	Univ. Rel.		
Organization	2.91	.92	.19	.19	Organ.	
Communication	2.91	.93	−.05	.18	.19	Comm.
Concern for Students	2.28	.98	.07	.33	.37	−.02

Next we considered whether these functions followed university patterns rather than disciplinary patterns. This concern applied equally well to departmental priority statements, to basic data, and to national reputation based on the Cartter report ratings. We analyzed our data to answer the following questions: How much of the variation associated with each of the above departmental functions is accounted for by differences in universities alone, and how much is accounted for by differences in disciplines alone? Do differences between universities account for a significant amount of the variation in each of the departmental functions over and above that which can be attributed to differences in disciplines? and Do differences between disciplines account for a significant amount of variation over and above that which can be attributed to differences among universities?

This analysis indicated that departmental authority operations, organization, student concerns, and university relations depend heavily on the university. Priorities presented a less clear picture. Development of the discipline nationally and development of junior staff are primarily university-determined, but undergraduate instruction is split between the two. Research activities (both basic and applied) and the service activities (nonmajor instruction internally and service to business and industry externally) are related primarily to the discipline.

The Cartter report,[1] one of the more frequently used assessments of quality in graduate education, at least for these ten universities, tends to be associated more with the university than the discipline. To explore further just what the Cartter report ratings meant for these universities, the significant correlations (.05) between measures of function and priorities and national ratings of the Cartter report were examined. Table 2 summarizes the findings.

Table 2.

DEPARTMENTAL FUNCTIONS AND PRIORITIES AS PREDICTORS OF
HIGH RATINGS ON THE CARTTER REPORT OF
GRADUATE PROGRAMS AND FACULTY
(All correlations are significant at the .05 level.)

	Correlation with Program	*Correlation with Graduate Faculty*
Functions		
Authority Operations		.22
University Relations	−.19	
Concern for Students	−.23	
Priorities		
Basic Research	.31	.30
Discipline Nationally	.27	
Graduate Instruction		.24
Junior Staff	−.21	
Undergraduate Advising		−.20
Undergraduate Instruction	−.20	−.18
Service to Business and Industry	−.21	

Departments that have a more democratic operation, that are more isolated from the rest of the university, and that have less concern for students tend to do better on the Cartter report ratings. Since these ratings are made on graduate programs and faculty, it

[1] Allan M. Cartter, *An Assessment of Quality in Graduate Education* (Washington, D.C.: American Council on Education, 1966).

is not surprising that high priorities on basic research, on developing the discipline nationally, and on graduate instruction correlated positively with the Cartter report. Undergraduate advising and instruction and service show negative correlations.

An analysis similar to that in Table 2 made for the basic departmental statistics showed that faculty size, faculty growth, and degrees granted are roughly equally determined by discipline and university. The percentage of faculty on tenure, degrees granted (undergraduate or graduate) per faculty member, publications per faculty member, service activities, and expenditures are related more to the discipline than to the university.

It is evident that a number of variables are more directly associated with the university than with the discipline. The remainder of this chapter will deal primarily with those department functions which are strongly influenced by university policy.

ORGANIZATION AND OPERATION

Consultants looked at the title of the chief administrative officer of the department and any formal statements of what his duties and responsibilities were. Mode of selection, term of office, types of assistants, and the departmental committee structure were major points of interest. The range of department organization went from very simple (in which the department chairman had no formal committees) to complex (in which a chairman and associate chairman had an elaborate committee structure with scheduled meetings and also met regularly with the entire departmental staff). Most typical was the pattern wherein the chairman met regularly with several key faculty members and had established a series of other advisory committees on such matters as graduate student affairs, curriculum, library, and research.

Three comments on three separate departments at three different universities illustrate the range of the organizational patterns. The first was simple and straightforward:

> Committees are ad hoc as needed. He, as chairman, does the administrative or managerial work of the department. He says, "I clutter up the time of the members as little as possible."

The second was typical of most departments:

As in other departments in the university, the head of the department has the title of chairman, and in this case the position generally rotates on a five-year basis. By tradition it goes to the most
recently appointed full professor, indicating again that it is more
a chore than an honor. There are no formal committees in the
department, though the chairman appoints ad hoc committees as
the need to solve specific problems arises.

The third comment describes one of the more complex operations:

There are two assistant chairmen, one in charge of undergraduate
and graduate students and studies (his responsibilities are prin-
cipally for the enrollment of these students), and one in charge
of building, equipment, and laboratories. The department has an
elaborate committee structure comprising sixteen standing committees.

It was noted by the consultants that there was often little
relationship between the complexity of the organization and the
democracy of the decision-making process of the department. One
chairman operating with few committees would seek the advice of
many members of his faculty, while another with elaborate committee structures would not even ask for recommendations from the
committees on important issues.

We asked our consultants to make a judgment on whether
the department was autocratically run, paternalistic, an oligarchy,
a bureaucracy, a democracy, or laissez-faire with little organization
and maximum freedom of the individual to determine his own role
and carry it out as he wished. Most departments organized themselves into a democratic bureaucracy, with some interesting distinctions by discipline, illustrated in Table 3.

Departments in professional schools tended more toward the
autocratic and paternalistic pattern, those in chemistry, history, and
psychology preferring the democratic bureaucracy, and mathematics
and English departments representing a mixture between an oligarchy and democracy.

The characterization of the operational style was the easiest
for consultants to make. The following statements are typical:

The best descriptive term for this department is that it is, in fact,
autocratic, with the head making many of the decisions and rely-
ing upon very few people for advice, which he may or may not
follow. The department is not a closely knit group.

Table 3.

OPERATIONAL PATTERNS OF SIXTY-NINE DEPARTMENTS

Number of Departments Operating in Each Pattern

Discipline	Autocratic-Paternalistic	Oligarchic	Democratic Bureaucracy	Laissez-Faire
Chemistry	2	0	7	1
History	1	2	6	1
Psychology	1	2	6	1
English	0	5	5	0
Mathematics	2	5	3	0
Business	5	1	4	0
Electrical Engineering	5	1	3	0
Total Departments	16	16	34	3

Perhaps it can be classified best as a working democracy with a considerable organization. Decisions are made by a variety of persons, at a variety of levels, individually and collectively. I would deem the chairman to be ubiquitous, an aggressive manager-leader.

The organization for management is minimal and casually administered. The department might be said to be "democratically laissez-faire," consensually oriented, and permissive regarding itself and others, and to place a low value on management processes.

CONCERN FOR STUDENTS

Perhaps the most significant comment made by consultants was that a depth of concern for the individual student was seldom evident. In certain departments, particularly in professional schools, there was very little instruction of nonmajors. Major programs were carefully prescribed and few electives possible. In other departments, most notably history and English, there seemed to be at some institutions a genuine concern for the responsibility of nonmajor instruction and some attempts to provide a system for close personal advising of students. On the whole, however, departmental patterns were related to institutional policy. Reports of consultants left the clear impression that some institutions emphasized faculty-student interactions and the departments were expected to develop procedures to implement these policies.

Where graduate programs have not yet started, there is still the possibility that the department seriously attends to its undergraduates. This point is well illustrated in the following observation from one consultant:

> The department expects to have a graduate program within two or three years. The department insists on a close faculty-student relationship, and works closely with its majors to plan advantageous programs involving individual research. Also, the department has been unusually successful in designing and offering courses for nonmajors that attract excellent students.

More typical, however, is this comment:

> While the undergraduate committee is said to be conscientious in the advising of undergraduates, this function is quite obviously performed as an obligation and so regarded by a large portion of the faculty members.

> A senior professor observed that "promotion depends almost entirely on research productivity. Too many complaints against a man's teaching would *probably* keep him from being promoted."

In spite of the fact that consultants detected little apparent concern for students, the highest priorities, as *stated* by deans, chairmen, and faculty, were in the areas of undergraduate and graduate instruction. It was fairly typical for chairmen to rate instructional activities higher than did the deans, but consistently highest ratings were given to this activity. Yet these ratings are not altogether believable, unless one is prepared to accept a dubious view about what makes for good undergraduate education. It was clear that many deans and chairmen felt the best way to produce quality undergraduate instruction was to develop a quality research and graduate program which would attract a good faculty. Yet universities that had highest ratings on quality of graduate programs and the graduate faculty, as judged by the Cartter report, tended to place least emphasis on undergraduate instruction and showed lowest concern for students.

Correlations found between instruction and other departmental priorities are revealing. There were significant correlations among undergraduate instruction for majors and nonmajors and the undergraduate advising program, but the undergraduate program was unrelated to graduate instruction. As noted above, emphasis on undergraduate instruction was based partly on university concerns and partly on the discipline. Advising activities of departments appeared to develop out of college and university patterns, although this conclusion is more subjective than statistical. Advising of majors, however limited in its conception, was clearly accepted as a necessary departmental obligation.

Relationships of the graduate instructional program are difficult to summarize, since it is difficult for faculty to identify clearly when they are instructing graduate students, when they are training someone to become a staff member in a department, when they are advancing the discipline, and when they are training someone to become a research worker. Although graduate instruction receives high priority and a great amount of emphasis in all the universities, it remains, in this study, a relatively isolated and elusive activity. Developing of junior staff, however, is correlated with the department's advising program and basic research activities of faculty, and with developing the discipline on the national scene. Yet the data show that development of junior staff and of the discipline nationally is more university- than discipline-related.

FACULTY SIZE AND GROWTH

One characteristic most directly related to institutional policy is the pattern of faculty size and growth of the last ten years. As can be seen in Table 4, faculty size and growth are directly related to general funds provided. Departments with large general funds have experienced the largest growth in faculty over the past ten years. Distribution of faculty in these departments includes more nontenured faculty and fewer tenured faculty than do other departments. That is to say, the largest growth has occurred in those departments that now support a large number of graduate students. Perhaps because of larger size or perhaps because of subsidy of graduate students, these departments tended to do better on the Cartter report. The number of B.A. degrees they produced per faculty is less than for departments without large general funds.

Table 4.

Significant Correlations (.01) of Some Basic Data Indices for Seventy Departments

	General Fund	Grants	Faculty Growth	Per Cent Tenured Faculty	Per Cent Non-tenured Faculty	B.A. Growth	B.A. Granted/ Faculty	Ph.D. Granted/ Faculty	Publi-cations/ Faculty
Faculty Growth	.70								
Per Cent Tenured Faculty	−.45	−.37							
Per Cent Nontenured Faculty	.47		.32	−.85					
B.A. Growth			.33						
B.A. Granted/Faculty	−.38		−.36			.51			
Ph.D Granted/Faculty		.55		−.55	.40	−.42			
Publications/Faculty		.59		−.34				.57	
Cartter Rating	.48	.31	.30					.39	.34

Another significant characteristic relating to department size and growth is the amount of grant funds the department is able to attract. Although there is no significant correlation between grant funds and faculty growth, it is important to note that departments with large grant funds produce more Ph.D. degrees per faculty member and significantly more publications per faculty, and do very well on the Cartter report.

Departments which have experienced a rapid faculty growth over the last ten years have experienced an accompanying growth in the number of B.A. degrees produced, but with fewer degrees produced per faculty. These departments tend to have a smaller percentage of their total personnel in clerical and technical positions, and do not produce as many Ph.D.'s or publications as those departments with large grant funds.

OUTPUTS AND FINANCES

One of the easiest measures to collect on departmental output is number of degrees produced at various levels. The university with the smallest departments, based on the number of faculty members, produced over 65 per cent more doctorates in these departments than any other of the universities. It also produced over 40 per cent more master's degrees and about an average number of baccalaureates. For this university, the ratio of graduate to undergraduate degrees produced approached unity. Variation in this ratio was very great among the different universities, ranging down to .22. Departments and universities with lower ratios were large public universities handling large numbers of undergraduates. Larger ratios tend to be characteristic of institutions rating high in the Cartter report. There was a negative correlation between baccalaureates per faculty and publications per faculty.

Disciplines, too, varied greatly in the average number of doctorates produced, with chemistry well in the lead. Not surprisingly, the average annual grant expenditures in chemistry were over twice that of any of the other six disciplines represented.

General fund dollars per faculty member, as would be expected, showed considerable variation over the seven disciplines, with chemistry again far out in front at $20,000 per faculty member. Mathematics, electrical engineering, English, and history were grouped close together at about $15,000, with psychology and management winding up sixth and seventh respectively. Psychology, like chemistry, mathematics, and electrical engineering, was the beneficiary of significant grant funds.

Attempts to estimate degree costs were abandoned because of great variation in numbers and levels of degrees granted. However, it did appear that faculty productivity, represented by degrees produced per faculty member, would be a factor in costs. Disciplines of English, history, and management produced double or triple the number of degrees per faculty member, as compared with remaining disciplines. One major disadvantage of degrees granted is that these may lag behind increasing faculty support by several years. Accordingly, it has seemed wise to make only passing allusion to this aspect of the data.

DEVELOPING JUNIOR STAFF

Two priorities that are more influenced by university practices than by discipline affiliation are: developing junior staff and developing the national stature of the department through the discipline. Although development of junior staff was not considered a very high-priority item, it seemed to be more related to developing of teaching and research assistants among the graduate students than did the developing of the careers of instructors and assistant professors in the tenure pattern. The character of this activity appeared to depend on institutional pressures rather than disciplinary ones. It was significantly related to nonmajor instruction, graduate instruction, and the development of the discipline nationally. A high emphasis on this activity was characteristic of departments with large graduate programs who used graduate students as teaching assistants and research assistants in programs leading to publications that would advance the discipline nationally. Thus, developing junior staff was related to basic research also, as this tends to advance the discipline.

The questionnaire data also provide some insights into the kinds of departments which place a relatively high emphasis upon the development of junior staff. Communication tended to be relatively high within the department, especially with the chairman, with the heads of department committees, and among the faculty. There tended to be relatively little communication across departmental lines to either faculty or chairmen in other departments, or to deans or other university administrators. Similarly, the influence of the members of the department was relatively high, while those outside exerted relatively little impact upon activities within the boundaries. Both the dean and university administrators were reported to have little influence when the faculty reported that developing junior staff was a high priority. The orientation of the faculty was to the department as opposed to the university or the discipline.

The overall picture that emerges of departments where career development of junior staff is given a high priority is one of a relatively compact and self-contained unit where the chairman acts as a linking pin or gatekeeper of information and influence to the rest of the university. When faculty seek special consideration about such matters as promotions and tenure, salary increases, leaves of absence, travel, and even extra funds for research, they turn to the chairman rather than other faculty or university administrators. The tightness of the department tends to cloak much of the influence of the chairman because many important decisions are made in consultations with other tenured faculty or by vote of the entire staff. For example, there are indications that such matters as promotions, budgets, office space, and requirements for majors are not made by the chairman acting alone or arbitrarily, but rather in consultation with others.

DEVELOPING THE DISCIPLINE

Certain universities have made a commitment to national stature, which is often interpreted at the departmental level as a commitment to advance their own discipline nationally. In these departments, it is easier to get funds to attend national meetings, recognition is given to services performed for national associations, and publications which advance the discipline nationally are rewarded. As already noted, this activity has a significant positive relationship to development of junior staff and is also significantly related to the research programs of the departments. Service to business and industry is negatively correlated with an emphasis on developing the discipline nationally. Departments do not see the application of research to the problems presented by business and industry as contributing to the development of the discipline.

Advancing the discipline nationally also has consequences for the internal structure of departments. Unlike those departments which stress the development of junior staff, those seeking to advance the discipline are much less cohesive and the influence of the department chairmen is relatively nil. For example, departments of this type had relatively little communication within their own departments or across departmental lines. Although the influence of the faculty and its committees and of the graduate students was considered relatively high, the influence of the department chairman and all other members of the university community was considered relatively low in internal departmental affairs. Except for the matter of salary increases, faculty did not report seeking the department chairman for anything requiring special consideration. And, when it came to describing how decisions were made in these departments, there were no consistent patterns as to whether the chairman, executive committees, or members of the faculty participated or exercised influence.

It may very well be that departments in the throes of developing themselves nationally focus primarily upon individual faculty enterprise and do not identify or affiliate with others with whom they have daily contact. One might expect that such departments are very uneven and divided as to the proper degree of stress or the amount of resources which should be allocated to the pursuit of national stature. This divisiveness would occur because some members recognize their inability to partake and contribute to national advancement; they came to the department and were promoted when other priorities prevailed and now they must adjust to the fact that their own contributions are no longer heavily rewarded.

NATIONAL IMAGE

The national image of the department relates in part to the development of the discipline and its standing among groups who rate graduate programs and faculty. The Cartter report is an example of such a study.

Perhaps it is unfair to use the ratings on the Cartter report for the departments and universities selected for this study. Its disadvantages of emphasis on the graduate program and the subjective nature of the ratings themselves certainly do not make for either a reliable or a complete estimate of the national image of departments used in this study. However, it seemed that some profitable exploration might be made of the relationship of the emphasis departments place upon certain of their activities and their rating on an external measure, such as the Cartter report.

Institutions as a group fell a little below the acceptable-plus rating for the graduate program and averaged acceptable-plus for their graduate faculty. The following statements describe departments that tended to do well in the Cartter report.

Faculty in departments mentioned in the Cartter report responded quite differently to our questionnaire than those not listed. Perhaps the major difference between departments mentioned in the Cartter report and those which were not is the amount of emphasis they gave to different missions. For example, consistent with our consultant reports, faculty whose departments were mentioned favorably in the report placed a relatively lower emphasis upon undergraduate instruction of both majors and minors. On the other hand, it is clear that departments mentioned in the report placed a relatively higher emphasis on research, whether it be basic or applied. They also gave a relatively higher emphasis upon developing the junior staff and advancing the discipline nationally. The instruction of graduate students was emphasized almost equally by both types of departments, although there is a tendency for those mentioned in the report to give a slightly higher stress to this mission of priority. In terms of the relationship of the department and the university community, we found virtually no difference between the emphasis given by those departments mentioned and those not mentioned.

When respondents were asked to indicate what *should* be emphasized in their departments, faculty of departments mentioned in the Cartter report stated basic research and graduate instruction, whereas those of the nonmentioned departments clearly stressed undergraduate instruction. As we shall see throughout this report, there is generally great consistency between what is actually a departmental mission and what department members feel should be a priority.

Perhaps the most clear-cut generalization which can be made about departments mentioned and those not mentioned in the Cartter report is that the former place a relatively lower emphasis upon nondepartmental matters within the university as affecting their behavior. For example, on the question asking what determines departmental autonomy, there was relative agreement between members of the mentioned and the nonmentioned departments that the chairman was relatively unimportant. However, members of departments which were mentioned in the Cartter report were more likely to say that departmental size and departmental enterprise in obtaining outside funds determined autonomy; whereas departments which were not mentioned in the Cartter report were much more likely to say departmental prestige and overall college policy determined autonomy.

When one examines the question concerning influence over departmental matters, the same pattern emerges as was found in the autonomy question: units within the department, except for chairmen, were seen as expressing relatively high influence by those members of departments which were mentioned in the Cartter report. For example, compared to members of the departments which were not mentioned in the Cartter report, faculty in the highly rated departments stated that the faculty, departmental committees, and graduate students all exerted relatively high influence over departmental affairs. On the other hand, university administration, the dean, and the chairman of the department exerted relatively low influence over departmental affairs. Interestingly, when faculty were queried about their own personal influence over departmental affairs, there was no difference between the faculty in either the mentioned or the nonmentioned departments. In summary, then, faculty within departments mentioned in the Cartter report tend to see autonomy and influence generated within the department and not

outside of it. Also, it is a peer phenomenon, and the chairman of
the department is excluded from participating in this activity.

We assumed there would be different patterns of communication within departments which were mentioned and those which
were not mentioned. We assumed that in departments mentioned
in the report, there would be more internal communication and
relatively little external communication. However, we found absolutely no differences between departments mentioned in the Cartter
report and those not mentioned when it came to communication
across departmental lines, across university echelons, or within departments. Similarly, we found no differences between departments
mentioned and nonmentioned in terms of clique formation and degree of conflict within the departments. And finally, we expected
to find that members of departments mentioned in the Cartter report would have a reference group which was external to the department and members of nonmentioned departments would have
a reference group within the university or within the department.
However, there was actually no difference in terms of reference
group in the mentioned and nonmentioned departments.

One consistent difference between departments mentioned in
the Cartter report and those which were not is the procedures faculty reported they would use to receive special consideration on
problems confronting them. For all of the problems we asked the
faculty how they would handle, members in nonmentioned departments indicated that they would go to one administrative unit above
that which was reported by faculty in departments mentioned in
the Cartter report. For example, when we asked to whom they
would go for special consideration about a salary increase, members
of departments not mentioned in the Cartter report responded in a
relatively high frequency that they would go to the dean, whereas
those in departments mentioned in the report responded that they
would go to the chairman of their own department. Similarly, when
asked to whom they would go for special consideration about obtaining more graduate students, members of departments not mentioned in the Cartter report said they would go to their chairman,
whereas those in the mentioned departments said they would go to
the faculty in their own department. This pattern was extremely

consistent and reached across such problems as obtaining more money for research, for which those in nonmentioned departments would go to the dean and those in mentioned departments would go to the chairman; obtaining a change in teaching assignment, for which those in the nonmentioned departments would go to the chairman of the department and those in mentioned departments would go to some of the faculty within the department.

This perception that a lower echelon controls the fate of members within departments mentioned in the Cartter report also carries across into the item which asked the faculty to tell us how some major decisions were made in their departments. Here again we found a relative consistency between the mentioned and non-mentioned departments. For example, when it comes to deciding upon promotion and tenure, the faculty of departments mentioned in the Cartter report were more likely to say that a vote of the tenure faculty decides the matter. In matters of salary increase, the members of mentioned departments were less likely to say their chairman decides it rather than saying an advisory committee does so. On the question of teaching assignments, members of departments mentioned in the Cartter report were less likely than those in non-mentioned departments to say the chairman decides it and more likely to say that an advisory committee decides it. And on the question of the requirements for major and graduate students, the members of faculty in mentioned departments were relatively more likely to say that a vote of all the faculty is required to set these standards and less likely to say that it is decided by an advisory committee.

Some insight into the departments mentioned favorably in the Cartter report is given by the reports submitted by the consultants on the project. They reported that even the deans and chairmen of the departments favorably rated in the Cartter report saw these departments as engrossed in their own programs and somewhat isolated from the total university community. Frequently these administrators would report that these departments tended to operate in a more democratic manner, but it was never made clear whether or not this was so because autonomy and authority were delegated by the administrators to the departments because of their national rating or whether these departments had been able to acquire such privileges and then achieved national standing. On the basis of the data we can report, one would be very hard pressed to make recommendations for national prestige. Correlational data do not permit statements inferring causality.

As consultants for this study visited with department chairmen, faculty, deans, and chief academic officers, certain observations were reported about relationships between departments and central administration. Some departments were found to be deeply involved in university affairs and were regarded as effective working units by the rest of the university. Some departments sought involvement but were not effective. A few departments seemed willing to be involved in university affairs but were ignored by the rest of the university, whereas other departments had deliberately isolated themselves from the rest of the university. The most frequent pattern was that of a department with one or two faculty members active in university affairs, but with the department as a unit seldom taking a position on all-university matters.

Various levels of involvement are well documented by consultants' reports. A department which views freedom as noninvolvement with the rest of the university was summarized as follows:

> As in the case of most departments interviewed, there is the feeling that central administration does not really affect faculty members in a palpable way. They are satisfied with their freedom in instruction and freedom in research, and while the department head is currently serving as president of the University Senate, other members do not seem deeply involved in university affairs.

The more typical department was reported by consultants as follows:

> The department is viewed by the university as being strong, really distinguished in research productivity. Many of its members are active and concerned about all-university affairs, but the department does not take departmental stance, per se, on university issues.

The few that were deeply involved with the university had departmental relations with the rest of the university similar to these:

The department has provided an imposing array of administrators, including the present chancellor. It is usually well represented on elected university committees as well, and exerts an important influence in university affairs that extends well beyond merely departmental concerns. The department is highly regarded inside and outside the university.

The questionnaire responses of faculty contribute additional information about university-departmental relationships. Specifically, we asked about the amount of influence university administration exercised over departmental affairs. Interestingly, university administration was ranked fifth among the eight positions we listed. (See page 60 for the complete listing.) In general, when the university administration was viewed as highly influential, the department faculty, its committees, and graduate students were perceived as possessing relatively little influence. The personal influence of faculty was also low; but the influence of university committees and the dean was viewed as relatively high. Autonomy in the total university was described as determined by university policy as opposed to the efforts of the department chairman or the faculty. And not surprisingly, when the university influence over department affairs was perceived as high, faculty reported that they considered themselves as members of the university rather than as members of the department or their respective disciplines.

The questionnaire data suggest that when university influence is high, the department chairman has little say over events and occurrences under his purview. For example, on *all* of the matters requiring special consideration which we asked about, there were negative correlations between going to the chairman for assistance and the influence of the university. (Four of these correlations were statistically significant, and they included some of the most important items, such as promotions, tenure, and salary increases.) Similarly, some type of established policy within the department seems to control such matters as recruitment of new faculty, salary increase, awarding of assistantships, and requirements for majors. The faculty reported they had relatively little decision-making power in this area either as a whole or through tenured staff or the executive committee. Generally, they reported that the chairman made these decisions, but he too was limited by university practices and policies.

Communication patterns in departments which are heavily influenced by university administration are interesting because they tend to flow across departmental lines rather than within and among faculty. Thus, we found a significantly positive correlation between university administration influence and discussing problems with chairmen and faculty of other departments. Perhaps when university administration influence is high, faculty seek coalitions in other departments in order to effect policies which have a direct bearing upon themselves. Interestingly, we found no correlation between university administration influence and the amount of communication between departments and the upper echelons. Neither was expressing departmental views to the upper administration perceived as a high priority; it received little emphasis.

The correlation of priorities with the influence of university administration over departmental affairs was all negative or nonsignificant. Graduate instruction, basic research, advancing the discipline, and the career development of junior staff were all significantly and negatively related; that is, as university administration influence over departmental affairs increased, emphasis upon these four items decreased. In terms of what faculty thought *should* be emphasized, undergraduate instruction was positively related to the influence of university administration. Although faculty did not report that emphasis *was actually* placed on undergraduate instruction, our basic data show a significantly positive correlation between the influence of the university administration over departmental affairs and the number of B.A.'s per faculty produced in 1967. One must conclude from these data that when the university administration is perceived as influencing departmental affairs to a relatively great degree, faculty do not feel they can get anything done by themselves. Interestingly, even when ideal missions (in this case undergraduate instruction) coincide with reality (producing B.A.'s), the faculty are apparently unaware of the situation (they do not report a high emphasis upon undergraduate instruction). Perhaps one function of the department chairman is to mitigate the influence of the central administration to the faculty and thereby give the latter a feeling that they are represented and have a spokesman who can defend their interests. In our study, however, weak chairmen seemed to exist with strong central administrators.

The communication systems between departments and deans varied greatly. Some deans felt it was their role to make policy decisions and then persuade chairmen to implement decisions as effectively as possible. Others felt that policy should be originated with each department, approved by the dean, and forwarded to central administration. Chairmen almost always viewed the dean as part of central administration, or at least as the means of communication with central administration. Instances of chairmen deliberately circumventing the dean were rare, and these cases usually reflected a completely ineffective dean. In some instances elected faculty advisory committees competed with the chairmen in supplying two-way communication between dean and department.

The intradepartment communication process was more varied and again seemed to depend more on personalities than on either the university or the discipline. Consultants' reports were primarily focused on whether or not the communication was one-way or two-way between the faculty and chairmen. Sometimes a wide variety of communication modes (bulletin boards, meetings, news letters, and the like) was used to inform the faculty of decisions, with little opportunity for faculty to respond or take part in those decisions. Other times faculty seemed to know what was going on, were aware of decisions that had been made, felt that they had participated, and yet no formal communication system was apparent. Our consultants were able to gain some insights into how communication problems are solved or created. In one case, the consultant reported:

> There is abundant consultation by persons affected by decisions which are made, but this consultation is informal. The meetings of committees and the departmental faculty which ratify decisions are limited in number. The department has one regular meeting per year and approximately six per year on call. Approximately 100 pages of memoranda material are sent to staff in the course of the year. A brief biennial report is submitted to the dean.

From another institution a consultant reported:

> The department does not have a newsletter and makes some use
> of bulletin boards as well as memos to the staff. Communication
> seems to be very ineffective within the department, and it is evi-
> dently designed to be that way. It is up to the individual member
> to keep informed by the grapevine or gossip, since there is no
> system of communication.

The communication process ranged from one in which faculty members sat in small groups with the chairman, to one which
had only formal written communication with no opportunity for
feedback. The typical department used regular or occasional department faculty meetings as the primary method of communication. Generally, all faculty were able to participate in the departmental meetings, but in some cases, after the routine announcements
had been made, nontenured faculty members were excused, leaving
tenured faculty to discuss and decide new issues. Although departmental communication often seemed independent of college and
university communication patterns, it was affected by departmental
organization, which was in some cases partly determined by university policies. Thus the existence in a department of an executive
or advisory committee certainly affected communication, although
it might have either restricted or broadened it, depending on the
committee, the chairman, and the policies developed.

Once again we can turn to the questionnaire data to extend
and amplify the consultant reports. Examination of the two items,
frequency of communication to deans and to university administration reveals very different patterns, with one notable exception:
when communication from faculty to these two levels of the university is relatively high, there is a greater number of joint appointments held by members of the respective departments. This pattern
does not imply that it is the faculty with joint appointments who
actually have the contact to higher administration, but the mere
existence of these links to other parts of the university probably acts
as a stimulus to cross-departmental lines and seeks assistance with
departmental problems. In departments with many joint appointments, there is probably more difficulty handling certain kinds of
staff problems, and higher authority is required for resolution of

the concerns. Our data indicate that there seems to be little difference between departments with many joint appointments and those with few—except for communication to upper echelons.

Communication to university administration is not consistently related to other variables we measured in this study. As one might expect, departments reporting relatively more communication to central administration also report that this activity receives relatively high priority from the staff. Undergraduate instruction also receives a relatively high priority.

Patterns of communication to the dean are more revealing than those to central university administration. The dean seems to be the link between the department faculty and other units within the university. Thus, we find that departments reporting relatively high communication to the dean also report high communication to faculty and chairmen of other departments and to the central administration. Contact with the dean also provides faculty with a sense of control over their own departmental affairs, as they report high personal influence. (Interestingly, these same departments do not report that faculty influence in general is high.) Perhaps one reason for this finding is that faculty can influence their own chairmen after they have had access to the dean. The truth of this comment is reflected in the finding that communication to the dean is correlated with communication to the department chairman; but the influence of the department chairman is negatively related to faculty communication to the dean. When communication to the dean is relatively high, there is also less likelihood that faculty will seek their chairman for special consideration in such matters as tenure appointments, salary increments, leaves of absence, and so forth. However, in matters of teaching assignments, they will still go to their respective chairmen.

High communication to the dean is related to departmental emphasis upon applied research and service to the community. However, there was no relationship to any aspects of undergraduate instruction or advising; and there was a negative relationship to an emphasis upon basic research.

High communication to the dean, then, is indicative of practical departments; that is, departments have joint appointments to increase their staffs without having to pay for the entire salaries; they produce more B.A.'s per faculty although they put little emphasis upon this activity; and they have a relatively higher proportion of senior staff who know their way about the university and can make contacts with other departments. One might assume these departments are also more interested in advancing the total university because their reference group is the university (as opposed to the discipline or the department), and a relatively higher proportion of their members serve on college and university committees.

INFLUENCE OF THE DEAN

Universities vary greatly in the amount of influence which they concentrate at different levels in the hierarchy. For example, some universities maintain faculty bylaws which stipulate that many major decisions shall be made at the faculty level with a great deal of discussion and staff participation. Other universities concentrate most of the decision-making power at the dean's level (or higher), and delegate very limited authority to the department.

No university is entirely consistent, and there are many differences in the decisions which are delegated and those which are centralized. Departments also differ in how their decisions are reached, but here our concern is primarily with the influence on the department of university forces external to it. Some of the differences were reported to us by the faculty members in answer to the question: In general, how much say or influence does each of the following have over what goes on in your department?[2] Eight different positions within the university were rated by the faculty, resulting in the following rank order of influence over departmental affairs:

1. department chairman
2. department faculty as a whole
3. special department committees
4. dean of the school
5. university administration

[2] For another study using this item, see Winston W. Hill and Wendell L. French, "Perceptions of Power of Department Chairmen by Professors," *Administrative Science Quarterly*, 1967, *11*, 548–574.

6. respondent personally
7. all university committees
8. graduate students

This order offers no great surprises other than the fact that it reflected a rather high degree of consistency over all disciplines and universities, regardless of size, national stature, or source of support.

We expected to find that strong deans would seek department chairmen who dominated their departments, but there was a negative, though not statistically significant, relationship between these two positions as perceived by faculty. Low negative, though statistically significant, relationships were found between the influence of the faculty and the department chairman and between faculty and deans. These findings do not convincingly support the frequent contention that the faculty are influential only when chairmen and deans are relatively passive; rather, the low correlations suggest that each has a sphere of influence, and one does not deprive the other to any great extent.

Some relationships between the roles of deans and chairmen were of special interest. For example, departments of business management and electrical engineering tended to see the influence of deans as quite high; chemistry and mathematics ranked the dean's influence as relatively low. English and history ranked their chairmen relatively high, whereas psychology and business management ranked chairmen low.

The dean's influence on departmental mission or goals was examined and found related to the emphasis faculty perceived as being given to service to business and industry. This relationship is of particular significance to a dean in professional schools. Emphasis on undergraduate instruction was also related to the influence of the dean, whereas the emphasis faculty gave to instruction of graduate students was not. Two areas, career development of junior staff and basic research, were actually negatively correlated with the dean's influence. It is not surprising, then, that when department faculty saw the dean as influential, they also believed that their department placed little emphasis upon advancing the discipline and profession nationally. In short, when departments perceive the dean as relatively influential, there seems to be a consistent picture of the department as being engaged in local activities (service and undergraduate instruction) rather than having a national orientation. Of course, the dean may be viewed as more or less influential by various departments in his college.

Faculty members were also asked to indicate which three of the ten missions the department *should* emphasize. On this item, three responses accounted for over 75 per cent of the answers: undergraduate instruction, graduate instruction, and basic research. Of these three, none was related to dean's influence. In those departments where the dean was perceived as influential, the faculty, whether from satisfaction, apathy, or lack of influence, had no consensus as to desired mission priorities.

In general, the perceived influence of the dean was positively related to the proportion of faculty in the tenure track. The faculty were also oriented generally to the university rather than to the discipline or even the department. Influences of the university administration and all-university committees were positively related to influential deans.

In those departments where the dean was perceived as influential, the faculty members reported that they discuss the departmental matters with him and with faculty from other departments, as well as with the chairman. Another question asked that individuals indicate to whom they would go for special consideration about nine different problems they might face. The overwhelming response was always the department chairman, but the proportion of respondents within each department who mentioned the department chairman as the contact for a particular problem was unrelated to the influence of the dean except for three items: salary increase, leave of absence, and funds for research scholarships, which showed negative correlations.

Faculty members were also asked to respond to the question: How are decisions reached in your department for each of the following? Respondents were given ten different items, and were asked to check one of four alternatives which approximated their understanding of how decisions were made in their departments. A score of *1* was arbitrarily assigned to the most concentrated form of decision making (department chairmen acting within an established policy), and a score of *4* for the most delegated form of decision-making responsibility (the vote of all members of the departmental staff). On this crude decision-making responsibility scale, all ten items were negatively related to the perceived influence of the dean. Five of the ten correlations were statistically significant: recruitment and selection of new faculty; promotions and tenure; salary increases; award of assistantships, fellowships, and scholarships; and requirements for majors and graduate students.

The responses to these items clearly indicate that when deans are perceived as influential, decision-making responsibilities within the respective departments are perceived as undelegated. They tend to be executed by department chairmen either acting within an established policy or in consultation within an advisory group, rather than by a vote of tenured faculty or vote of all members of the department staff. An interesting question emerges at this point: Is it the lack of delegation of decision-making responsibilities within a department that contributes to the perception of the dean as influential over departmental affairs? Unfortunately, correlational analysis does not provide a ready answer for this interesting question.

In general, deans and department chairmen agreed on priorities assigned to instruction (both graduate and undergraduate), basic research, developing the discipline nationally, and nonmajor instruction. They also agreed that applied research and service to business and industry should receive the least emphasis in the department. Differences in emphasis were found on undergraduate advising, development of junior staff, and advancing the discipline within the university. Deans tended to place more emphasis on undergraduate advising, whereas chairmen felt that more emphasis should be placed on developing junior staff. Deans saw the function of advancing the discipline within the university as being more critical than did department chairmen.

UNIVERSITY AS REFERENCE GROUP

Faculty members responding to our questionnaire were asked whether they thought of themselves primarily as members of the university, the department, or of the discipline. About 15 per cent indicated that they thought of themselves more as members of the university; these respondents tended to be full professors who have served the department for a long time. They were not interested in moving to another university for higher salaries or prestige. They tended to believe—more than their associates—that the dean has influence in the department and that certain key faculty members are also influential. This view was not held by those oriented toward the department or discipline, who tended to view the chairman as more influential than the dean or other faculty members. The faculty member with university orientation tended to discuss problems with the dean and other university administrators at the vice-presidential or presidential level, and saw his opinions as sought by deans and other administrators. As a group, these faculty members valued undergraduate instruction, applied research, and service to business and industry much more than did faculty with disciplinary orientations. They were more likely to be involved in service roles and be influential in national organizations. They produced more B.A. and M.A. degrees than did their colleagues. This group can be viewed as implementing the teaching and service responsibilities of the university and as less dependent on the department than their colleagues. This group may be the most influential link between central administration and department faculty. Yet some members of this group in departments which have recently developed a research orientation may be threatened thereby and may, in fact, be much less influential than they think.

PUBLIC VERSUS PRIVATE SUPPORT

Although the literature is filled with commentary about differences between public and private universities, little systematic investigation has ever demonstrated that faculty behaved differently in one as opposed to another. Perhaps the one exception to this rule is the Lazarsfeld and Thielens volume, *The Academic Mind*.[3] One of their most interesting findings was that social scientists in private universities felt better protected by administrators against Mc-

[3] Paul F. Lazarsfeld and Wagner Thielens, Jr. *The Academic Mind* (Glencoe, Ill.: Free Press, 1958).

Carthy-type incursions of academic freedom than their counterparts in public-supported schools. The explanation for this seems to be the political legislatures' control over funds and the susceptibility of state universities to public pressure.[4]

Aside from this unique research, departmental operations in the two types of schools remain open to much speculation. By dividing our data between public and private universities, we were able to ascertain a number of consistencies which clearly delimit the two types of schools. Our sampling procedures caused us some initial concern because we feared that the departments mentioned favorably in the Cartter report might tend to fall into either the public or the private domain. However, analysis of this problem showed that the Cartter report was independent of both the private and public schools we studied.

When the faculty were asked to report what determined departmental autonomy in their respective universities, we found little difference between the public and private schools. However, one dimension, university policy, was definitely more pronounced as a determinant of departmental autonomy in public schools. There was little difference for the other dimensions. Because university policy was more important in public schools, we immediately assumed that the influence of the university administration and all-university committees would also be greater in public schools; however, we did not find any differences between the amount of influence exerted by university levels or even the dean over departmental functioning. The differences we did find in influence over departmental affairs were all located within the confines of the department. For example, faculty in the public university departments felt that they personally had less influence over departmental affairs, and the faculty as a whole had relatively less influence than their counterparts in the private universities. In contrast, the faculty in public universities reported that others within the department, such as the chairman and graduate students, exerted relatively high influence when compared to the faculty in private universities. Exactly why faculty in public universities should perceive themselves and their peers as ex-

[4] Ibid., pp. 180–187.

erting relatively little influence is difficult to ascertain from the data we have. Perhaps one clue can be found in the difference between the faculties of the two types of schools in the amount of communication in which they engaged. As a general rule, faculty in public universities reported much less communication than those in private schools. The differences between the two types of schools were most noticeable when the faculty were asked to report the amount of communication to their respective chairmen, deans, and university administration. However, even in such areas as communication to other faculty within the department, graduate students, special faculty committees, and chairmen and faculty outside the department, we found a consistent, if statistically nonsignificant, difference between the two types of schools.

Faculty in public universities reported the existence of cliques in approximately equal frequencies to those in private universities; but the extent of disagreement among cliques within departments was much greater within public schools. The disagreements may be greater in public schools because there is a greater tendency for faculty to use the department as a reference group than in the private universities. In the latter, the university or the discipline is the reference group for faculty, and perhaps the direction the department takes is slightly less meaningful and, consequently, less worthy of conflict and social disruption.

We assumed that departmental missions would be quite different in the public and private universities, but our data did not support this idea. The major missions—undergraduate instruction, graduate instruction, and basic research—were all the same. When we examined responses to our questions about what the department *should* emphasize, here again there was no difference between the public and private schools. In fact, the only difference we found was the emphasis which was placed upon advancing the discipline nationally: faculty in public schools tended to feel that their department emphasized this goal more than faculty in private schools.

We have mentioned that the faculty in public universities felt relatively less influential than their counterparts in private schools; and that the chairmen and graduate students were perceived as possessing greater influence in the public schools. When we examined how decisions were actually made concerning such matters as promotion, salary, and leaves of absence, we found no difference between public and private schools. In fact, the only difference reported was in the area of decisions concerning promotions: faculty in public schools said that the chairman was likely to decide this matter, whereas those in private schools reported that a vote of the tenured faculty was required.

In response to our question about where faculty would go for special consideration of specific matters, we found that promotion, salary, and leaves of absence were more in the domain of the chairman in public schools than in the private. On all other matters we asked questions about, such as travel or obtaining funds for graduate assistants, there was little difference between public and private universities.

The conclusion we must reach, then, from analysis of the data, is that few important differences exist between the public and private universities. Faculty in the former do consider themselves less influential than those in the latter, and they perceive less communication with various points within the total structure; but in terms of how the department is actually run or the emphasis that the department places upon different goals, the two sources of support for universities do not affect operations. Certainly, these conclusions run contrary to some of our most cherished myths.

In summary, perhaps the most striking differences in conception of a department are found in the critical relationship between the dean and the department chairman. If the departments belong to a professional college where the distinctions between disciplines are not clear and the college is dedicated to a relatively unspecialized degree, the dean may exercise much more authority than where he has to deal with widely divergent disciplines. The national tendency for large universities to split traditional arts and sciences colleges into small, more homogeneous administrative units —although based partly on size—tends to bear this conclusion out. The dean is more aware than faculty or chairmen of what the image of a department might be nationally. He must translate departmental aspirations into operational procedures of a university within limited funds. Many times seeming inconsistencies in department organization and/or operation within a college were explained by a dean reporting on how he was able to justify departmental aspirations and support the department within existing university patterns.

A fairly clear picture has emerged of several different kinds of departments in several different kinds of institutions. Some institutions are committed to providing graduate education and supporting necessary research. Other institutions try to preserve the integrity of the undergraduate program and encourage close relationships between the academic faculty and the student body. Departmental priorities tend to reflect these institutional commitments.

The picture that emerges across disciplines is also pertinent. Variables associated with the discipline are those dealing with the traditional role of faculty instruction, research, and service. Research and service are defined differently, depending upon discipline, but departmental attitudes toward pure and applied research and toward service are strongly influenced by prevalent disciplinary attitudes on a national basis.

One major dimension in a department is its orientation to its university and its discipline. Certain functions and activities follow university policy. It is not appropriate to ask: How do chemistry departments across the country function, and how much emphasis do they place on undergraduate advising? These are university matters, and it is more appropriate to ask: How do other departments at this university function and advise undergraduates? Likewise, a university policy for all disciplines on research emphasis or service to business and industry is inappropriate.

A department should relate its desires for a high rating on a national study of graduate programs and faculty to its own goals and concerns and to university commitments. If departmental interests are basically related to concerns for undergraduate instruction and advising, it should ignore ratings which value basic research and graduate instruction. If the university encourages graduate education, research, and national prestige in a department, then decreased attention to undergraduate education must be expected. Each department should evaluate its own interest in serving instructional needs, university demands and operational needs, the discipline, applied research, and service to society. The evaluation depends in large measure on whether the department views itself as representing a discipline or as an agency for forwarding university goals.

4

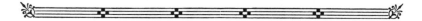

Internal Structure and Perceptions

Even within a single university, great variations exist among departments in conduct of their affairs because faculty members accept various missions and assign to each different priorities. The nature of their tasks vary (men who work in laboratories are obviously not quite like those who write poetry or novels). Faculty members are influenced by different policies set by their chairmen or committees.

Not only do departments vary in their missions, but individuals within these departments also have specific objectives which do not necessarily coincide with those of the department, or of the university. Faculty objectives may, in fact, be highly personal and even unrelated to the discipline. Confusion is added to this picture by the fact that there is little agreement as to what the missions *should* be for different units. Even apparent agreement is misleading because of different specification of appropriate means. Thus universities work at cross purposes to disciplines, departments, and individuals, with agreements and conflicts in objectives obscured rather than clarified by the fact that all use the same abstract and ambiguous terminology. Everyone agrees to a concern for high-quality undergraduate education, but interpretations are readily adjusted to encompass other goals. Some professors even argue that departmental or university objectives exist only as vague composites of individual faculty objectives. In the extreme, this means that, in the name of academic freedom, each faculty member must be permitted to do his own thing.

When faculty members, department chairmen, and deans indicated on a five-point scale the emphasis they felt the department placed on ten different goals, the following rank order resulted:

1. instruction of graduate students
2. basic research
3. undergraduate instruction
4. advancing the discipline and profession nationally
5. advising undergraduate majors
6. instruction of undergraduate nonmajors
7. expressing departmental views in the university
8. career development of the junior staff
9. applied research
10. service to business and industry

Since respondents rated each mission on a five-point scale, it was theoretically possible to rate all the ten equally high (or low). However, such rating was generally not the case; departments which ranked undergraduate instruction high, tended to rank basic research relatively low. Those departments where undergraduate instruction ranked high also believed that it *should* be so, and did not regard basic research as a major departmental mission. When faculty members were asked to indicate which three of the ten goals the department *should* emphasize, the initial three missions again were chosen most frequently.

Disciplines varied greatly in priorities of goals. English and history ranked undergraduate instruction higher than did mathematics and psychology. Chemistry and mathematics ranked basic research high, whereas management and English ranked it relatively lower. Graduate instruction was given high emphasis by psychology and chemistry, but relatively little by management and history. The overall lowest-ranked item, service to business and industry, was ranked higher by management and electrical engineering than by English and history. These findings are not surprising, but they do demonstrate empirically the conflicting priorities which appear in the modern university. Each discipline pulls in its own direction and compromises have to be made while overall policy issues remain unresolved.

Graduate Instruction. Although graduate instruction ranked above all the other missions in priority, it did not correlate with emphasis upon either basic research or undergraduate instruction. We would have predicted that those emphasizing graduate instruction would also emphasize basic research as an essential and closely related mission. Similarly, we would have expected a correlation between graduate and undergraduate instruction because of a general concern for teaching and the development of educated persons. Neither of these expectancies materialized in the data.

The correlates of emphasis on graduate education revealed no consistent pattern. As expected, departments emphasizing graduate education reported that influence of graduate students was relatively high, and communication to them was also. No other groups were depicted as involved in departmental affairs. The chairman was not viewed as important in any manner whatsoever and was not sought for any special considerations, nor was he depicted as making decisions which affect departmental affairs. No other group of faculty emerged as important in handling decisions that must be made. In fact, no clear picture emerged of the manner in which anything gets done in departments that emphasize graduate instruction. Indeed, there is little indication that anything really does get done in these departments: there is no correlation between the emphasis upon graduate instruction and the production of B.A.'s, graduate students, publications, or service to the university on committees.

This anomalous role of graduate instruction justifies focus upon undergraduate instruction and basic research as indicative of two distinctive patterns which faculty members or departments may select for their overall goals. Departments emphasizing one of these missions differed markedly from those emphasizing the other. They definitely exhibited different patterns of production. For example, for our gross measures of publication activity there was a small but negative correlation with attention to undergraduate instruction, whereas a positive correlation was found between publication activity and emphasis upon basic research. The ratio of advanced degrees given in 1967 to the number of B.A.'s given in 1967 yielded a significant negative relationship with emphasis upon undergraduate instruction, and a positive one with the basic research emphasis. Data for 1957 yielded the same results. These relationships exhibit consistency, but hardly suggest cause-effect in either direction.

Undergraduate Instruction and Basic Research. Departments emphasizing undergraduate instruction exhibited a relatively greater dependency on the university. For example, the positive correlation of the percentage of all funds spent for tenure track faculty in 1967 with emphasis upon undergraduate instruction and the negative correlation with emphasis on basic research apparently result from the fact that departments emphasizing basic research obtain grants and employ nontenured personnel with these funds. However, the proportion of operating funds for supplies and services from the general fund was correlated positively with emphasis on basic research but not with emphasis on undergraduate instruction, indicating that departments which obtain outside money also obtain more institutional funds.

Departments emphasizing undergraduate instruction seem to

undergo less change in personnel than those emphasizing basic research. For example, both the proportions of resignations and of new appointments in 1967 for the tenure track faculty were negatively correlated with emphasis upon undergraduate instruction. No relationships were found between resignations and appointments with emphasis on basic research. Thus there is no evidence here that the research emphasis increases mobility.

Faculty members who felt that the department placed much emphasis on basic research identified themselves with their department. Faculty members who placed emphasis on undergraduate instruction tended to identify themselves more with the university and believed the department placed a lower emphasis on basic research. In departments where the faculty as a whole placed an emphasis on basic research, few faculty members served on committees. If, however, a department placed emphasis on undergraduate instruction, the members of that department were very likely to devote time to university committees.

The internal structures of the departments which emphasized either basic research or undergraduate instruction were also different. Those emphasizing undergraduate teaching tended to use the department chairman as a means for obtaining many of their needs and wants, including tenure, travel, changing teaching assignments, introduction of new courses, and additional graduate assistants. Those emphasizing basic research approached the department chairman primarily for salary increases, leaves, and research funds. Perhaps the availability of outside resources permits greater autonomy for the investigators, and they may even look to outside sources for many of their needs rather than to the department. The undergraduate instruction orientation was also characterized by more discussion of problems with both chairmen and university administrators than was found with the basic research emphasis. Emphasis on undergraduate instruction seemed to permit or encourage a more open operation, with a good deal of personal influence vested in the department chairman, but with all-university committees also having influence.

Departments which emphasized basic research, delegated more decision-making powers to the faculty. For example, the greater the emphasis upon basic research in the department, the more likely it was that decision making would be delegated for recruitment and selection of new faculty; promotions and tenure; salary increases; teaching assignments; office and research space; awarding of assistantships, fellowships, and scholarships; and requirements for majors and graduate students.

Since faculty members in a basic research department show a tendency to avoid university involvements, one might assume they would much prefer to have a departmental chairman make decisions, but active committees (especially for awarding assistantships or determining employment for majors and for graduate students)' were reported in many departments. It was not surprising to find that in departments emphasizing basic research there was more likelihood that a vote of tenured faculty or a vote of all members of the departmental staff would be required for many decisions. It was evident that in these basic research departments the faculty was not so devoted to research as to be unwilling to participate in departmental affairs. In fact, the emphasis placed on basic research was correlated positively with the influence that faculty exerted, with the influence exerted by graduate students, and the influence of department committees. These relationships reflect the democratization of a decision-making process.

Negative correlations were found between the degree of emphasis on basic research and the amount of influence exerted by the dean and the university administration. These findings support earlier evidence that departments with this orientation are or at least see themselves as relatively independent of the central university and its functionaries. It should not be assumed that the chairman is neglected within the departments emphasizing basic research: faculty members in departments emphasizing basic research reported a tendency to consult the chairman for special consideration about salary increases, leaves of absence, and money for research. The importance of these items indicates that the chairman is not relegated to an inferior role, but rather that the research faculty has a distinctive priority of concerns.

Apparently undergraduate instruction and basic research represent two distinctive missions which go far to determine the en-

tire character of a department. Some faculty members perceived
them as nearly antithetical; certainly high priority on one meant
relatively low priority on the other. The differences in missions also
are reflected in the output: graduate degrees, basic research, and
publication, on the one hand, and baccalaureates, instruction, and
university involvement on the other. The goals or the self-defined
missions of the department are distinguishing features which determine its organization and role in the university.

Other Missions. It was mentioned earlier that emphasis on
undergraduate advising and instruction of nonmajors were positively correlated with undergraduate instruction. The only other
item which correlated positively with undergraduate instruction
emphasis was that of expressing departmental views to the college
and university. This seems to be another indication of the degree
of interaction and dependence of the instructionally oriented department in relation to the larger university system.

Although career development of younger faculty members
was found to be more a matter of university than disciplinary determination, it was also correlated with emphasis upon basic research.
Emphasis upon basic research was also highly correlated with emphasis upon advancing the discipline and the profession nationally,
whereas undergraduate education, advising, and applied research
were negatively related to emphasis upon basic research.

The two departmental missions which were ranked lowest
in priority were applied research and service to business and industry. When a department emphasized one, it also tended to emphasize the other. Both missions were negatively related both to
emphasis upon basic research and the emphasis a department should
place upon undergraduate education. The few departments with
these emphases tended to be oriented toward the university as a
reference group and to have a larger proportion of their staff promoting the department outside of the university. Deans and university committees were seen as more influential than the department chairmen. There appeared to be little delegation of decision
making from the chairman to the faculty on such matters as delegation of recruitment, promotions, salary increases, and leaves. All
were negatively related to emphasis upon applied research or serv-

ice. Apparently many of these matters are handled by the respective deans rather than by the chairmen. Discussion of departmental matters with the dean was also positively correlated with these missions, suggesting again the centralization of influence and authority. There were positive correlations between both emphasis on service and applied research and discussing matters with members of other departments. These correlations suggest that departmental structure is a less rigid and confining one in the professional college where service and applied research are emphasized.

The two disciplines which tended to give higher priorities to applied research and service were the professional departments: management and electrical engineering. However—and despite the preceding paragraph, which suggests common patterns in such departments—there appeared to be differences between the fields apparent in the interviews but not captured by the instruments used. Applied research and service to business and industry seemed less clearly differentiated in the management departments. The tendency seemed to be to regard any noninstructional venture yielding a written report (survey, consultation, or published paper) as research. In colleges of business, the degrees seemed to represent more a college product than a departmental one, even though some specialization was permitted. Even at the graduate level, the M.B.A. and D.B.A. were not departmentalized. Thus, common commitment to a joint product may explain why the dean and the college rather than the department were found to be highly influential.

The situation found in engineering was somewhat different. Chairmen generally asserted that the traditional specialties of electrical, mechanical, civil, and chemical engineering were no longer meaningful. Undergraduate degrees have become largely nonspecialized, and graduate study may involve research on a problem cutting across several of the traditional fields. In electrical engineering, much of the research was theoretical and heavily mathematical. Service to business and industry, for these persons, was viewed as productive of significant problems for research.

INTERACTIONS WITHIN THE DEPARTMENT

Three distinct aspects of interpersonal relationships within departments are salient: the reference groups of the faculty, influ-

ence exerted by chairmen and faculty, and amount of disagreement
among the staff.

Faculty members were asked to indicate how they thought
of themselves: as members of the university, of their departments,
or their disciplines. The faculty responses were well distributed over
the three groups, although only about 15 per cent indicated the
university orientation. As noted in the previous chapter, the group
oriented toward the university tended to be senior faculty members,
professors with some years of tenure at the university. Younger men
tended to orient themselves toward the discipline more than older
men.

Discipline as Reference Group. After the university, the
remaining two reference groups are the discipline and the department. In order to focus on departmental differences, departments
were ranked according to the proportion of men who chose each as
their major reference group.

We found some variations in orientation among the faculty.
For example, although there were wide variations among universities and the proportion of faculty who chose each reference group,
the variation among disciplines was even greater. Approximately 10
per cent of the mathematics faculties chose the university as a reference group, whereas 35 per cent of the business administration staff
did so. Psychology had the highest proportion of staff selecting discipline as a reference group, with approximately 55 per cent doing
so; only 30 per cent of electrical engineering faculties chose discipline. About half of the electrical engineers chose the department
as their reference group, whereas only 15 per cent of the staff of
business administration did so.

These same data can be examined in another fashion, that
is, the amount of disagreement within each discipline. Here we
found that history and chemistry seemed least agreed on their
proper orientation, whereas psychology and business administration
had the most internal agreement.

Reference groups tend to shift as a faculty member gains in
rank: the highest proportion of discipline-oriented faculty are found
among the assistant professors, and the highest proportion of university-oriented faculty are found among the full professors. Inter-

estingly, the assistant and associate professors are almost even in selecting the department as a reference group; however, the associate professors edge ahead slightly. These data suggest that there is a progression from orientation to discipline to department to university as one rises in rank. Part of the explanation for this finding can probably be found in the sources of support and friendship patterns among faculty. The young assistant professor has few friends in his new job and must seek standards of performance from his discipline; he is probably most ambitious and seeks to advance himself professionally. As he gets older he makes more friends; at first they come from the department and then from the larger university in which he works. As he publishes fewer papers than anticipated, and receives less acclaim from his discipline, he turns to others with whom he daily interacts for job-related rewards. Thus his attachment to the discipline weakens as he is pulled into the social web of the university.

Faculty with the highest discipline orientation tended to be found in departments which have both a relatively high proportion of new appointments and a relatively high proportion of resignations of tenure track faculty. The proportion of faculty members indicating that the discipline was their major reference group was correlated significantly with the proportion who reported the prestige of prospective departments as a primary reason for accepting another position. No relationship was found between "having more time to pursue my own interests" or "making more money" and the disciplinary orientation.

The orientation to the discipline was negatively correlated with the amount of emphasis that these departments placed upon undergraduate instruction, undergraduate advising, instruction of undergraduate nonmajors, expressing departmental views to the university, and furthering the careers of younger staff. There was also a negative correlation between the discipline orientation and the feeling that undergraduate instruction *should* be emphasized, but both graduate instruction and basic research were positively related.

Faculty oriented toward the discipline rated low the influence of both the department chairman and of all-university committees.

There was a negative correlation with discipline orientation and discussion or communication with faculty and chairmen outside the department, and the discipline-oriented faculty members were not attracted to committee service within the college or university. Apparently the guidelines for behavior of the discipline-oriented faculty members are based in the discipline rather than in the university.

The two areas of decisions which were consistently handled by the faculty when orientation to the discipline was strong were recruitment and promotions. The discipline-oriented faculty thereby controls the departmental character. The discipline reference group and assignment of priority to basic research are simply different ways of characterizing the same pattern.

Department as Reference Group. The rank order of departments whose faculty selected the department as their primary reference group was, necessarily, negatively correlated with the ranks for the selection of university and discipline. This finding is partly a statistical artifact because respondents chose but one of the three alternatives in answer to the question. Yet it is noteworthy that a higher negative correlation was found between department and discipline than between department and university. This suggests that departmental and university reference groups are less distinctive than department and discipline.

When the department was the reference group, the influence of the dean and university administration was perceived as relatively low; while the influences of departmental chairmen, faculty and its committees, and graduate students were perceived as relatively high. The department chairman was also seen as one capable of providing special consideration for promotions and tenure, salary increases, leaves of absence, travel expenses and money for research and scholarship. Perhaps the ability of the chairman to provide these benefits increases the importance of the department to its faculty. In those departments where the faculty was oriented within it, there was no relationship to the amount of decision-making delegation to faculty except in the one case of budgetary matters. This suggests that delegation to the staff of more responsibility (as some human-relations advocates suggest) is not an essential element in increasing orientation to the department. However, involvement in the budgetary matters would surely bring the faculty very close to the heart of departmental operations.

Faculties with a strong departmental orientation also placed great emphasis upon basic research, but there was no relationship with either graduate or undergraduate instruction. However, these same departments also indicated that they should place more emphasis upon undergraduate instruction. These departments also produced a relatively high ratio of graduate to bachelor degrees, and the departmental orientation was negatively related to the number of undergraduate degrees per faculty. Thus, these relationships might suggest that a departmental orientation was associated with a desire to change certain aspects of teaching responsibilities and research orientation. However, there was no evidence to indicate conflict or excessive tension because of disparity between what is done and what ought to be done. In fact, faculty members reporting a departmental orientation also reported a relatively low degree of disagreement within the staff. Partially in support of this perception is the fact that the proportion of resignations among the tenure track professors was relatively low in 1967. One might speculate that these departmentally oriented faculties are relatively comfortable in their surroundings but are troubled by tendencies toward increased research and graduate study, which constitute something of a threat to the existing pattern.

Influence of Department Chairman. The position and the influence of the department chairman varied greatly throughout the departments and universities. In some, the department chairman, sometimes called a head, controlled virtually all aspects of departmental affairs. He made the departmental budget, assigned teaching loads, recruited and hired, promoted and rewarded or disciplined individuals with little or no consultation. At the other extreme, the chairman was little more than a coordinator who was expected to garner resources from the dean to carry out the decisions of the faculty. In between were the vast majority of chairmen who worked within a set of policies or bylaws and operated through or with faculty committees. These are the chairmen who are besieged by both the dean and faculty to represent and reconcile the often divergent interests. As such, they are like foremen, men in the middle, who are besieged by both management and workers to represent and promote the divergent interests of both parties. To be successful they must win and maintain the confidence of both groups by compromise or by less straightforward means which threaten their own integrity.

The position of department chairman in many universities today is regarded more as an obligation and duty to be assumed for a period, even at personal sacrifice, rather than as an honor and position of influence. Yet we found relatively few chairmen of this type in our sample. There were many more examples of scholars selected—even imported—to develop the department and move it into national stature based on research and graduate programs. Undoubtedly, this reflects the developmental character of many of the universities in our sample. It was evident that the increasing size of departmental staff, diversity in faculty interests, and the difficulties of recruiting qualified students have made the job of the department chairman more a burden of administrative detail than one in which imagination and originality can prevail. It is not that department chairmen are always constrained by the university systems in which they work (although this is often the case), but rather that the staggering amount of routine activities required and the diverse expectations of the dean on the one hand and the faculty on the other greatly limit the chairman's authority and deprive him of satisfaction in his work. Meanwhile, his scholarly career, which was partly responsible for bringing him the assignment, is seriously jeopardized.

Our interviews with the chairmen and faculty indicated that a scholar is not expected to seek or enjoy the position of chairman. Those who do apparently enjoy it and maintain the assignment for a long time may be suspected of leaving the community of scholars and seeking the shelter of an administrative post in which routine duties justify cessation of scholarly activity. Some departments, in order to make the transition between faculty member and chairman easier, have developed the practice of rotating chairmanship. All senior professors (even associate professors in some cases) are expected to participate, thus leading to an oligarchic or committee pattern of administration. Another aid for department chairmen that we noted frequently was the appointment of an assistant chairman, often a minor scholar or nonscholar chosen from within the department to absorb some of the heavy administrative routine.

Whatever the particular configuration of administrative influence emanating from the department chairman's office, the position still possesses some connotations of prestige and power. For example, when faculty were asked to whom they would go for special consideration of eight problems which they might confront, the department chairman was overwhelmingly chosen. All eight problems which a faculty member might face were positively correlated with the perceived influence of the department chairman and six were statistically significant. From such important matters as promotion or tenure action to more mundane considerations such as a change in teaching assignments or acquiring of office space, all were considered as under the jurisdiction of the department chairman. Despite departmental variations based on priorities and faculty orientation, faculty members still seek the chairman's advice and influence on matters that trouble them.

Some other findings about the chairman are of interest, although they cloud as much as clarify the total picture. Faculty reported that undergraduate instruction *should* be emphasized when department chairmen were considered influential. An influential department chairman and the college policy were both perceived of as a contribution to departmental autonomy. Departmental prestige in the scholarly community and enterprise in obtaining outside fundings were not seen as determinants of departmental autonomy. Our data also indicated that departments where the chairman was perceived as most influential were not oriented to the disciplines. Thus a negative correlation was found between the influence of the department chairman and the proportion of faculty who chose the discipline as their primary focus of identity.

University orientation in those departments where the chairman was influential can be inferred from other findings. For example, in departments where the chairman was influential, faculty gave a high priority to teaching undergraduate nonmajors and to career development of junior staff.

Less influential chairmen were found in departments that

delegated decision making, had productive faculty, and promoted the department nationally (for example, serving on journals as editors or consulting government or industry). From these findings we would conclude that the most influential chairmen are found in departments where faculty are relatively inactive.

This section on the influence of department chairmen is ambiguous, and the data are not easily explained. It supports an assertion we made earlier that the position of the department chairman is vague, often misunderstood, and not clearly perceived. Certainly, we found no marked positive relationships between the so-called strong chairman and certain faculty productivity variables, such as publications, graduate or undergraduate students, or the promotion of the department within the discipline and/or university. Yet other evidence accruing from observations and interviews suggests that the chairman's influence is often the key factor in determining the quality of a department.

Influence of Department Faculty. In the departments studied, faculty involvement in department or university matters was established primarily in two ways (or a combination of them). In some, the entire faculty raised issues, discussed them thoroughly, voted on what should be done, and then outlined the tasks for a subgroup to carry out. Other departments depended on committees to do the work or to develop policies for the approval of the faculty. Committees were organized around other subdisciplinary interest groups or administrative functions. For example, in some chemistry departments special committees were formed around organic and inorganic chemistry; in psychology interest groups had developed around clinical and experimental specialties. Committees on curriculum, admissions, tenure, and promotions, which are basically administrative functions, represented another pattern of organization, alternative or supplemental to the interest groupings. In some departments, a single administrative, executive, or advisory committee assisted the chairman on almost every phase of departmental operations.

A number of correlates of faculty influence in a department help to characterize the situation. Faculty influence was positively correlated with the influence exerted by special department committees and by graduate students. There was some indication that faculty influence was partially a function of communication, not only with the chairman, but also to department committees and to other faculty within the department. Graduate students were not left out of these communication networks because significant positive relationship was found between an influential faculty and discussion of departmental matters with graduate students. These communications may help to bring faculty members into a greater identification with the department.

In the faculty perceptions, the department chairman's influence, the dean's influence, and the university administration influence over departmental affairs were all negatively correlated with the influence of the faculty. Undergraduate instruction and basic research were correlated equally with faculty influence, but departments in which the faculty as a whole was influential also gave high priority to basic research. Departments in which faculty exerted relatively high influence received a relatively high level of support, as measured by operating funds for clerical help and supplies from the university. They tended to have a relatively high proportion of tenure track professors, but the rate of adding new professors was relatively low, perhaps because of increasing use of graduate assistants. Thus it may be that tenure track members of the faculty perceive themselves as being more influential over departmental affairs because there emerges a large and visible group of persons who are of lower status. Whatever the case may be, it is clear that those faculties perceiving themselves as relatively influential also believed that dcision making about recruitment practices, promotions, and awards of assistantships to graduate students should be made by the staff. Thus departments where faculty considered themselves influential saw themselves as controlling their own fates as well as the students within a department. It is noteworthy that administrative matters (for example, budget, travel, leaves, and the like) were not related to faculty perceptions of their own influence.

Influence of Graduate Students. In the past few years students have demanded increased influence in university and departmental affairs. Although much of this pressure has come from the undergraduates, graduate students have also raised their voices.

We asked our respondents to indicate how much influence graduate students have over departmental affairs, and then we examined their answers in terms of the correlates of influence. In departments where graduate student influence was perceived as high (by faculty), communication with students about departmental affairs was also perceived as high. These departments also tended to emphasize graduate student education and basic research, and to give reduced priority to undergraduate instruction. Although one might also expect a disciplinary orientation, this was not the case; there was no relationship between graduate student influence and the reference groups of the faculty. In those departments where faculty are secure and relatively stable, students can be influential without disruption of the department or their own education. For example, the influence of graduate students was positively related to our productivity (or publication)' index and also to the proportion of full professors in the department. The faculty members had received sufficient recognition and stature so that they were not threatened by student demands. Another indication of the stability of the departments with relatively high graduate student influence was found in the lack of disagreement: there was a negative relationship between graduate student influence and perceived disagreement in the department.

Department chairmen also seemed to play a greater role in those departments where graduate student influence was relatively high, as indicated by a positive correlation between graduate student influence and department chairman influence. A positive correlation also was found between high graduate student influence and going to the chairman to discuss personal concerns or departmental matters. Thus student influence seems to fit into rather than disrupt established channels. One reason for this may be that the faculty also feel influential, as indicated by a positive correlation between graduate student influence and perceived faculty influence. However, there was little relationship between student influence and the influence of the dean or the university administration. To summarize, the departments with high graduate student influence are characterized by stability and high mutual influence among faculty and chairmen; they are relatively self-contained governing units.

Communication. Our questionnaire asked respondents to indicate the amount of communication they held with different persons about departmental affairs. The responses indicated that most communication took place within departments, and then across departmental lines to peers, and finally to university administrators. The different kinds of communicattion were ranked as follows:

Communication with:
1. Faculty in own department
2. Chairman of own department
3. Chairmen of special committees
4. Graduate students
5. Faculty of other departments
6. Dean of school or college
7. Chairmen of other departments or institutes
8. University administrators

The pattern of correlations among the communication variables is unlike those for other variables. For example, we found that departments emphasizing basic research were not likely to emphasize undergraduate instruction. One emphasis denied or negated the other. But the communication variables are not so structured. A number of relationships indicated that departments discussing their affairs with one group were also likely to do so with others. Thus we found that those department members discussing matters with the departmental chairmen were also likely to do so with their faculty associates, with the dean, and with the graduate students. Even the lowest-ranked item, university administrators, was positively related to discussion of departmental affairs with chairmen. Communication with faculty was not highly related with as many other positions as with chairman, so peer interaction does not have the same significance as communication with chairmen. One must conclude, then, that those departments which communicate effectively with their chairmen also can do so with other units and persons in the university structure. This conclusion suggests that if one wanted to improve overall communication within the university, it could be

done by encouraging the use of the chairman as an initial clear-
inghouse.

Departments with relatively high communication with chairmen also tended to have faculties which felt a sense of influence
over departmental affairs. There were significant correlations between communication with chairmen and the personal influence
perceived by faculty. Interestingly, communication to chairmen was
not related to the influence of chairmen. In fact, there was some
indication that decision making was more widely distributed when
communication to chairmen was relatively high. A high level of
communication with the chairman apparently results in his role being that of acting for the group rather than for himself.

A somewhat different set of relationships emerges from relatively higher level of communication with the dean. The approach
to the department chairman for special consideration in such matters as promotion, tenure, or salary increments is negatively related
to discussing departmental matters with the dean. Thus, it would
appear that deans who utilize the open door policy in some ways
undermine the authority of departmental chairmen. This observation is supported by the negative correlations found between the
influence of departmental chairmen and the amount of communication with deans.

Curiously but consistently, the influence of faculty members
was positively related to communication with the dean. Perhaps
direct contact with the dean, bypassing the chairman, provides a
feeling of exerting influence, but it is also true that when communication with deans was high, there was a tendency toward communication with faculty of other departments, with chairmen of one's
own and other departments, and with university administrators.
The possibility of contact with the dean seemed to enhance the
range of contacts outside the department. However, prestige in the
field as measured by recognition in the Cartter report or by the
publication record is not in any way related to communications with
deans.

In departments characterized by a relatively high pattern of
intradepartmental communication there were very few clear-cut relationships which would help in understanding the significance of

these peer interactions. However, faculty members did perceive greater faculty influence in departmental affairs and a delegation to the faculty of decision making about most important matters.

Disagreement. We had assumed that the more disagreement among the staff, the greater the influence of administrators or the greater the discrepancy over goals. However, neither of the speculations proved true. None of the basic data gathered from records were related to the amount of disagreement. This result would suggest that, although faculty might believe that disagreement affects their behavior, it has no measurable effect upon their performance. Within these departments, disagreements did not seem to cause sufficient tensions or problems to have any great consequences and require special attention. This finding does not completely square with observations and interviews, which would suggest that disagreements are, at times, destructive of morale and of productivity. The resolution appears to lie in the fact that minor disagreements are common and taken in stride, and that serious ones occur infrequently.

It is not easy to summarize this discussion of departmental self-perceptions. Part of the difficulty lies in the impact of the university on the department. Also, differences in the stage of development of departments and in their position in the university obscure possible relationships. A department located in three colleges, spread widely over the campus, and with a chairman reporting directly to a vice-president will not operate in the same manner in respect to communication or decision making as another department of the same size and same discipline housed in a single building and reporting to a single dean. Departments in colleges of business are typically less structured and have less autonomy than departments in the arts and sciences.

The various relationships examined are weak or modest even though statistically significant. Departmental organization and patterns of communication did not turn out to be nearly as important as we had anticipated. The reference group—university, department, or discipline—seems to provide the most meaningful approach to the understanding of departmental differences and at the same time effectively relates these to the university. The fact that in a department the faculty members may be spread over these three orientations means that no department is necessarily typical of the ideal, but the spread may indicate the transitional nature of the department or suggest the existent unresolved problems with regard to departmental priorities.

Faculty Reactions
and Concerns

In the preceding chapters we viewed departments globally, that is, in terms of the social processes which seemed to characterize their several operations. However, individual faculty, chairmen, and deans often impose their personality characteristics upon departments, thereby giving a relatively unique flavor to each unit. In this chapter,[1] we focus upon some faculty perceptions and show how they

[1] Donald J. Reichard made the major contribution to this chapter.

91

are related to departmental processes and even university relationships. First, we discuss problems and their resolution as faculty report them; then we analyze the intricate problem of departmental autonomy from the staff's perspective.

In a study including departments from several disciplines operating within the disparate frameworks of some fifteen universities, great diversity in departmental problems and in faculty views about them is to be expected. Therefore, in order to allow as much freedom as possible in the statement of problems, we included two open-ended questions in the faculty questionnaire.

NATURE OF PROBLEMS

We asked first: "What are the two or three major problems or issues which you see in the operation of your department? Are these generated by internal or by external factors? How might these be resolved?" Responses to the question were categorized in regard to the nature or type, the source, and the resolution of each problem stated. The nature or types of problems fell into ten general categories: (1) Inadequate facilities—lack of or poor quality of libraries, laboratories, equipment, or space. (2) Need for improved faculty (quality)—the need for upgrading the caliber of persons within the department, elimination of deadwood or narrow provincialism. (3) Need for more faculty (quantity)—evidenced by references to the existence of large classes, or to lack of time because of heavy teaching loads. (4) Lack of funds—this category included the need for additional state, federal, or foundation support, as well as the need for outside research funds or auxiliary research (clerical or technical) support. (5) Need for better salaries for faculty (not graduate assistants). (6) Interference or influence from sources outside of department but within the university—this category included problems ranging from too much administrative control to lack of administrative leadership, as well as problems concerning promotion standards or policy questions set by the college or university. (7) Operational deficiencies—this category included problems such as favoritism, inadequate communication, lack of social cohesion, weak leadership, or lack of agreement upon departmental goals. (8) Need for improved graduate or undergraduate programs—this category included the need for higher graduate assistant stipends, as well as the need for more graduate assistants with greater competence. (9) Other. (10) No response.

Categories for classifying problems in regard to source or cause included (1) internal (controllable by the department), (2) external (not controllable by the department), (3) both, (4) uncertain or do not know, and (5) no response. Departmental deficiencies are internal to the department but may originate from outside. Thus weak leadership may be imposed by external selection of the chairman. Each problem was also categorized in regard to the resolution offered. The categories for the resolution of a problem were basically the same as the categories for classifying the nature or type of a problem, for the resolution was often implied in the statement of the problem. Thus, if an individual responded to our question with "Need more space—build a new building," the problem was classified in regard to nature or type as "inadequate facilities," in regard to source as "external" (to the department), and in regard to resolution of the problem as assignment of more "facilities." If, however, the individual stated the problem as "Need more space—resolution money," the nature of the problem was classified as "more money." This distinction seems to reflect a faculty differentiation between priorities in assignment of funds and lack of funds.

Some problems were unique and therefore difficult to classify. The University of Southern California faculty member who noted that little communication existed among faculty members within his department because the smog caused the exodus of most faculty by early afternoon indicated a problem which was classified in regard to nature as lack of communication. In regard to source, the problem was classified as "external," and after some hesitation the resolution to the problem was classified as "other."

Because the responses were at times quite complex, determination of the number of problems stated was difficult. Largely because one rater might recognize a larger number of problems in an individual's response than would another rater, the inter-rater reliability for classification of problems as to nature or type was moderate (.72). The inter-rater reliability for classification of problems in regard to source was somewhat higher (.84). Terse responses—often a simple listing of problems—provided no indication as to source or resolution of the problem, although the resolution of the problem was often inherent in the problem statement. Thus, when an individual mentioned the lack of outside research funds, the inference of "more funds" seemed obvious as a resolution to the problem. Disagreement as to when this inference was appropriate accounted for the relatively low inter-rater reliability (.69 for classification of problems) in regard to their proposed resolutions. All intra-rater or inter-rater reliability calculations were based upon a random sampling of the responses offered by 5 per cent of our subjects.

Responses. Table 5 indicates that 2,320 problems were noted by 1,121 (84 per cent) of the respondents, an average of 2.07 problems per respondent. The remaining 212 (16 per cent) faculty members did not answer this particular question. Approximately 2 per cent of the respondents indicated that no problems existed within their department. Operational problems accounted for more than one fourth of all problems noted, and the need for improved graduate or undergraduate programs, the need for less interference from external sources, and the need for more funds each accounted for more than 10 per cent of all problems noted.

The source of the problem in the majority of cases (51.5 per cent) was classified as external to or beyond the control of the department, whereas for 43.0 per cent of the problems noted, the source of the problem was within the internal control of the department. Respondents were more inclined to recognize the existence of problems than the resolution of them. Thus the 1,121 individuals who noted 2,320 problems (2.07 problems per person) noted only 1,969 problem resolutions (1.76 resolutions per person). Table 6 indicates the resolutions to problems suggested by respondents.

The improvement of internal operations within a department, the supplying of more money, and lessening of influences from forces external to the department are listed far more frequently as resolutions to problems than any other factors; of these, improve-

Table 5.
Nature of Problems

Nature of Problem	Rank	Number of Times Problem Indicated	Percentage of Total Indicated Problems	Percentage of Individuals Indicating Problem One or More Times
Operational	1	639	27.5	39.3
Need Improved Grad or Undergrad Programs	2	396	17.1	26.0
External Influence	3	301	13.0	20.9
Need More Funds	4	284	12.2	21.0
Need Improved Faculty	5	214	9.2	14.8
Need Facilities	6	174	7.5	12.9
Need More Faculty	7	172	7.4	12.5
Need Better Faculty Salaries	8	93	4.0	7.0
Other	9	47	2.0	3.4

Table 6.

RESOLUTION OF PROBLEMS

Resolution	Rank	Number of Times Indicated	Percentage of Individuals Indicating Resolution	Percentage of Total Resolutions Indicated	Percentage of Total Problems Indicated
Better Internal Operations	1	656	37.7	33.3	27.5
More Money	2	488	24.9	24.8	12.2
Less External Influence	3	438	26.6	22.2	13.0
No Response	4	317	16.1	—	—
Improve Faculty	5	116	7.9	5.9	9.2
Improve Grad or Undergrad Program	6	78	5.4	4.0	17.1
Other	7	70	5.0	3.6	2.0
Improve Facilities	8	57	4.2	2.9	7.5
More Faculty	9	50	3.8	2.9	7.4
Improve Salaries	10	16	1.1	0.9	7.5

ment of internal operations is by far the most frequently suggested resolution.

Analysis of data.   Table 7 indicates the twenty variables based on other responses in the Faculty Questionnaire or other available data by which the open-ended-question responses were analyzed.[2] The chi square technique was used as an aid in pointing out characteristics or factors in institutions or departments which might influence faculty responses as to the existence of a problem, its source, or resolution. The twenty control variables were each associated with twenty-three dependent variables—nine categories of problems, five source classifications, and nine modes of resolution. The detailed results are not provided here, but Table 7 does indicate the total number of significant findings at each significant level for each variable.

The greatest number of differences occurred in relation to whether or not the graduate program of a department or its graduate faculty was rated in the Cartter report. Responses also differed significantly, particularly in regard to the respondent's discipline, to his reference group, and to whether the respondent saw his department to be affected by a department chairman, university administration, or departmental faculty of high, medium, or low influence. We were most concerned with the patterns of differential response, regardless of whether or not the findings were "significant."

Faculty members in private institutions were more inclined than faculty members in public institutions to report problems in regard to facilities or space, the improvement of the quality of instruction at the graduate or undergraduate level, and interference from sources external to the department but within the institution. On the other hand, faculty in private institutions were less inclined to cite the need for adding more faculty to the department. The source of problems was seen as external to or outside of the control of the department more often in private than public institutions.

Certain problems had greater relevance to faculty in particular disciplines. The chemistry departments in our sample tended

[2] A more detailed explanation of how variables were constructed from data in the Faculty Questionnaire is available in Chapters Three and Four and in the appendices.

Table 7.

NUMBER OF STATISTICALLY SIGNIFICANT RELATIONS BETWEEN
FACULTY INDICATIONS OF NATURE, SOURCE, AND RESOLUTION
OF PROBLEMS AND OTHER VARIABLES

	Level of Significance			
Variable	*.05*	*.01*	*.001*	*Total*
Public or Private Status of University	3	1	2	6
Discipline	1	4	5	10
Size of Faculty	3	2	1	6
Cartter Ratings of Graduate Program	5	1	5	11
Cartter Ratings of Graduate Faculty	1	3	4	8
Faculty Rank	1	0	1	2
Years in Department	1	0	1	2
Joint Appointment Status	1	0	1	2
Autonomy of Department	4	0	1	5
Influence of University Administration	2	1	2	5
Influence of Dean	4	1	2	7
Influence of Department Head	5	1	2	8
Influence of Department Faculty	0	3	6	9
Influence of Individual Faculty Members	3	1	5	9
Reference Group—University	1	1	2	4
Reference Group—Department	2	7	3	12
Reference Group—Discipline	3	3	2	8
Emphasis on Basic Research	0	3	1	4
Emphasis on Graduate Study	3	3	1	7
Emphasis on Undergraduate Instruction	1	2	1	4
Totals	44	37	48	129

to be rated favorably in the Cartter report in regard to the effectiveness of graduate programs, and graduate faculty more often than were departments in other disciplines. Faculty members in chemistry departments placed a high emphasis upon basic research and tended to mention the need for facilities, more funds, and concerns relating to their department's academic programs more frequently than did faculty members in other disciplines. Chemistry faculties tended to regard the department rather than their university or discipline as their reference group, perhaps because a higher percentage of chemistry faculty members had been in their departments for fifteen years or longer than was true with faculty in other disciplines. Chemistry professors were less likely than faculty from other disciplines to note the existence of internal problems within their department or to cite the lessening of internal conflict as a key step in the resolution of departmental problems. Across all disciplines, chemistry departments were probably the most democratic with the personal influence of each faculty member and the influence of the departmental faculty as a whole. Chemistry faculties tended to note more diverse solutions to departmental problems and also tended to cite, as did engineering faculties, the obtaining of more funds, presumably for research, as aiding in the resolution of their department's problems.

History departments in our sample were rated in the Cartter report less often than departments from the other disciplines represented in our study. Their faculties tended to regard the university as their reference group, whereas their departments were characterized by a low degree of autonomy and a relatively high percentage of problems relating to internal operations.

The English departments in our study presented the clearest profile. They tended to be of large size (31–81 members) more often than departments from other disciplines; they failed to express a strong commitment to either the university or department as a reference group; and they were definitely not oriented to their discipline as a reference group. These departments tended to have influential department chairmen, and they placed relatively less emphasis upon graduate study or basic research than most other disciplines. Individual faculty members and the faculty as a whole were viewed by the faculty as having little personal influence in their departments. These departments were characterized by a low degree of autonomy as viewed by the faculties, yet the English faculties presented a reasonably compliant image in failing to report, relative to other disciplines, problems of great concern. Indeed, the only manner in which the responses of English faculty diverged from faculty in other disciplines was that the needs for improved facilities, increased departmental funding, and more faculty were less commonly mentioned.

Psychology departments, like chemistry departments, presented an aggressive image. Psychology faculties expressed extremely strong commitments to their discipline as a reference point, as well as great emphasis upon basic research and graduate study. Very few faculty members saw the university as a reference group. Problems of an operational nature apparently plagued psychology departments, whereas the incidence of operational problems or discord was remarkably low in chemistry departments, where the reference group was primarily the department rather than the discipline or the university. The incidence of joint appointments was relatively high in psychology and engineering departments. However, as a general rule, faculty with joint appointments tended to cite problems of an internal nature significantly less often than faculty without joint appointments. Faculty in the departments of psychology noted the need for improved facilities relatively often but cited the need for lessening external administrative interference relatively infrequently. The improvement of facilities and the diminishing of internal problems were regarded as the most crucial factors in resolving these departments' problems.

A third department, generally of relatively large size, was mathematics. A low commitment to the university as a reference group was apparent, but a strong emphasis was placed upon basic research. Mathematics faculties saw their departments as characterized by a low degree of autonomy, but at the same time, the influence of the university administration and the deans of the colleges within which these departments operated was regarded as slight.

Mathematicians stressed the need for a higher-caliber faculty and the need for improving the department's instructional programs, as well as the quality of graduate students. The relatively high percentage of faculty members in mathematics departments who failed to indicate the source of stated problems suggests relative unconcern for and perhaps relatively little knowledge of university operations. The need for expensive laboratory facilities or extensive research support was shown not to be as great in mathematics as in the natural sciences. The mathematics departments' relative noncompetitiveness for what may be the prime determinants of autonomy— facilities and large-scale research support—may account for their relative lack of autonomy as well as the lack of external administrative influence in departmental operations.

Electrical engineering faculties gave their primary allegiance to their department rather than their university or discipline. A larger than average percentage of engineering departments in our study were rated favorably by the Cartter report in regard to the quality of graduate faculty. Joint appointments were more common in engineering than in other disciplines. These departments were found to be more heavily represented in public rather than private institutions and generally possessed a good deal of autonomy. The source of problems noted by these faculty was regarded as internal or under the control of the department less often than was the case with other disciplines. As prime competitors for funds, the engineering faculty regarded the obtaining of additional funds as beneficial to the resolution of departmental problems.

The management departments in our study were small in size and several were well rated in the Cartter report in regard to the effectiveness of their graduate programs. Respondents professed a high degree of departmental autonomy within the context of strong external influence by the university administration and the dean of the college and a weak department chairman. Individual faculty members generally felt that they had a high degree of personal influence, although, strangely enough, the influence of the departmental faculty as a whole was perceived as low. The university served as the primary reference group, but great emphasis was placed upon graduate study. Management department faculty cited particularly often the need for reducing interference from sources outside of the department but within the university.

Apart from the profiles obtained of the departments from various disciplines, differential response patterns were evident among departments of large (31–81), medium (20–30), or small (5–19) size. Most notable was the frequency with which problems of an internal nature were noted in large departments as compared to departments of moderate or small size. The larger the size of the department, the more frequently was the source of problems designated as internal and the less frequently was the improvement of the quality of faculty members cited as an aid in resolving the department's problems.

Marked contrasts were presented in the nature, source, and resolution of problems noted by individuals in departments rated favorably in the Cartter reports.[3] Faculty from departments rated highly in regard to their graduate programs responded in much the same manner as faculty in departments with highly rated graduate faculty. Faculty in favorably rated departments cited the need for improved facilities and increased funding. Since faculty in rated departments expressed less concern for increased faculty salaries or for improvement of the quality of their faculty, it must be presumed that the needed funds were of research activities. The existence of and the need for resolution of inner conflicts was indicated as necessary significantly less often than in nonrated departments. The source of problems was external or outside of the control of the rated departments much more often than with nonrated departments. All in all, faculty responses from individuals in rated departments appear to validate a criterion of quality identified in *Conversations Toward a Definition of Institutional Vitality* as purposeful energy.[4]

We had thought that there might be considerable variation

[3] Allan M. Cartter, *An Assessment of Quality in Graduate Education* (Washington, D.C.: American Council on Education, 1966).

[4] R. E. Peterson and D. E. Loye (eds.), *Conversations Toward a Definition of Institutional Vitality* (Princeton: Educational Testing Service, 1968), p. 25. See also JB Lon Hefferlin, *Dynamics of Academic Reform* (San Francisco: Jossey-Bass, 1969).

in responses of faculty with different rank and degrees of seniority in their departments. In fact, however, very few diverse response patterns were evident. Only two consistent findings emerged. One finding in regard to seniority within a department was that the need for more faculty was cited more often as the seniority of members in a department increased from 0–3 to 4–8, 9–15, and more than 15 years. The second finding in regard to rank was that the resolution of departmental problems through the lessening of internal conflict was noted most often by assistant professors, less often by associate professors, and least often by full professors.

Seeking additional insights as to the nature, source, and recommended resolution of departmental problems, we classified each department as high, medium, or low in comparison to other departments in regard to the amount of autonomy enjoyed by the departments. We also used the same threefold classification in rating the influence on departments of the university administration, dean, department chairman, departmental faculty as a whole, and individual faculty members. The analysis of responses in regard to our measure of departmental autonomy yielded results which were difficult to interpret. Faculty from departments with a medium degree of autonomy, primarily chemistry and psychology, noted the need for facilities and funds most often, whereas the need for reducing the influence of elements external to the department but within the university was indicated less often by faculty from departments with high or low autonomy. The need for improved faculty and the citation of problems in the department's instructional program seemed to increase as the degree of autonomy decreased.

External influence by central administration or by the dean tended to occur at the same level and have the same perceived effect on the department. Several strong relationships were evident. As one might expect, the stronger the influence of the university administration or the dean of the college, the more frequent was the mentioning of problems resulting from excessive external influence. However, it was also true that the stronger the influence of the dean or university administration, the greater was the incidence of problems of an operational nature. The reduction of internal conflict as well as external interference was thus seen as crucial to the departments operating within a framework of a strong dean and strong university administration. Also, we found that the frequency of the stated need for increased funds and the resolution of departmental problems through the addition of more faculty members was inversely related to the influence of the dean. The need for improved facilities or space was cited less frequently when the influence of university administrations and deans increased. In view of our finding that a favorable rating in the Cartter report was often associated with the perceived need for improved facilities and more money, one might question whether satisfaction with departmental resources is desirable, as it does not seem conducive to favorable recognition by one's peers in the academic community. One might ask, "What price tranquility?"

In examining the responses of faculties in departments with chairmen of high, medium, or low influence, no consistent relationships emerged between the influence of the department chairman and the tendency to indicate problems of a particular nature, source, or resolution. The most prominent tendency was for faculties in departments with chairmen of medium influence to note problems in regard to the lack of facilities and funds, as well as the need for additional faculty. Faculty members in this type of department stressed increased funding and the upgrading of faculty quality as needed to solve departmental problems. The frequency with which problems of an operational nature were mentioned was substantially lower in departments with chairmen of moderate influence than in departments with low- and particularly high-influence chairmen. We hazard as explanation for this curious fact that mediocrity may eliminate tensions, but seldom begets excellence. It is possible, too, that unobtrusive chairmen, as with several chemistry departments in our sample, allow for the fulfillment of individual capabilities.

We asked faculty members how much influence they, as a whole, had in their departments' activities. Their responses, interpretable as rough indicators of democracy-autocracy, revealed a considerable number of clear relationships. The greater the influence of the faculty as a whole, the greater was the percentage of individuals citing problems relating to the need for improved facilities, increased funding, and improved instructional programs. Money was proposed as an important factor in the resolution of departmental problems, but the source of departmental problems was often regarded as external to or beyond the control of the department. Problems of an operational nature which were internal in source and which required internal resolutions decreased as the influence of the department's faculty (democracy) increased. In short, faculty in these departments felt they had greater control over their own destiny and were aggressive in pursuing their interests.

Departments where individual faculty members felt they had a high degree of personal influence also regarded the source of their problems as primarily external to rather than within their departments. Internal conflicts or operational problems were noted relatively seldom in comparison to departments with faculty of medium or low personal influence. Increased funding and improved facilities were mentioned frequently as a resolution to problems, whereas a reduction of operational problems was regarded as relatively unnecessary in solving departmental problems. Finally, we detected a slight tendency for faculty in departments where individuals perceived high personal influence to cite a need for additional faculty and higher salaries.

We felt that departments with high, medium, or low commitments to the university, department, or discipline as a reference group would indicate different patterns of need. In regard to faculty in departments with high, medium, and low attachment to the university as a reference group, few consistent findings were noted. The stronger the orientation to the university as a reference group, the greater was the percentage of faculty members within a department who noted problems in regard to excessive external influence in departmental affairs. It also appeared that faculty in departments with the lowest orientation toward the university were most likely to indicate the need for additional faculty.

A departmental orientation was associated with a pronounced tendency to place relatively little emphasis on perceived existence of or need to resolve problems of an operational nature or the need to improve the department's instructional programs. The perceived need for improved faculty salaries appeared to increase, however, in direct proportion to the degree of faculty orientation to the department as a reference group. Faculty in departments with a high orientation to the department feel that departmental problems could be solved best through the improvement of facilities, instructional programs, and the quality of the department's faculty.

Finally, in regard to reference group orientation, we found a disciplinary orientation to be associated very strongly with a high incidence of problems of an internal or operational nature. If harmony was the by-word in departments with a strong departmental orientation, conflict and disharmony were certainly apt descriptors of departments that adopted the discipline as their reference point. The inverse relationship between a disciplinary orientation and the perceived need for the improvement of a department's instructional programs may not have indicated the quality of or attention paid to instruction as much as it meant inattention to instruction and a strong emphasis upon basic research.

The last group of variables used in our analysis of response patterns was the relative emphasis placed upon basic research, graduate study, and undergraduate instruction. We found that faculty in departments which placed a high degree of emphasis upon basic research (in general, chemistry, mathematics, and psychology departments) were much more likely to note the need for improved facilities and increased funding. The source of problems in these departments was found to be external or outside the control of the departments more often than in departments less oriented to the seeking of research monies from outside funding agencies.

Possibly because departments placing high emphasis upon graduate study may already have obtained high-quality faculty, the frequency of the stated need for the upgrading of faculty was inversely related to the emphasis placed upon graduate study. However, emphasis upon graduate study was positively related to the incidence of problems classified by nature and source as operational. Thus, reduction of operational problems as well as improved facilities were seen as major keys to resolving the problems of this type of department, but less evident was the need for reducing interference from sources external to the department but within the university.

The higher the emphasis placed upon undergraduate in-

struction, the less frequently noted was the need for additional monies or the likelihood to cite additional facilities as a help in resolving
departmental problems. Low emphasis upon undergraduate instruction, on the other hand, was understandably associated with the
need for facilities, funds, and the reduction of internal problems.

EFFECTS OF AUTONOMY

Another primary focus of our study was the examination of
the effects of autonomy upon departmental operations. We asked
faculty members this question: "It has been said that the autonomy
accorded to departments leads to a gradual commitment of a university's resources rather than a rational plan developed for the
university as a whole. Do you see this as true with your institution?
Can or should anything be done to correct it?"

At the time when this question was phrased, it seemed clear
to the study staff and others who reviewed it. In retrospect, the
wording might have been improved, for a number of persons re-
fused to respond on the grounds that the question was meaningless.
Those who responded, however, indicated by their responses that
they fully comprehended the issue raised. Agreement or disagreement with the statement that autonomy leads to the gradual commitment of a university's resources rather than a rational plan for
the university as a whole is indicated in Table 8. The intra-rater
reliability for classification of these responses was quite high (.94).
Also recorded in Table 8 are the responses to the question as to
whether or not anything should be done to correct the situation.
Here the intra-rater reliability was found to be .97.

In addition, we classified the reasons offered by those who
responded either "Yes" or "No" to the question "Can or should
anything be done to correct it?" These responses, indicated in Table
9, had an intra-rater reliability of .89.

Table 10 indicates the twenty control variables by which
each one of our twenty dependent variables (responses) were analyzed and the number of times each control variable contributed
statistically significant results in respect to faculty responses. In examining the perception of impact of departmental autonomy and
the recommended solutions, the variables of rank, influence of the

Table 8.

EXISTENCE AND DESIRABILITY OF DEPARTMENTAL AUTONOMY

"It has been said that the autonomy accorded to departments leads to a gradual commitment of a university's resources rather than a rational plan developed for the university as a whole. Do you see this as true with your institution?"

Response	Number	Percentage of All Respondents	Percentage Response Represents of Usable Responses
Yes	394	29.4	44.7
No	406	30.3	46.1
Uncertain	81	6.0	9.2
Do Not Understand Question or Not Qualified to Answer	96	7.2	
No Response	359	26.8	

"Can or should anything be done to correct it?"

Response	Number	Percentage of All Respondents	Percentage Response Represents of Usable Responses
Yes	314	23.6	45.6
No	284	21.4	41.2
Uncertain	91	6.8	13.2
Do Not Understand Question or Not Qualified to Answer	95	7.1	
No Response	552	40.8	

Table 9.

CAN OR SHOULD ANYTHING BE DONE TO CORRECT IT

Yes, something can or should be done to correct it.

Solution	Rank	Number	Percentage of Responses Indicated
Better Planning	1	89	25.1
Better Administrative Leadership	2	85	24.0
More Faculty Involvement in Decision Making	3	58	16.4
Better Cooperation Among Departments in Planning	4	40	11.3
Flexible Adherence to a Plan	5	34	9.6
Other Organizational Forms (Centers, Institutes)	6	29	8.2
Other	7	12	3.4
Limit Term of Department Chairman	8	4	1.1
Emphasize Teaching Instead of Research	9	3	0.8

No, nothing can or should be done to correct it.

Reason	Rank	Number	Percentage of Responses Indicated
Autonomy Generally Works Out Well	1	104	48.8
Departments Have Better Idea of Needs	2	46	21.3
Administration's Solutions Would Be Worse	3	33	15.3
Rational Planning Impossible	4	30	13.9
Other	5	3	1.4

Table 10.

EXISTENCE OF AND SOLUTIONS TO AUTONOMY:
SUMMARY OF STATISTICALLY SIGNIFICANT FINDINGS BY SOURCE

| | *Level of Significance* | | | |
Variables	.05	.01	.001	Total
Public or Private Status of University	4	1	0	5
Discipline	6	0	0	6
Size of Faculty	2	0	0	2
Cartter Ratings of Graduate Program	2	2	0	4
Cartter Ratings of Graduate Faculty	2	0	0	2
Faculty Rank	4	2	2	8
Years in Department	0	3	3	6
Joint Appointment Status	1	1	0	2
Autonomy of Department	4	1	1	6
Influence of University Administration	2	1	0	3
Influence of Dean	2	0	0	2
Influence of Department Head	3	3	0	6
Influence of Department Faculty	0	2	0	2
Influence of Individual Faculty Members	5	2	1	8
Reference Group—University	1	0	0	1
Reference Group—Department	6	3	0	9
Reference Group—Discipline	2	3	2	7
Emphasis on Basic Research	1	0	0	1
Emphasis on Graduate Study	1	1	0	2
Emphasis on Undergraduate Instruction	1	1	1	3
Totals	49	26	10	85

department chairman, discipline, time in department, and degree of perceived autonomy in the department produced the greatest number of statistically significant findings. Once more, however, it was the pattern of responses which concerned us most.

Analysis of Data. In general, we found that autonomy, like beauty, was in the eye of the beholder. Faculty observers in private institutions apparently had a sharper eye and a greater awareness of the impact of departmental autonomy than was the case among observers in public institutions. Furthermore, faculties in private institutions were more inclined to dislike what they saw and therefore urged that something could and should be done to correct problems stemming from departmental autonomy; that is, they believed that a rational plan for the university should be constructed.

As might be expected, a faculty member's disciplinary orientation had some bearing on the manner in which he reacted to the extent and effect of departmental autonomy. English professors, perhaps because of their own perceived lack of autonomy, were least likely to indicate that departmental autonomy existed within their institutions. Management department faculty apparently recognized the influence of the dean, for an extremely high percentage of faculty in these departments indicated the lack of departmental autonomy. Management faculty were much more likely than English faculty to recommend university planning as an alternative to excessive autonomy. Although they did not recommend systematic planning specifically as an alternative to autonomy, engineering faculties felt that more decisive administrative leadership could serve to keep some departments from becoming too autonomous. History faculty members were more inclined to stress the need for greater faculty involvement in the planning process.

In examining the reasons offered by those who found the existing pattern acceptable, we found that English faculty were more likely to indicate that "autonomy generally worked out pretty well" than were faculty from other disciplines, particularly management and history. Psychology department members, strong in their disciplinary orientation, offered the rationale that "planning is virtually impossible" more often than faculty in other departments, whereas history faculty members, more prone to adopt the university as a reference group, were least likely to express the opinion that the administration in attempting to solve the problems of autonomy would devise a less desirable situation that already existed.

The size of the department in which an individual worked had some influence in a faculty member's attitude toward departmental autonomy. Particularly in small departments of five to nineteen members, there existed a relatively strong belief that something could and should be done to correct excessive autonomy. In this regard, faculty in small departments recommended stronger administrative leadership in planning.

Faculty in departments rated by the Cartter report in regard to effectiveness of graduate programs were much more likely to respond to our question than were faculty in nonrated departments. They agreed that autonomy existed within their institution and were more inclined than their colleagues in nonrated departments to endorse that situation. Faculty in rated departments felt that if steps were to be taken to lessen the autonomy of departments, there should be more faculty involvement in the decision-making processes. If a rational plan were to be adopted by the university, faculty members in rated departments also stressed the need for flexible adherence to the plan.

A number of interesting variations in response patterns occurred in regard to rank. We found that as rank increased, so did the perception of departmental autonomy within the institution. Of greater interest, however, was the direct relationship between an increase in rank and an increase in the percentage of faculty members who felt that something could or should be done about controlling the excess autonomy of certain departments. Thus, full professors were more likely than associate professors and associate professors were more likely than assistant professors to indicate the need for the adoption of some sort of rational plan and the need for greater efforts at interdepartmental cooperation, as well as for a flexible adherence to a plan. Assistant professors, in part because of their lower response rate, appeared to be least willing to place their trust in university-wide planning as initiated by central administration.

Findings in regard to time spent in a department and rank were quite similar. Thus, the longer the time spent in a department, the higher the percentage of faculty indicating the existence of autonomy and the more likely were faculty with increased time within a department to indicate that something could or should be done to correct the situation. Faculty who had been in their departments for only up to three years, again partly because of differential response rates, were least likely to indicate planning as a workable alternative to autonomy, whereas faculty in departments for a period of nine to fifteen years were most likely to advocate increased planning efforts as a feasible solution to the problems of autonomy.

We found faculty with joint appointments to be much more sensitive to the impact of departmental autonomy than those without joint appointments. They were also more inclined to recommend that steps be taken to reduce autonomy. The main steps recommended were increased efforts at obtaining better cooperation among departments and increased use of other organizational forms such as interdisciplinary centers or institutes. Both solutions could entail increased numbers of joint appointments and presumably indicate favorable commentary on the experiences of those with half or quarter-time appointments.

In our examination of the nature, source, and resolution of departmental problems, we found departments perceived as having moderate autonomy (chemistry and psychology were overrepresented in this classification) to be aggressive in the pursuit of outside funds and improved facilities. Faculties in departments with moderate autonomy as compared with faculty in departments where autonomy was high or low, were also more likely to indicate that nothing should be done to restrain departmental autonomy. Reasons most frequently offered were that autonomy generally worked pretty well, departments had a better knowledge of needs than did central administrations, and rational planning was most difficult if not impossible within complex universities. Flexible adherence to a plan was particularly stressed by professors in departments with moderate autonomy. Apparently lack of complete autonomy does not impede the effectiveness of these departments, as some of the most vigorous and highly rated departments in our study functioned with only a moderate degree of autonomy as perceived by the faculty. Perhaps, too, some autonomy only whets the desire for more of it.

Various attitudes toward departmental autonomy were displayed by faculties in departments operating within the context of deans, department chairmen, and faculty of high, moderate, or low influence. Analysis of our data in regard to the amount of influence attributed by faculties to their university's central administration yielded no easily interpreted patterns of response to questions concerning the existence of and solutions to autonomy. We found faculty in departments dealing with deans of high influence significantly less likely to indicate the belief that something need be done to restrict autonomy, perhaps partly because little autonomy was apparent to faculty working in a strong-dean setting.

The existence of autonomous departments was most apparent to faculty in departments with chairmen of moderate influence —perhaps a reflection of an apparent overloading of professorial responses, for they generally tended to attribute less influence to the department chairman than did associate or assistant professors. A department chairman of moderate influence was also most frequently associated with advocacy of rational planning, flexible adherence to a plan, and the use of other organizational forms as alternatives to autonomous departmental operations. In comparison with the response of faculties from departments with perceived high or moderate faculty influence, we found faculties in departments characterized by a low degree of faculty influence least likely to indicate that nothing should be done to correct autonomy. Departments in which the personal influence of faculty members was found to be highest were on the average of slightly smaller size than departments where individual faculty tended to be of lesser influence. Our original premise that autonomy was in the eye of the beholder was confirmed by the fact that the existence of departmental autonomy was most often recognized by faculties in departments enjoying the highest degree of personal influence. The belief that excessive autonomy required attention was also stronger in this type of department.

Differential response rates to the question of the existence and desirability of departmental autonomy made some of our findings in regard to the use of university, department, or discipline as a reference group difficult to interpret. However, it was quite apparent that faculty members adopting the university as a referent were much more likely to perceive the existence of excessive autonomy than those oriented to the department or discipline. University-oriented faculty were also most inclined to recommend that something, most often the development of a rational plan, be undertaken to restrain autonomy.

Similarly, in regard to the emphasis placed by faculty upon basic research, graduate study, and undergraduate instruction, many respondents failed to indicate if anything should be done to correct the evils of autonomy. The presence of or lack of intense commitment to either basic research or undergraduate instruction was associated with low response rates to this item. The response rate was, however, fairly uniform among faculty in departments with a high, low, or medium degree of emphasis upon graduate study. Here, we found a higher percentage of faculty in departments placing a high degree of emphasis upon graduate study, recommending increased efforts at interdepartmental cooperation and flexible adherence to a plan.

FACULTY COMMENTS

Faculty members found no difficulty in identifying problems in their departments and displayed no difficulty nor reluctance in identifying the source of difficulty and some possible solutions. The issue of possibly excessive departmental autonomy touched a much sorer point, and responses varied from refusal to respond to such a ridiculous implication, to expressions of deep concern coupled with explicit suggestions for restraints on departmental autonomy. A sampling of the responses will, on the one hand, demonstrate the nature of the material on which this chapter is based and, on the other, reflect something of the concern, insight, humor, and frustration exhibited.

Some faculty members found evidence of external control rather than departmental autonomy:

Myth or reality? The administration sets the departmental budget, picks the chairman, sometimes appoints new faculty members, fixes the history requirements for all undergraduates, and in some colleges determines the year in which the student will fulfill them—does all this without prior consultation with or the approval of the chairman and/or faculty. On the other hand, the department can indicate the fields into which it would like to expand. It can set the language requirements for its graduate students, and it can approve or disapprove applications for admission to the graduate programs and for assistantships and teaching fellowships. Naturally, the administration has the final word on hiring new faculty members. Aside from the basic courses required of all freshmen and sophomores, the chairman can determine teaching schedules within the limitations set by the university registrar. The department receives a budget from the director of libraries, and it can assign priorities to purchases. Do we have autonomy? Again, the administration has the final word on promotion, tenure, leaves of absence, and travel authorization. There is on paper a rational plan for the development of the university as a whole, but short-term considerations actually seem to determine the allocation of the university's resources. The administration and not the department commits the resources of the university.

Quite to the contrary, the administration so consistently has taken the department's voice from it in budgetary matters that it has not been able to contribute to the university as a whole what the students deserve in terms of education. The lack of rational plan seems to me to be from the point of view of the purpose of the department in the university. The many sometimes trivial inadequacies that could be overcome by greater voice of the department members are being invested in superfluous trinkets that are at best on the periphery of the university's purpose. This *can* stop. The taxpayer's money *is* available, but the decision as to its use is invested in too few people with too many special interests other than genuine education. I believe that if the president and treasurer were to sit down with the department as a whole, some greater understanding might develop. I sincerely believe that these men would not listen, however, because their minds are already made up about what the voters want of *their* universities. We have a lot of bread and plenty of circuses. The voters really like it too.

Some faculty members recognized the existence of a high degree of departmental autonomy and strongly defended it:

Yes. Nothing should be done. The university as an entity is less important than the departments severally.

The value of "a rational plan developed for the university as a whole" depends on who develops the plan. Personally, I feel that autonomy of departments and of individual scholars and teachers is much more stimulating, attractive, and valuable in the long run than a university planned by academic bureaucrats. Academic freedom is the value which overshadows all the others, and it should not be abrogated in the name of planning, efficiency, money, or anything else.

In my opinion, the departments *are* the university (in a large university, at least); each represents a section of the faculty, the students, research, and of the body of knowledge. The main problem is therefore better communication between departments, and planning on an interdepartmental level. It should be the function of the university administration to support these processes to as great an extent as possible, rather than take them over.

No great university was ever created by crippling able departments to bolster weak ones. Any "rational plan" I ever heard of in such a situation was simply a way for people who know budgets but not disciplines to answer spending requests with "No" in advance. I'll risk the empire-builders in return for their leaving me alone. Keep your rational plans.

Leave control in hands of intelligent faculty, as per our greatest (best) universities. Keep administrators and their plans to a minimum level necessary to process paychecks and parking tickets.

Nothing should be done to correct departmental autonomy. If it was not for the unbelievable uncanniness of our department chairman in thwarting the moves of central administration, nothing would get done.

However, there were as many responses expressing concern about the undesirable effects of departmental autonomy as there were responses completely endorsing it:

It is quite true that departmental autonomy causes Balkanization of a university; however, in my experience individual departments within the university always have clearer-headed developmental plans than the vague, empty, and grandiose ideas of the middle administrative levels. Rather a federation of effective departments, with interdisciplinary cooperation between individuals, than a portentous front of institutes for this or that nebulous purpose. The only preventive for intellectual middle-age spread in administration, research, or instruction, at any level, is leadership at the top. Let us all pray for excellence in university presidents and department heads.

I don't think all wisdom lies with departments; far more power than wisdom is in them. On the other hand, in the American academic world of the 60's, a department is a clear rock to stand on. I'm not sure a university-wide plan can help, but a strong liberal arts interdisciplinary curriculum might (does) help to mitigate departmental provincialism.

The statement is almost universally true—certainly here. The problem arises because of Parkinson's law, because department chairmen are almost inherently empire builders, and because higher authorities don't have the breadth, wisdom, and guts to do their jobs of keeping unjustifiable expansions under control. Something does need to be done about the problem—mainly by administrators above the department chairmen, especially in budget decisions. They need to take the broad view, budget according to justifications given, and (when unconvinced) say NO.

It is largely true. Why should my department (a large, powerful, and influential one in physical science) be favored, as it is, over those which train people for equally important fields, such as music, literature, or philosophy? So long as American priorities remain what they are—poverty in the midst of plenty, a war-primed economy—the desired changes cannot be expected to come. The subject should be faced more openly on a country-wide basis, helped by organizations such as the AAUP.

I agree with the statement. Solution: assign all of the faculty to committees outside of the department as well as inside the department. If a department becomes too big or powerful—divide it into two or more smaller units. Have a fixed length of appointments to chairmanships and important committees. Keep everyone in the university informed of all important activities within each department. Sponsor university-level projects and activities which could attract the interest and cooperation of the faculty. Keep all channels of communication open as much as possible.

And finally there were a few faculty statesmen who sought some balanced resolution of departmental initiative and autonomy, and recognized the need for overall university direction.

I see this as true here. Certainly something can be done about it, and I think we all feel this may be the contribution of the new president. It is a difficult task because I see myself in two communities—the community of my discipline which moves across institutions, and the university community which does not. These incumbencies seem to be in conflict mostly now, although I feel they need not be. The key to it, I feel, is an understood and accepted role of the university as an institution in the professional community outside.

This is true if the university's concept of development is basically in conflict with departmental autonomy. It does not have to be in conflict. If the policy approves of diversity, and if there is adequate control of resources, the department grows with the university. The ideal goal is not a finished puzzle of interlocking fixed-shaped pieces, but a living community of interaction, shifting balances, changing structures. This will be healthy or chaotic depending on the individuals involved.

These faculty responses portray quite well some of the views and problems which provided the incentives for producing this volume. The final two responses may be accepted as suggesting a path to resolution of some of the issues raised in this chapter and even as providing a preview of some of the conclusions reached in our final chapter. It is encouraging to find that some faculty members within departments recognize and forthrightly express many of the same concerns that are regularly noted by administrators and competent observers of the current higher education scene.

The Institute

One of the most startling recent developments in the university is the proliferation of nondepartmental units, which demonstrate such variation within and among institutions in origin, purposes, names, budgeting, and administration as to constitute a crazy-quilt patchwork, attractive to the eye, but bewildering in its lack of design. Our experience is that the very existence of these units is unknown to many faculty members and administrators. Often they are located in rundown houses or other remodeled facilities just off the main campus—hard to find, entered through side doors rather than main entrances, and so informal in operation as to communicate an impression of bumbling and pointless operation. In one institution

studied, the number of these units grew from nineteen to forty-five
in the five years from 1961–1962 to 1966–1967. The personnel involved increased from 92 to 276 (total of academic and nonacademic employees). Another major university lists over two hundred
such units.

The range of terms used gives some clue to the disarray:
institute, center, program, committee, laboratory, office, bureau,
council, services, clinic, organization. Certain terms are more popular on some campuses than on others, but there is no consistency in
usage of the terms, even on a particular campus. *Institute, center,*
and *laboratory,* however, are by far the most common terms used for
nondepartmental units engaging in some combination of instruction,
research, and service. Terms such as *office, bureau, services,* or *clinics*
are more likely to be used to designate university services, but some
units using one of these titles are also extensively involved in research,
instruction, or public service.

A sample of actual titles gives further indication of the dif-
fuse nature of the array: Poetry Center; Poisoning Control Infor-
mation Center; The Center for Study of Man in Contemporary
Society; Institute for Research on Land and Water Resources; In-
stitute of Human Sciences; Space Institute; Institute of Outdoor
Drama; Institute for Saline Studies; Failure Analysis Laboratory;
Laboratory for Research on Human Performance; Laboratory of
Tree Ring Research; Bureau of Business and Public Research; and
Bureau of Recreation. Both very narrow and impossibly broad com-
mitments are apparent in this sample.

ORIGIN AND PURPOSE

Because of the varied designations, the lack of knowledge
our campus contacts had about such units, and our own ineptness
in describing our concerns, the range of units contacted in our visits
included some of little real concern to us. A Computer Center or a
unit with some equivalent title is an established unit on most university campuses. A Bureau of Business and Economic Research is
a long-established feature of most schools of business. An Audio-
visual Service or its equivalent is found on all campuses. Centers for
Continuing Education are well recognized. So, too, are Counseling

Centers, Reading Clinics, and Testing Bureaus. Despite the confusion of terminology, these various titles all indicate service units which, in some form, are essential to all institutions of higher education. At an entirely different level, but likewise of no interest to us, are the independent research institutes or foundations loosely affiliated with some universities by physical proximity and administrative overlap. Confusion in terminology and function was found with each designation. Thus we found that the term *institute* is used to cover conferences, short-term education programs, and even a continuing program of monthly discussion meetings.

With experience, we narrowed the focus of our concern to units characterized by the following purposes: development of interdisciplinary studies and research not readily accommodated in the departments (Latin American studies); development of new fields of study or research (Electron Acceleration Laboratory); a combination of research, training, demonstration, and service (Institute of Higher Education), with emphasis on practical applications and problem solution; and training for graduate students, faculty field experience, research and methodological training (Social Science Training and Research Laboratory).

Such purposes make the institute (hereafter used as a generic designation of all such units) somewhat like a department, which is why we found them of interest. In fact, they reveal the inadequacies of departments which, by their devotion to a discipline, to carefully demarked areas of concern, and to preservation of disciplinary fences, find that interdisciplinary activities and a direct concern with social or applied problems are inappropriate, distasteful, or impossible. There are, however, other reasons for the existence of such units. Some have obviously been formed by faculty and administration agreement in the hope (not always realized) of attracting foundation or federal funds; some have been introduced simply to provide a title and status to attract or keep a widely recognized scholar or researcher, or to assuage the chagrin of an individual passed over for, or just relieved of, an administrative assignment. Some institutes have resulted from the entrepreneurial efforts of a single individual who obtained a grant, initiated an income-producing service, or sold one or more administrators on an idea.

One institute director reported that he developed the inspiration at lunch, and had a presidential letter authorizing the institute by 3:00 p.m. Obviously, the actual motivations for setting up these units are often very different from the avowed purposes.

Great variation is apparent in the characteristics of the individuals involved, in the programs carried on, in the mode of appointment and operation, and in the sources of funds. The executive head of such units is most commonly called a *director,* but *chairman, executive officer,* and *dean* are also used. Directors have status varying anywhere from assistant chairman of a department to vice-president. The units may be initiated by governing board action or by administrative order of administrators ranging from president to department chairman. Appointments of directors follow a similar pattern. In a department of sociology, we found a research institute which primarily served as a device (literally so) to account for reduced teaching loads, not necessarily involving research, and headed by a director appointed by the chairman. At the other extreme, we found the director of an institute appointed by the governing board operating at the vice-presidential level and empowered to seek funds, initiate new programs, and introduce new institutes.

Between these extremes are institutes established and directors appointed by joint agreement of several departments, usually approved by the dean or deans concerned, and often formalized by presidential order or governing-board action. The last sanction is highly prized, and is usually necessary if the unit is to be granted a budget of its own from institutional funds. One university encourages the development of such units and occasionally provides them with immediate help, but generally prefers joint departmental or college sponsorship on an informal basis for a period of years. If the unit demonstrates its worth and viability, it may then be designated as an official institute, and thereafter it operates under university statutes covering this type of unit.

ORGANIZATION AND ADMINISTRATION

Most of the institute directors interviewed were first incumbents and hence were unable to be definitive about how a new appointment would be made; obviously, it depends on the status and level of the assignment. For those holding their title by board action, the usual approach suggested was that of recommendation by the deans or department chairmen concerned to the academic vice-president. Some units have an executive committee of administrators rather than institute staff, reflecting a common pattern in which the institute has no full-time staff other than possibly the director. Seldom did we see institute staff other than the director, and when we did (even an acting or associate director), we were almost invariably told that only the director really was in a position to answer questions about the full scope and mode of operation of the institute. We came to suspect that the prototype of the modern institute director is found in the old-time department head who was the only professor and who regularly issued the orders of the day.

The character and problems of institute staffing are closely related to its budgetary sources. A director of a Latin American Studies Institute, who coordinates for several departments a doctoral program using staff and courses from these departments, may actually have no staff or budget of his own. He may be privileged by the good will of the chairman and/or the dean to have a say in new appointments, tenure, curriculum development, and degree requirements. His influence on the curriculum and degree requirements is enhanced by his influence with those faculty members in the several departments who teach courses designated as part of the Latin American Studies program. If the director is a scholar of some repute and the initiator of the program, he may have extensive influence. If he is an untenured faculty member, he will be fortunate if his own department reduces his teaching load by one course and the dean provides him with a part-time secretary. Nevertheless, the title, the sign on the door, and the privilege usually accorded of sitting with the department chairmen at meetings called by the dean offer some recognition which an enterprising operator can, by grants or politics, promote to something more impressive in a few years.

However, seldom does the institute director achieve significant stature and power until he gets a budget and a staff of his own. The easiest and quickest route is to obtain funds from external sources. The director who accomplishes this can then appoint staff members, secretaries, and graduate assistants whose jobs emanate from him and whose loyalties are, therefore, clearly to him. If funds are sufficient to import some scholars whose stature commands departmental recognition, courses can be developed, even though offered through departments; graduate assistants can write dissertations under institute direction; and, ultimately, the institute may achieve departmental, school, or college academic prerogatives.[1] And surely the instructional contribution deserves a permanent lien on the general fund budget.

Another route to permanent and possibly enhanced status (which can be pursued simultaneously with the first) is through providing a service to students and possibly to faculty members. This service (counseling, testing, statistical assistance), originally offered for a fee or possibly developed as a by-product of research, becomes the basis for obtaining continuing annual support from the university. By either route, the anomalous and dubious endeavor becomes a fixture. Some directors are sufficiently influential to acquire that status for their institutes at the beginning.

The research institute in the sciences seems to be more satisfied to concentrate on research. The recognized researcher can, if he wishes, have a departmental connection. He may have little interest in instruction, and, for those who have, an occasional seminar or the direction of a doctoral dissertation seems to relieve the urge. Even the research institute, however, seeks for a foothold in the general fund budget so that hiatuses in external support can be bridged without endangering the security of the director and other key members of the institute staff. The wise institute director, like the university president, seeks for support from several sources, with a degree of flexibility in their allocation so that the continuance of major programs is assured.

The institute which attains significant support from external sources usually appoints several types of personnel. Persons with academic degrees are sometimes given the usual academic titles in

[1] For an analysis of how this process has worked itself out in the case of federally supported language and area centers, see J. Axelrod and D. N. Bigelow, *Resources for Language and Area Studies in the United States* (Washington, D.C.: American Council on Education, 1962).

accord with experience and scholarly stature, but outside of tenure rules in order to alleviate the university having to take over salaries if external support fails. One university has defined three levels and types of appointments in institutes. The first includes teaching and research faculty with the usual ranks. These individuals are assigned to the institute, but appointed to one of the university departments and are subject to usual promotion and tenure procedures. The second group, designated as a Special Research Faculty, are called Faculty Fellows, with adjectival qualification as junior, assistant, or associate. The Junior Faculty Fellow is appointed from year to year, but is to be given three months' notice if he is not to be reappointed. Assistant, Associate, and full Faculty Fellows must be given six months' notice if they are not to be reappointed. Tenure is not given. The third group, the Special Professional Faculty, requires a minimum of a baccalaureate degree or its equivalent. Conditions of appointment are as for the Fellows, but the Professional Specialist is qualified as appropriate by addition of adjectives indicative of rank. Recommendations regarding Special Research Faculty and Special Professional Faculty are made by the director to the vice-president, but recommendations regarding teaching and research faculty proceed through the usual channels. Such distinctions are essential if the university wishes to avoid assuming additional obligations, and they also have the advantage of leaving decisions regarding the permanent faculty to the departments and colleges. One institute director (in an institution lacking such policies) characterized such institutes as paper tigers. His position was that the persons he wanted would not always meet departmental standards. He demanded and received complete freedom in making appointments under the usual tenure and rank pattern, and then negotiated with departments for dual status when that seemed desirable. This director reports to the president, who originated this particular institute and handpicked its director. Chairmen and other administrators in this institution expressed the hope that this pattern might be changed under a new president.

We found institutes so variously placed in the hierarchy that the director reported to a department chairman, to a committee of department chairmen, to a dean, to a committee of deans, to a vice-president, to a campus chancellor, to the president of a total state system, to a faculty committee from a single institution, or to a faculty committee with representatives from several campus units. This flexibility in the placement of the institute in the university hierarchy is undoubtedly one reason for its attractiveness, for the rapid expansion in numbers, and for the widespread suspicion and doubts expressed by both administrators and faculty. An institute operating directly under a system president is viewed with dislike by chancellors and lower administrators. One reporting to a campus head is viewed with suspicion by all lower echelons of authority. The ideal is not necessarily found—although some chairmen and deans would have it so—when institutes are imbedded in a department or jointly sponsored by several departments. A research institute with extensive funding is likely to be physically separated from a department, its staff may become sufficiently large to have what the rest of the departmental faculty regard as undue influence, and the institute director and his associates, having little concern about departmental matters, may run a tight operation to which others in the department—including its chairman—have no access and about which they have little information. So we were told in several cases by chairmen and departmental faculty members, even while deans and vice-presidents exulted in having kept institutes under control by their association with a department. Responsibility for an institute shared by several departments works well (from the departmental point of view) when the institute coordinates a program of instruction and research involving members of all departments and remains primarily dependent on the departments for its resources. Multiple departmental sponsorship cannot control the institute with extensive funding of its own, although the vesting in departments of all recommendations on positions under tenure rules does prevent an institute from getting completely out of hand.

BUDGET

The range of budget patterns has already been indicated. Some of those considered were entirely dependent on contracts or grants. Line item state legislative appropriations in the pattern of experiment stations and cooperative extension were found in several cases. Some were entirely dependent upon department or college contributions, whereas others had achieved a tight grip on regular allocations from the general fund. The preferred pattern, as indicated by the directors, was, quite naturally, a base of university support coupled with freedom to seek funds from other sources. None felt that the institute had really arrived until a basic operation was insured by direct university support. All of the institutes reviewed had some university support. The size of our sample makes it impossible to generalize with safety, but well over half of the units considered had support only from institutional sources.

PROGRAM

The variety of programs carried on by institutes is astounding. Some are engaged in a full range of instruction (undergraduate and graduate, although usually emphasis is on the latter), research, and service. The range of services includes: special libraries housed in institute facilities, seminars (credit and noncredit), colloquia, consultation, coordination of interdepartmental and intercollege research and field study, publication of journals, and the founding and subsidy of national organizations of persons with like interests. The usual pattern is that of continuing expansion, despite the fact that many institutes seem to have been initiated to explore and develop a new idea that might later be assimilated into the existing structure of the university.

Several administrators suggested that doubtful or high-risk programs, in terms of support or uncertain public reaction, had been started via an institute, with the expectation that the program could be later wiped out or absorbed if difficulty arose. Paper institutes introduced primarily to provide status for a particular individual have disappeared with the departure or retirement of that person. In several cases, an institute which was initially reported as discontinued was found, on further questioning, to have expanded into a more extensive operation with a new name. Two instances were found in which an institute initiated for research and service had, by successive stages, ultimately attained stature as a school offering specialized programs of undergraduate and graduate study.

We found profound differences of opinion as to whether these developments were desirable. Previously existing departments and colleges were likely to view these developments as an unwarranted dilution of scarce resources. Some administrators, including occasionally those instrumental in granting official approval, shared that view, but others saw these cases as examples of the successful use of institutes to explore and bring to fruition a new idea.

SUCCESSFUL INSTITUTE

The vast range of titles, functions, and administrative patterns makes it virtually impossible to say anything definitive about the successful institute. Much of the development has been due to the expediency, opportunism, and competition apparent in the operations of universities. It is expedient to set up an institute to provide a title for one who must be relieved of other duties or to keep a scholar chagrined because of failure to obtain some administrative assignment or honorific chair. It is opportunistic to set up an institute when it seems probable that foundation or federal grants may be attracted by the existence of such a unit. It is competitive to introduce institutes because other universities have done so. None of these motivations is necessarily bad, but, unless they are balanced by sounder considerations and by wide involvement of relevant segments of the university in the decision, the ultimate result may well be, as so many of our departmental interviewees indicated, a proliferation of units duplicating endeavors of existing departments and colleges, diluting the resources, and yielding a university structure so complicated as to be unmanageable.

Institutes, in the sense in which we are concerned with them, are introduced to undertake interdisciplinary studies and research not readily accommodated in departments, but in which several departments and members of their faculties are interested; to develop new fields of study and research not presently assignable to any discipline, department, or identifiable group thereof; to study and undertake to solve or alleviate some problem of our society; or to combine research, training, demonstration, and service in a manner not readily possible in disciplinary-based and highly structured departments. The successful institute, then, is one introduced to meet one of the four goals indicated in such manner as to permit accomplishment of that goal without unduly straining resources or impeding the operations of existing units in the university. Ideally, it should bring additional funds, and it should provide for individuals and units already affiliated with the university the opportunity to expand their activities and improve the quality of their programs. The use of the institute to provide autonomy and a wide range of operation for the unusual individual seems quite justifiable in some cases, but not at all so in others.

The difficulty is that institutes, once organized, tend to take on a character of their own which may deviate markedly from the original intent. In contrast to this too-common trend, the institute should be regarded as expendable and the long-term goal should be to unify and simplify the organization and management of the university rather than to fragment and complicate it. To attain this goal, it would be wise to deliberate at greater length about the need for any new unit, to consider the long-term implications of its introduction, and to provide for a recurrent review, which may lead to abandoning the institute or to incorporating it in some manner within the standard organizational pattern. In many cases, it might be desirable to initiate a new effort under a committee, with more formal designation awaiting evidence of the success of the initial endeavor. Thus the University of Chicago apparently has found the committee approach quite successful for some interdisciplinary programs. However, our observations do suggest that there are some types of interdisciplinary instructional, research, and service effort which justify institutes with a degree of permanency equal to that of the disciplinary departments and colleges. That does not mean they should become permanent fixtures, for, in a sense, any organization of the university is only a means. Colleges and departments, too, should be considered as temporary and subject to elimination, division, or combination as changing patterns in disciplines and in societal needs may indicate. Institutes, properly viewed, could be a means of exploring new patterns of organization rather than becoming bewildering additions to an increasingly complicated organizational pattern.

SUMMARY

Our pre-study concerns about institutes have been largely justified by our observations. We believe that some universities have rushed too hastily into the formation of such units without giving adequate attention to the long-term budgetary and organizational implications. We believe that institutions would benefit by examining the confusing array of designations used and by defining such terms as *institute, center, bureau,* or *laboratory* in some manner which would give indication as to the role, functions, and hierarchical placement of the units in the university. Confusion among faculty members, students, and even administrators would be eased thereby. Furthermore, it would then become possible to prescribe some policies for operation and budgeting of these units which would more clearly define their relationships to colleges and departments and fix responsibility for their supervision and review. The freewheeling operations of some academic entrepreneurs might thereby be brought under control, and many of the irritations of deans and department chairmen would be eased. On the other hand, successful institutes are not likely to result where their activities and personnel are defined and restricted by departments and colleges whose rigidities and disciplinary preoccupations originally generated the need for the institutes. Finally, we believe that the need for institutes should be considered as evidence of the general inadequacy and inflexibility of present university organization and used as a means of examining and remodeling that organization rather than introducing further complications into it.

Autonomy, Influence, Confidence

Autonomy is an overused and much-abused term in universities. Students, supported by many faculty members, demand autonomy in conduct of their own activities. Black students demand autonomous Black Studies programs. Departments call for autonomy in planning and carrying out their own programs. Individual scholars demand autonomy in what, how, and indeed whether they teach. In facing these demands, the university reaps a harvest of its own

132

sowing; for it too demands autonomy in deciding what it does and how it does it. Put most ungraciously (and nonnegotiable demands, whatever their source, are always ungracious), the university demands funds to support its ever-expanding programs but energetically resists any attempt to review the effectiveness of these programs or the need for them. When one source of funding proves inadequate for support of its aspirations, the university (administrators and faculty) scrambles for support elsewhere. Such support is often somewhat illusory because it may be only temporary, and it may not even cover all costs during the period of the support. Thus, more permanent sources of support—tuition, endowment, income, gifts, legislative appropriations—inherit the costs, and increases in these sources are sought. There is also always the hope that temporary support can, by continuing pressure, be made permanent and gradually increased in amount. Recent higher education pressures and expectations regarding federal government support are indicative of this hope.

We speak loosely of a system of higher education in this country, but there is no system. There is only a large and increasing number of institutions competing for status and for resources to sustain or attain status. Even at the state level, attempts to develop state systems with coordinating or control boards defining the roles of individual institutions are weakened and often thwarted by institutional aspirations buttressed by institutional lobbying, by political bargaining, or by funds from federal or other sources which support programs not included in the assigned role. Definition of institutional roles based on public interests is resisted by institutions confident that what is good for them is also good for the public.

Traditionally, institutional autonomy has been regarded as both a necessity and a virtue. Arguing from the ideal that freedom in research and instruction is essential to the pursuit of truth, the proponents of autonomy have viewed it as a necessity. In our culture, diversity and competition have been widely accepted as values, and thus autonomy which presumably permits and encourages these values is also a virtue. But a virtue carried to an extreme may become a vice. Surely autonomy in its traditional interpretation becomes a vice when it permits unnecessary program proliferation and waste. Competition, within limits, is a spur to quality, but it also encourages vainglorious competition for institutional status with little regard to costs or social needs. And, as both private and public universities increasingly feed at the same trough, it becomes essential, in the interests of national needs and limited resources, that some controls be placed on institutional autonomy. Such a view is not likely to be popular among universities. It may not even be popular among politicians, who often appear to enjoy the prestige and power which come from interminable hearings, pressures, and behind-the-scenes negotiations by which they gain publicity and some advantages for their own constituencies at the expense of a rational and efficient resolution of the issues involved. Accordingly, the thesis that autonomy requires control needs some elaboration and documentation if it is to be understood and given consideration.

QUALITY AND QUANTITY

The quality of a university (or of a department) is difficult to appraise. Furthermore, efforts to appraise quality have been generally, and sometimes bitterly, resisted by faculty and administrators. This is true whether one talks about instruction, research, or service. It is worthy of note that these three words (instruction, research, and service) which summarize the tripartite commitment of the university refer to processes rather than to results. The outcomes, benefits, or effects of education are seldom specified in evaluatable terms, so emphasis tends to be on the processes. The dubious assumption is that when these processes are carried on by conscientious persons, good results are inevitable.

The efficiency of a university is also difficult to appraise. It requires relating input to output or costs to benefits. Efforts in appraisal of effectiveness in universities have been even more limited than efforts to appraise quality. Institutions seek support in relation to the number and range of activities (processes) carried on rather than by documenting resource need by evidence of efficiency and effectiveness. Unfortunately, large expenditures are no more of an indication of quality than of effectiveness. For example, the organization and costs of undergraduate education vary greatly, but many educators have long suspected, and recent research tends to confirm, that any measurable difference in results depends more on admission policies than on processes and costs. Although there does exist reasonable disagreement regarding criteria of quality, the demand for evaluation tends to be rejected, both as an invasion of autonomy and as a questioning of professional integrity. This attitude is reinforced when one turns to graduate education, which is largely departmentalized and controlled by the faculty elite. Research, to some limited extent, is evaluated on a national market by other scholars, but most deans, department chairmen, and faculty members will admit that a large, though unknown, proportion of research has a limited audience and even more limited significance. The service activities of universities are commonly justified by the demand for them rather than by any evidence of their actual effectiveness.

In lieu of definite, tangible evidence of quality, there exists a tendency to equate quantity with quality. The number, range, and level of programs offered; number of volumes in the library; and number of publications, salary levels, and even of faculty members, students enrolled, and degrees granted have been used and accepted as indications of quality. The tendency to substitute quantity for quality has led to some amazing and dishonest actions by universities. Enrollments have been manipulated and even falsified to gain some imagined advantage of size relative to other institutions. One must sympathize and agree with a former state governor who remarked in confidence to a small group of eminent educators that he had learned never to believe data emanating from state institutions in support of a budget request. And, within institutions, administrators feel much the same way and for much the same reasons about departments.

Because of the confusion of quantity with quality, administrators and faculty have found that the quick route to recognition is in introducing new programs, especially at the graduate level. Although a proposed doctorate program is initially defended in terms of need, evidence that existing programs already find a shortage of qualified students may evoke the admission that the program is required to satisfy and maintain a strong faculty, to add to institutional prestige, or to compete on favorable terms with a nearby institution which already has the program. Probably no administrator has been so honest as to admit publicly (although some have done so in private) that *he* needed a specific program to demonstrate his leadership in raising the quality of the university. Departments in rapidly developing universities which have initially been given additional assistance to move to the doctorate level have found that assistance quickly diverted to move other departments to the same level, with apparently limited administrative concern for the difficulties generated or for the threat to quality that the action involved. In one rapidly inflating university, a mathematics department in such straits saw no alternative but to turn all freshman and most sophomore instruction over to unsupervised graduate assistants, many of whom were at the master's level. The only complaint these assistants made was that the professors were too busy to provide needed assistance in planning programs of graduate study or in directing dissertations. Yet both department and president were considerably irked by criticism of this situation. The department was turning out research and the president was busy with plans for a new college and a medical school.

This equating of quantity with quality becomes the basis upon which institutions resist regional, state, or federal planning that might define and preserve assigned roles. If status (confused with quality) is gained by adding new programs and moving to the graduate level, then autonomy is regarded as essential to the development of institutional character, and status (quality) is indeed jeopardized by agencies which insist on assigning institutional roles in a system of higher education. It sometimes appears that universities systematically promote confusion to avoid systematic planning.

AUTONOMY VERSUS LICENSE

The tendency of the academic to assume that he should be unhampered in developing his own interests and aspirations is amply apparent within institutions. Departments successfully demand an increased number of staff positions on the basis of increased undergraduate enrollment, and then use these resources to employ graduate assistants, simultaneously relieving the faculty of undesired undergraduate instruction, releasing time for research, and, not altogether incidentally, increasing the number of graduate students.

New programs developed in an experimental mode by a university, once staffed with a dean and faculty, have gone their own way, with little regard to the costs inherent in their pattern of instruction or their obligation to the university. Departments acquiring large grants from federal agencies have gloried in their independence of the university administration, although they usually expect and obtain increased general fund support also. Few grants and contracts cover all costs. And, at times, the general fund may have to pick up and support to completion some of the obligations incurred.

Administrators committed to the inauguration of prestigious graduate and graduate professional programs have not hesitated to introduce these despite lack of additional support. Resources have been stretched and the strength of existing programs sapped. In this context, public statements and actual intent may be at variance. A two-year medical school is requested with public indication of no immediate aspirations beyond this; meanwhile, staff is hired and plans laid for almost immediate expansion to a full program. Thus the university which aspires to set a model for society too often operates on the basis that the ends justify the means. Even if the ends were solely and clearly based on societal needs and goals, duplicity exercised for their achievement is hardly justifiable, and especially not in an institution committed to a search for truth. Worse yet, the public which ultimately provides the support for higher education sees through these antics and inconsistencies. The university becomes suspect as an agency committed to self-glorification and personal aggrandizement rather than to service to society. Students no longer accept the university as an earnest seeker after truth, for they see truth rejected when it interferes with university expansion. In this university context, it is not surprising that reciprocated confidence and exploitation of confidence approaching a swindle are central elements in university and department operations. Ordinarily, this confidence game is one of gentle persuasion, but it can become vicious.

Acquiring resources and the freedom to use them are the two central objectives of the game. Round one begins with the institution's request for funds. Universities exhibit complete confidence in their own essential worth and aspirations, and expect that this confidence will be accepted as sufficient evidence for full support—financial and otherwise—by the related clientele. They regularly request more dollars than they really expect, though not necessarily more than they need, and certainly not more than they would use. Institutional requests are inflated partly because of competition with other institutions and agencies, partly because of ever-expanding aspirations, and partly because administrators know that budget officers, boards, and legislators wish to demonstrate frugality by reducing requests without really jeopardizing institutions. Departments require no urging in assisting the university at this stage.

A high degree of autonomy also is regarded as a necessary secondary objective, even to the extent of using funds in ways not specifically indicated in original budget requests. The pattern fits well the sage advice of an often-successful seeker of research funds from foundations and government: "Phrase the proposal so that it fits the current prejudices of the grantor, but is sufficiently ambiguous to permit carrying out the interests of the recipient." In private institutions, budget formulation is less euphoric, since those who propose the budget may also find that they have to raise it. Furthermore, the entire budget-making and resource-allocation process seems to be much more closely guarded and controlled. To complete this round of the confidence game, administrators publicly complain if they receive less than they requested, yet not infrequently express private satisfaction that they received so much.

Round two moves to the internal budgeting process, with specific concern for the departmental level. University departments relate to higher administrative echelons in much the same way as institutions relate to their supporting clientele and governing boards. Resources and departmental autonomy are as necessary for departmental as for institutional effectiveness. For both, autonomy is meaningless without adequate resources. Departments observe the university administrators closely and display adeptness at imitating their gamesmanship. In initial stages of budget making, departments are seldom discouraged from inflating their requests, and those that do not may suffer in the final allocation. Departments do not typically provide detailed evidence of present resource utilization to support their requests for additional funds, and they do not find it expected. In fact, in many universities, neither departments nor central offices can provide relatively simple historical data. A demand for objective data by a dean tends to be regarded by the department as a lack of confidence in the department's program and judgment. Data may be hastily accumulated and carefully selected to support a specific request, but not to reflect the total operation.

The confidence game is not in itself undesirable. Indeed, in some form it is inevitable, for confidence is a key concept in the success of a department. The good department has confidence in itself and in the university. This confidence is reciprocated, and the department enjoys autonomy and support. Under these circumstances, the department may define its mission very narrowly, provided it performs it very well. The department that lacks confidence in its own worth is often beset with internal strife. It receives no confidence and obtains minimal support. It may be driven to isolation or to bitter and self-defeating attempts to improve its lot. It may, in some sense, have a high degree of autonomy, but this opportunity without capability condemns it to an existence like that of the eunuch in a harem.

Self-confidence, accompanied by sanctimonious attitudes and critical comment directed toward the rest of the university, is found in some departments, but self-confidence without mutual confidence between university and department is unhealthy and, in some degree, destroys the effectiveness of both. The autonomy of such a department may be threatened by administrative maneuvers. The department undertakes to justify and maintain its position by whatever combination of evidence and action may hold promise of success. A cold war may continue indefinitely.

INFLUENCE PROCESSES

To understand the conditions that produce or fail to produce departmental autonomy, it became apparent that it was necessary to pay very careful attention to the influence processes within the department and between the department and other administrative units within the university. The strategy and tactics of the confidence game, as practiced by all who participate in academic administration, were studied intensively, if not systematically. Among those employing various strategies, it was noted that at the extremes were two very different breeds of players. One breed was found in those departments that, by the nature of their discipline, found themselves heavily dependent on the university as their source of funds. In these departments, faculty looked to their chairman to provide the best possible working conditions. They cast about for the most articulate and powerful personality among their group and expected him to represent their interests to central administration. When the faculty were confident they had a strong leader, they were willing to entrust him with complete authority in virtually all matters except changes in the curriculum. Though committees existed in profusion, the chairman who succeeded in getting resources could run the show.

At the other extreme we found a breed of player who viewed the confidence game quite differently. In departments receiving extensive funding from outside the university, players displayed little concern and sometimes disdain for deans and central university administration. Here research priorities were based on national and international concerns, and faculty activities, mobility, and advancement were heavily affected by agencies outside the university. In these departments, the chairman maintained the confidence of his colleagues by virtue of his strong national credentials and his ability to guide younger faculty members into prominence on the national scene. These players were little concerned with maneuvering to acquire the confidence of central administration. Rather, they were confident of continued support, for they were producing research negotiable on national and international markets. Despite their aloofness and disdain for the usual maneuvering for support, they were quite successful in getting it.

On either extreme, and in the intermediate positions as well, the department chairman who had the confidence of both his faculty and central administration was virtually guaranteed as long a tenure in office as he wished. But, in order to maintain this dual confidence, the chairman had to proceed democratically enough to satisfy the departmental faculty, and yet be decisive and consistent enough to achieve results in accordance with goals mutually agreed upon between himself and the dean. Every chairman had his own administrative style by which he hoped to accomplish this. The outsider may have some difficulty understanding a department until he grasps the chairman's administrative style and the confidence he has developed with his faculty and dean.)

The chairman may play the role of honest broker, attempting to interpret accurately to both the department and the dean the concerns and dissatisfactions of the other. He may play one against the other to enhance his own position, in which case his days as chairman may be numbered. Or he may attempt to cater to the dissatisfactions of one, enforcing its demands upon the other, in which case the days of his life may be lessened by ulcers, high blood pressure, or heart failure. Only the honest broker role produces healthy reciprocated confidence. Diminishing or no confidence was demonstrated by frequent replacement of the chairman, by high rates of faculty turnover, inadequate support, and decline in quality of the departmental program.)

College deans provided some perceptive insights as they remarked on their efforts to understand the department through their contacts with its chairman. One dean said he wanted to know "what makes the faculty happy and what makes them unhappy. Unhappiness because of lack of research opportunities is very different from unhappiness because of pressure for more scholarly activity." Both the dean and the faculty looked to the chairman to interpret departmental needs in accordance with the goals and priorities of the institution, and thereby to obtain resources sufficient for the needs as actually seen by the department. Institutional patterns varying from highly structured and centralized university systems to others where a great deal of decentralization existed were reflected more significantly in the type of operation than were differences in disciplines. A man who had acquired the confidence of his faculty based on his accomplishments in his discipline, may have found it difficult to adapt to the reward structure of the university

but, having done so, he gained a higher degree of autonomy for his
department.

The tactics of the confidence game as played by successful
departments emerged from the data we collected. Departments were
looked at in terms of source of confidence, development of confidence, uses of confidence, and, finally, analysis of confidence and its
relation to autonomy and the securing of resources. To draw these
differences into sharper focus, eighteen departments with high ratings on the Cartter report were compared with eighteen rated low.

Sources of confidence were revealed by examination of departmental organization and procedures for selecting, appointing,
and reviewing the term of office of the chief department administrative officer. The title itself gave some clue. For example, if the
chief executive officer was designated as *department head,* he was
appointed by the administration to which he needed to maintain
allegiance while cultivating faculty confidence. If the title was *chairman,* it could be expected that he represented his faculty to central
administration and maintained the faculty as his source of confidence while developing that of the administration. The department
executive maintained confidence from administrative sources as long
as faculty wishes were translated into administrative action. Within
these extremes, there was much room for maneuvering and avoid-
ance of confrontation by all parties interpreting the wishes of each
to the other and by seeking satisfactory middle ground. The operating style of the eighteen low-rated departments tended to be oli-
garchical, whereas the eighteen top-rated departments were mostly
democratic.

Maintenance of confidence depended upon the style used by
the executive. An effective style was invariably based on and adjusted to direct experiences with the faculty and officers of central
administration rather than on some a priori pattern based on a
theory of administration. An analysis of communication provided
clues to the decision-making process, although one could not tell
how decisions were actually made. If it was found, for example, that
the communication process was essentially one-way—that is, if staff

meetings were used solely to inform the faculty—it was assumed that the decisions were made with relatively little or no faculty consultation. With some executives and faculties, this one-way communication was effective, and was interpreted as relieving faculty of time-consuming details. It may even be seen by the faculty and dean as democratic, although to the external observer it verges on authoritarianism or paternalism. In one institution, a dean, after characterizing a department as the most democratic in his college, stated that its chairman was the easiest of all to work with because he was decisive and his agreements with the dean were invariably supported by the department. Here the departmental staff also characterized the department as highly democratic.

FACULTY FEEDBACK

If opportunity for feedback existed and the departmental members had opportunity to respond and react to communications originated by the executive, it was assumed that a more truly democratic process was operating than in departments without such feedback. The data indicated that, even when faculty committees were extensively used, the executive was the person to whom most departmental members turned for decisions affecting their academic lives, so long as he got the results they desired. Faculty members who demanded committees did not always have faith in them when their own interests were at stake. "Going around" the chairman by referring matters of substance to others within the department or university was seldom encountered. When this did happen, the faculty members had lost confidence in their executive, either because they suspected his motivations, or they believed he was no longer capable of getting desired results. Analysis of the eighteen low-rated departments shows that they tended to have less opportunity for feedback from the faculty than did the eighteen top-rated departments.

The use of confidence also underlay the department's relationship to the rest of the university. The data indicated four general conditions. The first occurred when departments had made a conscious effort to gain the confidence of the rest of the institution, had been accepted, and were influential within the institution. A second condition arose when departments had tried to be influential in the university but had been rejected. A third occurred when departments were not influential and had made little attempt to influence university polity, although they may have been highly regarded because of their acknowledged quality. A fourth condition was encountered—primarily in professional schools—wherein the faculty deliberately isolated themselves from the rest of the institution, which may have resulted from highly specialized interests, self-consciousness about lack of acceptable academic qualifications, or physical remoteness. The eighteen low-rated departments were about average in their relations with the university. Of the eighteen top-rated departments sixteen were at the extremes—six were isolated from and ten integrated with the university.

INFLUENCE-CONFIDENCE PATTERN

Confidence and influence may be independent characteristics. A chemistry department may be regarded as excellent and have the full confidence of everyone; yet the department and its staff may, by choice, exert little direct influence in university affairs. Other departments that seek to exert influence may fail because of outsiders' doubts about the strength of the department and suspicions concerning its motives. In many of the universities studied, faculty influence in the university was exerted through capable individuals serving on faculty councils, rather than by departments operating as units. In a few cases, the prestige and knowledgeableness of such capable individuals had come to be something of a threat to the status of the department executive, who found individuals on his staff aware of university deliberations and decisions before they had been communicated to him.

Finally, an analysis was made of the influence and confidence patterns based upon agreement on departmental priorities. Faculty, department chairmen, and deans were asked to assign priorities to the same set of tasks. The agreement among deans, department chairmen, and the faculty "average" was greater than the agreement among faculty members themselves. This kind of analysis may be useful when one has an inkling that a particular department executive does not have the confidence of his faculty or his dean. A basic disagreement suggests that the chairman has not succeeded in achieving departmental unity. Disagreement between the dean and the department on priorities may lead to lessening of reciprocated confidence and to discontent, disillusionment, and budgetary difficulties for the department.

From this study certain tentative conclusions can be reached:

Autonomy is essential to effective departmental operation, but autonomy is meaningless without adequate resources, which, in turn, are dependent upon the existence of both departmental self-confidence and confidence reciprocated among the department, the dean, and the university. There is no simple prescription for attainment of this state, because the relationships among faculty, department executives, and the dean are based as much or more on personal relations as on systematic treatment of substantive issues. As one chairman said,

> We used to have a dean who urged us to prepare elaborate charts and tables to present a statistical picture of our problems. When he presented these to central administration, they did not give him anything because, basically, they did not trust him or his statistics. Now we have a dean who uses no statistics, but has the confidence of central administration. My job as chairman is to gain the confidence of the dean so that he will give me what I must have to satisfy the department.

The confidence game is a central element in university relations. The winners of the game are those departments with the financial resources, equipment, facilities, and autonomy necessary to support and reward the faculty members for those activities in which they wish to engage.

The outcomes of the confidence game are not always in the best interests of higher education. The major concerns are not so much with the game as with the manner in which it is played, and the ends to which it is directed. New rules and a different concept of winning are required, for what is regarded as good by the department is not always best for the institution or for higher education. And what is regarded as good for the university may not always be best for higher education or for society.

When autonomy becomes interpreted as license to do whatever an institution or a department desires and, therefore, as a justification for dissemblance or deception in attaining the necessary resources, negotiations based on mutual confidence degenerate into a confidence game in which higher education loses, even when an institution or a department appears momentarily to win. One has only to review the events of the past few years to determine that this is true.

8

Departmental
Self-Study

The combination of mounting costs, increasing numbers of students, and growing demands for service has forced colleges and universities to engage in self-study. Self-studies have also been encouraged by foundation support and by accreditation and review requirements of the various regional and professional accrediting associations. Self-studies vary in thoroughness and in extent. Some deal only with those phases of an institution which are closely re-

147

lated to a problem under discussion or to a decision that must be faced. Others include the total operation of the institution. Self-studies also vary in the approach used. Some are largely the product of committee discussions and hearings conducted by faculty members and outside consultants. Others involve extensive data collection on past history, detailed studies of the operation and effectiveness of a program, and planning for the future.

It is easier to conduct a thorough self-study in a small institution than in a large one. Since the small liberal arts college, for example, is unitary in nature, it is possible to study it as a single organism. In a large university, the size and autonomy of colleges and departments make it difficult to carry out a coordinated all-university self-study. The typical approach in the medium-sized or large institution has been to engage in a study of the purposes, objectives, and functions of the university as a whole, leaving it largely to the colleges and departments to review their own activities in the light of the general analysis and recommendations made by the self-study committee. Thus it happens regularly that, despite programs of institutional self-study and actual modification in policy or organization at the university level, many units in the university change little or not at all.

Under certain conditions self-study must begin at the smallest operating unit, the department. Previous chapters have suggested some of these conditions. The department commonly has its own operating budget and a great deal of autonomy in selecting staff, developing curriculum, and working out patterns of instruction. It may also furnish the greater part of the social life of many of its members, and it certainly furnishes the environment for professional growth. Single departments often have an impact on the educational policies of the entire institution, but a department may lack interest in the university's operations or disapprove of them and retreat from participation in all-institutional activity, finding solace in its own independence and self-sufficiency. Since the excellence of the university, especially at the graduate level, depends ultimately on the excellence of the departments, it is evident that some provision needs to be made for departmental review and self-study.

There are many reasons for conducting review and self-study. Increases in enrollment or the changing emphases in various undergraduate curricula may, within a limited period of time, throw heavy instructional loads on particular units. This may happen when money is not available or, because the budget is relatively inflexible from one year to another, cannot be transferred to the department accepting the increased load. An increased instructional load without appropriate increase in physical and human resources is a deadening influence on the department in many ways. It causes good faculty members to leave, and it makes it difficult to replace them. Moreover, those who stay are so burdened with instructional duties that other activities suffer. Even the instruction itself may become unsatisfactory. The department may shift the instructional load for freshman and sophomore courses to graduate students or other nontenured faculty without adequate provision for supervision and control. The imposition of new programs and services on a department, or its overenthusiastic development of them, also increases faculty load. For example, a new dean or chairman may change institutional policy by emphasizing research activity as the primary basis of promotion without adjusting faculty load to provide time for it.

When loads are heavy and financial support is inadequate in one department as compared with others, poor morale is inevitable, but morale may be low even in a department which has adequate resources. The difficulty may lie within the departmental administrative organization or activities, or with individual administrators who arouse doubts, concern, and antagonism in department members by unfairness, insensitivity, or failure to explain administrative policies. The department may be so demoralized that only strong intervention can bring about improvement.

Some departments, such as mathematics, English, chemistry, and history, offer courses that serve many other departments and units in the university. When a department is not responsive to the concerns and criticisms of other departments which it is presumably serving, dissatisfaction is likely to crystallize in a demand that it be forced to change its practices or that every college and department be made solely responsible for its curriculum. The service role of a department is not limited to courses and instruction. For example, departments of mathematics and statistics can promote research activities and instruction in other departments by providing consultation service for those who need to use mathematics and statistics in conducting their research or developing their courses. Unwillingness to provide such a service often results in lowered quality and increased costs in other units in the university. When duplicating or overlapping services are furnished, they may be inferior and more expensive than those which already exist.

As knowledge increases and the curriculum of the secondary and elementary schools changes, many departments should, but may not, make a complete restudy of the courses offered and the relation of these courses to each other. Elective offerings and course requirements for majors must be carefully balanced. The development of graduate programs should result in a careful restudy of the undergraduate curriculum.

The number of disciplines and departments is always increasing. The relations among departments and the placement of departments are also subject to change. Thus the issue of whether economics should be in the college of business or in the college of arts and sciences is resolved differently on different campuses. The question of whether new disciplines, such as biochemistry and biophysics, should be taught in separate departments has been answered affirmatively in many institutions. Large departments may find it desirable to subdivide their disciplines to coordinate courses and research. The demands imposed on a department may call for some restructuring so as to provide services without interfering with the activities of all members of the departmental faculty. The reorganization of a department, which may call for its division into two units or its assignment to another administrative unit, should be preceded by extensive self-study.

The conduct of a departmental review and self-study requires a study outline indicating the information that is to be obtained, as well as the means of obtaining it. The range of types of information requires a plan of organization, a set of procedures, and the assignment of personnel for carrying out the self-study. The following sections of this chapter present the study outline developed in connection with several departmental reviews at Michigan State University. Subsequently, the organization and procedures appropriate to self-study, as they have been developed in connection with several departmental reviews, are discussed. The outline and the procedures are not presented as final answers to the process of departmental review. The outline is comprehensive, and therefore contains much more than is likely to be required in any one departmental study. Experience in its use shows that it is necessary to adapt the approach to the specific department and to de-emphasize or omit points of little significance.

The departmental study outline has a number of major headings, with subpoints (see page 156).

Section 1, *Philosophy of the Department,* covers the basic purposes and educational objectives of the department. It also raises questions about the prevalent departmental points of view concerning the purposes of the university and the role of the department in the university at large. Since plans for the future presumably grow out of the philosophy current in the department, the purpose of this section is to find out whether there is a consensus in the department concerning the job it faces and the goals it seeks to attain. It becomes very important, therefore, to discover conflicts in point of view and to uncover unresolved or possibly unrealized disagreements between a given department and other departments or units in the institution.

Section 2, *Image of the Department,* covers not only the self-image, which is largely a summary or continuation of the first section on philosophy, but also the role of the department in the view of other persons and departments in the institution. This section also includes an appraisal of the department's graduate instruction and of research made by professors in the same discipline, but located in other universities with which this particular institution is closely associated. Finally, Section 2 raises a question concerning the national professional image of the department. What is the appraisal of the department by persons prominent in the various professional associations or in government, foundations, or business who are well informed concerning the merits of other departments in the discipline? Obviously, much of the information regarding Section 2 comes from sources outside the department. The various points of view expressed regarding the department may clash. The self-image of the department may conflict sharply with the outsider's image of it; and the outsiders may not agree. Such disparities reveal departmental emphasis and interests, as well as of strengths and shortcomings.

Section 3, *Human Resources,* calls for study of the faculty, the nonacademic personnel, the students, and the alumni. This section offers an opportunity to appraise the quality of the senior faculty by examining a variety of characteristics, and also to study the turnover of the senior staff. In a large department, the extent to which junior faculty members of various types are used and the amount of supervision they receive should be given particular attention. Departments vary widely in the number and quality of nonacademic personnel. Most of them are understaffed, but some— particularly those with numerous research contracts—have an excess of staff members. The quality and source of students, both undergraduate and graduate, and the students' appraisal of their experiences in the department deserve careful study. The extent to which the department maintains contact with its students who have obtained advanced degrees and the vigor with which it assists and supports outstanding undergraduates in the pursuit of graduate study or in placement in appropriate positions reveal the extent of departmental interest in individuals. The interaction of students, faculty, and nonacademic personnel has much to do with the morale and the image of a department.

Section 4 of the outline, *Financial Resources and Management,* suggests that the departmental budget and expenditures for the preceding five years be reviewed. Data on sums requested, sums allotted, and actual expenditures in several major categories may reveal disparities between plans, practices, and support. The participation of staff members, in addition to the department chairman, in drawing up the budget, and the bases upon which budgetary requests are made, may reveal the pattern of administrative operations. Some departments will have a number of different funds from which expenditures are made, and the established patterns for authorizing expenditures—particularly for travel—may also reveal something of the quality of administration in the department. Procedures in the assignment of priorities in the expenditure of funds often disclose whether the departmental administration is authoritarian or democratic in nature. The adequacy of departmental records on budget, faculty, students, committee activity, and university and college policies goes far to show whether a department is operated on a businesslike or a haphazard basis. The department's success in obtaining funds, fellowships, and research grants is another indicator of its quality and the effectiveness of its management.

In Section 5, *Organization and Administration,* the chairman's role and his interaction with various individuals and committees are examined. The adequacy and the nature of the departmental intercommunication system is an important aspect of the departmental administrative organization. The personnel policies of a department are in large part determined by the policies of the larger units of which it is a member, but there is usually flexibility in the interpretation of these policies. To a large extent, the decision whether to grant a request for sabbatical leave, a promotion, or a salary increase depends upon where the request originates and the degree of support it receives on the departmental level. Since decisions must be selective, the manner in which they are made and the information upon which they are based are fundamental, in the long run, in determining the quality of the department and the morale of its members.

Section 6, *Curriculum,* recommends a thoroughgoing review of all the courses offered in the department in relation to sound educational considerations: student needs, the faculty qualifications, and the demands of other departments. The alertness of the faculty to the need for continually reexamining and changing the curriculum in the light of new developments and new needs is a point of particular concern. Because of the importance of the curriculum in reflecting and shaping departmental views and programs, curriculum study is given more detailed treatment in Chapter Nine.

Section 7, *Instruction,* requires the collection of basic statistics on course enrollments, course repetition, and section size. These statistics are a clue to the efficiency of departmental planning of instruction, and offer a basis on which to suggest improvements.

Grade distributions from course to course, from term to term, and in comparison with those of other departments may suggest that the department is overgenerous or unreasonably rigorous in the grades which it assigns to students. The organization of instruction in the department usually reflects an adherence to traditional patterns, or alertness in adapting instructional patterns to objectives and using new learning technology in the improvement of instruction. The amount of supervision and coordination provided for junior faculty, especially as they relate to the definition of objectives and the development of examination procedures and grading practices in the teaching of multiple-section courses, demonstrates whether the department is actively concerned with the quality of teaching and with reasonable and fair standards for student appraisal. The opportunities it provides for honors and remedial instruction and its use of placement examinations reveal the sensitivity of the department to differences in individual needs and its willingness to adapt the program to meet these needs.

Section 8 calls for an examination of the *Physical Facilities, Equipment, and Supplies* of the department. The office space, research facilities, instructional facilities, and work space should all be scrutinized and a decision should be made concerning their adequacy, based in part on a comparison with facilities provided for other departments. Those who make the appraisal of the physical facilities and equipment, however, must bear in mind not only such matters as the amount of space, light, and heating, but also the acceptability of the facilities in relation to the purposes and the plans of the department, both present and future. In a review of space, it is important to consider whether the department is making the best possible use of the room available to it. Utilization statistics on classrooms and teaching laboratories should be available to all universities, but relatively little is known about utilization of departmental offices, conference rooms, departmental libraries, and research equipment and facilities. Of course, low utilization of offices may reflect their inadequacy as much as the inavailability of the staff. Equitable administrative procedures in the assignment of office space and a reasonable degree of organization in the arrangements and the housekeeping may be basic considerations in the determination of faculty morale. Equipment for nonacademic staff should also come under review to uncover deficiencies or faulty methods of distribution.

Section 9, *Liaison with Other Departments or Colleges,* deals with the relation of a particular department with other departments or colleges which it serves or depends upon, as the case may be. Data concerning the nature of the service and statistics on the numbers of students served are useful here. In large institutions, the problems of communication deserve particular attention. Extensive use of joint appointments may improve the liaison between departments, but it may also raise questions concerning the equitability of the load and the treatment of persons on joint appointments. The willingness of a department to cooperate in the teaching of courses or the conduct of research and the provision of means whereby such cooperation may take place are important in the development of interdepartmental rapport.

Section 10 takes a brief look at the *Role of the Department in the College or University.* A department which is strong in many respects may be opposed to many policies and goals of the institution, indifferent to them, or actively committed to them. The role of the department in the college or university may be unsatisfactory to the department itself or to other departments in the institution. A major undertaking, then, is to determine what adjustments can be made to bring about a change of role.

The various sections of the outline will disclose many specific points of strength and weakness which need to be analyzed. A mere statement of isolated strengths and weaknesses is not adequate; it should be accompanied by an examination of their interrelation, prior to the presentation of specific recommendations for reorganization and for new or revised policies. The final section of the outline recognizes that the department under examination may need additional resources and support. Little is gained by engaging in an intensive study of a department unless there is advance assurance that additional resources and support will be forthcoming if it is demonstrated that they are necessary.

The process of study would include examination of documents; committee review and analysis of practices and policies, and preparation of reports; and interviews with students, faculty, staff members of the institution outside the department, and possibly even with persons from other institutions. A great many data would be collected, and facilities would be toured and, in some cases, examined by experts on matters of heating, lighting, and ventilation. Outside consultants would almost certainly be called for. A recurring need is likely to be gaining access to statistics, norms, or judgments for like departments in the same and other institutions.

Most departments in most institutions could use more resources than they have, but resources are limited. Even if a self-study discloses that a particular department is in great need of assistance, it cannot be given a disproportionate share of the university's total resources. Departmental studies do not provide a simple formula which will enable every department to rank among the top ten in the country.

The study outline developed in connection with departmental reviews at Michigan State University is as follows:

1. Philosophy of Department

    1.1   Purposes: relative emphasis on research and publication service, and instruction

    1.2   Objectives
          1.21   Educational goals toward which students are expected to progress
          1.22   Professional goals toward which academic personnel are expected to progress

    1.3   Points of view about education and role of department in the university, including service and liberal-education obligations

    1.4   Plans: specific aims for the future, such as course expansion, faculty increase, extension of graduate work, and research expansion

2. Image of Department

    2.1   Self-image in relation to instruction, research, and service functions

    2.2   Intrauniversity image of undergraduate and graduate instruction

2.3 Interuniversity image of graduate instruction and research

2.4 National professional image

3. Human Resources
   3.1 Faculty
      3.11 Senior faculty (instructor, assistant professor, associate professor, professor)
         3.111 Rank, salaries, age, degrees, institutions, tenure status, awards
         3.112 Professional-society memberships, offices held, and participation (meetings attended)
         3.113 Research activity and publications
         3.114 Public service, consultation (private or university-sponsored)
         3.115 Role and status in university (research or teaching)
         3.116 Interests and qualifications in relation to departmental role in the university
         3.117 Stability (turnover) of senior staff
      3.12 Junior faculty (assistant instructor, graduate and research assistant, lecturer, specialist, and so on)
         3.121 Numbers and types of part-time junior faculty used
            3.1211 Number, classification, qualifications, and function
            3.1212 Relation to departmental organization and administration
   3.2 Clerical personnel
      3.21 Number, classification, qualifications, and function
      3.22 Extent of service available to faculty members
      3.23 Technical aides
         3.231 Number and function
         3.232 Relation to faculty and clerical personnel
   3.3 Students
      3.31 Enrollments by levels, undergraduate and graduate (last five years)
      3.32 Number of majors, undergraduate and graduate

8. Physical Facilities, Equipment, and Supplies
    8.1 Office space for faculty
        8.11 Adequacy of space, lighting, and heating
        8.12 Convenience in reference to location: distance, levels, and so on
        8.13 Equipment
        8.14 Privacy
        8.15 Utilization
    8.2 Research facilities
        8.21 Adequacy
        8.22 Location in relation to office
        8.23 Equipment
    8.3 Seminar rooms, staff room, and so on
    8.4 Classrooms and teaching laboratories
        8.41 Adequacy of size
        8.42 Location
        8.43 Equipment
        8.44 Utilization
    8.5 Work space for nonacademic help
        8.51 Adequacy
        8.52 Location
        8.53 Equipment: typewriters, duplicating machines, calculators, and so on
    8.6 Departmental library, reading room
    8.7 Arrangements and housekeeping
    8.8 Supplies and services
        8.81 Adequacy of supplies
        8.82 Adequacy of services for
            8.821 the faculty
            8.822 instruction
            8.823 research

9. Liaison with Other Departments or Colleges
    9.1 Departments serving this department
        9.11 Nature of service
        9.12 Size of load and level of service
    9.2 Departments served
        9.21 Nature of service
        9.22 Size of load and level of service
    9.3 Patterns of communication with units serving or served
    9.4 Use of joint appointments

      9.5   Interdepartmental cooperation in course offerings, research, and so on

10. Role of Department in College or University
- 10.1 Awareness of and commitment to the goals of the college or university
- 10.2 Involvement in college or university planning
- 10.3 Clarity of definition of role of college or university
     10.31   Acceptance of role
     10.32   Possibilities of changing role
- 10.4 Factors external to the department to be considered in appraising or altering departmental role and functions in the university

11. Summary of Findings and Recommendations
- 11.1 Major strengths
- 11.2 Major weaknesses or areas for improvement
- 11.3 Specific recommendations regarding
     11.31   reorganization
     11.32   new or revised policies
     11.33   resources and support required

As the outline indicates, no adequate self-study of a department can be made except as the role of the department in the institution is studied and the quality of the department is compared with that of departments in like institutions. This means that the study committee itself must include persons who are not members of the department and that in all likelihood it will wish to have recourse to a number of outside consultants. Departments do not always welcome a study of such dimensions. Their natural preference is to conduct their own study and then report to deans and other administrators what additional resources they need. A department can, of course, recognize that it has difficulties in its relations with other units and that it is perhaps not fulfilling its anticipated role, but it is difficult for the members of a departmental staff to get a frank appraisal of the department from outsiders. Therefore, outside consultants should report to the dean, the vice-president, or to the study committee rather than directly to the department. It is even more difficult for departments to be objective about their own inadequacies and strengths. The tendency is to assume that the acquisition of more resources, rather than better use of existing resources, will solve all their problems.

A thoroughgoing self-study, such as is summarized in the outline, requires time and money. Money for it is not likely to be available in a departmental budget, and a department in difficult circumstances may not have available staff time to invest in it. Out of these circumstances, Michigan State University has developed a pattern for initiating and carrying on a departmental self-study:

1. The department, the college dean, and the academic vice-president or provost agree that a detailed analysis of the operations of the department is desirable. A normal condition of this agreement is that any sizable increase in resources will be withheld until the self-study is completed. It is also a part of such an agreement that funds to support the self-study will be made available.

2. A self-study committee is then appointed, composed of five kinds of representatives: the department chairman, a respected senior member of the department, a representative of the college, a representative of a department extensively served by the department under study, and a representative of the provost's office. It may or may not be deemed appropriate to add to the committee a representative of the Office of Institutional Research. This office always makes its staff and facilities available in the collection of data for the study. In the case of large departments, a liaison faculty member who is not on the committee may be useful in coordinating data-collection procedures.

3. Using the self-study outline as a basis for collecting and reporting data,

   a. The department chairman writes a report on the status of the department as he sees it. For this purpose he may draw upon any data he has or request that additional data be collected by the committee or the Office of Institutional Research to assist him in the preparation of his report.

b. The departmental staff, under the leadership of the faculty member on the committee, prepares a detailed report of the status and aspirations of the department. Usually the department faculty form subcommittees to handle various parts of the outline. The faculty leader, who may be either a senior departmental member on the study committee or the liaison faculty member mentioned previously, is given time to supervise the development of the report.

c. The nondepartmental members of the committee interview all the staff members of the department under study and of those departments it serves. They may also interview administrators and other members of the college or university whose opinions may be valuable. The interviews with staff members of the department will ordinarily include graduate assistants. Frequently graduate and undergraduate students are also interviewed and receive questionnaires to fill out.

d. The chairman and the faculty member visit and study several comparable departments in other universities which seem to have problems similar to those of the home department. It would probably be desirable to have the entire committee, or at least one member outside the department, join in this field-study phase of the analysis, but, in the interest of reducing costs, this has not been done.

e. The department and the committee jointly agree on the outside consultants invited to study the department, asking them to limit their study to particular sections of the outline instead of attempting to cover all aspects of the department's operations in a three- or four-day stay.

4. Each of the reports (the chairman's report, the reports of the two or three consultants, the field-study report, the department reports, and the report summarizing the interviews) is then analyzed and codified in relation to the departmental study outline, which may have been

modified somewhat to meet special departmental problems or concerns. If faculty and student questionnaires
are available, these are related, generally by plan, to
points in the outline, so that there is minimal difficulty in
using the questionnaire results in the preparation of the
summary report.

5. The codified materials from the various reports and the
questionnaires are then brought together in the outline
for committee study and comment. The committee works
through the study outline, considering every suggestion
and criticism which has been made.

6. The committee writes its own report, including a series
of recommendations, and the final report is organized almost exactly in accordance with the departmental study
outline. The entire contents of the final report, and the
language in which it is couched, are approved by consensus in the committee. No statement in the report is
ever subjected to a vote.

7. Finally, the report is submitted to, discussed by, and ultimately (perhaps with some revisions) accepted by the
department and the provost. Assignments are then made
to the various units, such as the provost's office, the college, and the department or department chairman, for
carrying out its recommendations.

8. The report may call for a marked increase in the staff
and in the budget of the department. If so, this increase
is usually contingent upon the department's taking action
to modify or develop its program. The report may call for
for extensive continuing study of certain problems, and
staff time and money to carry it on. It may also call for
a single major allotment of funds for purchasing equipment, space, and so on. The department responsible for
putting the recommendations into effect is required to
give the committee an account of the steps it has taken
in accordance with the major proposals in the report.
Annual reports of progress may be required to justify

increased resources projected over a period of several years.

In general, the conduct of comprehensive studies of individual departments is a salutary experience for all concerned. Administrators learn that although it is easy to be critical of a department's operations and cynical about its attitudes, departments do, nevertheless, face serious problems. Self-studies have demonstrated that many improvements can be made in the departmental operation. Recommendations for such improvements are not always welcomed by the departments, but increased appropriations can be made contingent on their acceptance. On the other hand, it is equally clear that the departments which face a number of acknowledged problems require help to resolve them. It is clear also that the inadequacy of communication among departments and colleges on a university campus is a major source of tension, misunderstanding, and suspicion. Departments must learn that if they are to receive the kind of support they wish from the university, they must indeed become contributing members of the university. A study may also prove to other departments that a given department does have special problems created by the demands of its discipline and by the multiplicity of services which it provides to many different units of the university. Administrators may learn that budgeting procedures have not always been equitable in relation to the shifting load and varying quality of departments, and that failure to recognize this inequity compounds problems which become increasingly difficult to resolve when they go unrecognized for a long period of time.

Perhaps the most telling evidence in favor of the pattern of departmental self-study described in this paper is that some departments have requested self-studies instead of having to be persuaded to accept them. Furthermore, experiences with this type of self-study led to broader study of the departments reported on in previous chapters. The self-study outline and experiences with its use provided the background for selecting much of the data collected and the various analyses made. A revealing fact about the situation of the university department is that despite serious problems in some of the departments in our sample, no self-study of the depth described here had been made in any of them.

Curriculum Review
and Control

Even in those universities in which the faculty role in governance has continued to be somewhat limited, contacts with departmental faculties repeatedly reveal the conviction that the faculty—and ultimately the department—must determine policies, requirements, and offerings in the interlocking areas of curriculum and instruction. The weakness in this situation is that faculty members seldom display any concern about the financial implications of their curricular and

166

instructional policies. Furthermore, their curricular interests are narrowly departmental (or professional) and often not in the best interests of students, particularly the undergraduates. Dissatisfaction among graduate students is also quite common, but the student's dependence on the department (often even on the same professor) for his stipend and his progress on a degree has, until recently, effectively prevented open expression of grievances or of revolt. Graduate assistants or teaching fellows on modest or starvation stipends find it difficult to understand why they have heavier teaching assignments than many of their professors or why they should contribute significantly to research with small recognition, pecuniary or otherwise. Marked inequities in expectations or demands of professors to whom assistants are assigned, even within the same department, add to the dissatisfaction. Sheer inability to get the ear or the eye of his major professor is a common complaint of the graduate student, even at the dissertation stage.

Regarding the undergraduate major, the department's preoccupation is usually with the number of students and their caliber, as revealed by continuance into graduate study, and all too often with encouraging the student to take an unreasonable number of courses in the department. Although the major selected by an undergraduate is often but an incident (and accident) which has little relation to his future career, either vocationally or educationally, the major is, for the department, the only significant element in the undergraduate program.

The preceding remarks state circumstances so widely prevalent that many professors express more surprise than resentment when these circumstances are questioned. Their view is that it is a privilege for a student to be accepted by a department, and that whatever happens thereafter must be accepted as necessary puberty rites to attain maturity in that discipline. However, the concern of this chapter is with the curriculum, and the sole purpose of the preceding comments is to indicate some reasons why departmental control of its curriculum, its instruction, and its major requirements must be brought recurrently under examination by administrators or committees with a broader and less biased view of university resources, goals, and policies, and of student educational satisfactions and needs than departments seem to have.

Professors—and even administrators—have a natural tendency to take pride in having a great number of courses, even when few students are enrolled in many of them. There is also a tendency to assume that quality instruction and learning are possible only when classes are small, although extensive studies by many researchers over a long period of years have produced little evidence that class size makes any significant difference in the kind or amount of learning which takes place. These findings may only mean that an instructor's behavior has little relationship to the number of students he faces, but, in any case, the need for many small-enrollment courses can hardly be justified by professorial preference; some other justification must be sought if the resulting high costs are to be defended.

Over a period of ten years, one major university found that the number of separate courses at the undergraduate and graduate levels combined had increased by approximately 500 courses, from 3,100 to over 3,600. Among the 3,600 courses were some that had not been offered in five years, and others that had not been offered in the entire period since they had been added to the curriculum. Departments, however, resisted pressure to eliminate any course on the grounds that in the future a professor might be found who would wish to teach the course, or that a number of students might turn up who should take it. Such nonfunctional courses hardly have any impact on the efficiency of operation of an institution, except for the minor expense of keeping track of them and printing them in the catalog. There is, however, an ethical consideration involved in indicating the presence of courses which have not been and are not being offered, and the existence of such courses is certainly an indication of a lack of adequate review and control of the curriculum.

Of the 3,600 courses mentioned, approximately one-third were at the graduate level, leaving approximately 2,400 undergradlate-level courses. Of these undergraduate courses, only 11 or 12 per cent had an annual enrollment of over 150 students, and most of these courses were offered, two, three, or four times during the year rather than in a single quarter. On the other hand, approximately 42 per cent of the courses had an annual enrollment of 20 students or less, and among these were 211 courses at the freshman and sophomore levels. Despite an overall university enrollment approaching 30,000, it was evident that the number of courses spread student enrollments so widely that there were very few large-enrollment courses and a relatively large number of courses (55 per cent of the total) with annual enrollments so small that offering the course but once a year would still not yield an unreasonably large class.

Although the commitment to year-round operation may require the repetition of courses enrolling only five or ten students, the evidence certainly demonstrates that this situation does not account for all small-enrollment courses, many of which are not essential for any curriculum. Since instructional load tends to be based upon credit (or contact hours), small-enrollment courses result in a lowered level of productivity or efficiency for the instructors teaching them. The diffusion of enrollments over many courses also results in inability to organize efficient combinations of large lectures and small discussion groups because of the relatively few large-enrollment courses.

LOW-CREDIT COURSES

A frequency distribution of the number and percentage of courses by credit showed that nearly 71 per cent of the courses carried three credits or less. Actually, there were 25 which carried no credit, 71 which carried one credit, and 60 which carried two credits. Some of the results of such low-credit courses are clear, even though the quantitative evaluation of the impact is difficult. Interviews with students suggest that, when loaded with five, six, or more courses, they tend to build a program that includes several "snap" courses in which they can get by with minimal preparation. Registration, scheduling, and grading problems are multiplied.

Another element of inefficiency arises from reduced faculty loads. Responses to questions about typical loads indicated an increasing tendency to define load in terms of courses rather than credits. Obviously, a two-course load (a common pattern) composed of two- or three-credit courses is less productive than a two-course load composed of four-credit courses.

Attempts to reduce the number of low-credit courses incur resistance from the faculty. In certain departments, low-credit courses obtain large enrollments because they are used by students to fill out a schedule. The argument is usually presented that this broadens the student's cultural horizon, but one suspects that the department is more concerned about the total enrollment and the budgetary implications. Low-credit courses also lend themselves to dividing up knowledge into smaller pieces which coincide with particular interests and specialties of faculty members, whereas larger credit blocks may force a faculty member to teach a segment of his discipline in which he is not especially interested.

CLASS SIZE

We made a tabulation of the number of credits taught in classes of specified size for one particular term in order to examine class size more closely. This tabulation involved determination of the various patterns of instruction in each course and the section size and credit corresponding to that particular pattern. Thus, a course meeting with a lecture of 300 students once a week and ten sections of 30 students each twice a week would be recorded as one credit taught to 300 students and two credits taught in classes of 30 students. On this basis, it was found that over 90 per cent of the graduate-level credit-hours were offered in classes of 20 or fewer students, and 80 per cent to classes of 10 or fewer students. This finding is not too startling considering the nature of graduate study. At the undergraduate level, 42 per cent of the credit-hours were found to be taught in classes of 20 or fewer students, and 19 per cent in classes of 10 or fewer, a rather more startling finding considering that, in a large university, the usual characterization is that classes are very large.

Most institutions have established some procedures whereby classes of exceptionally small enrollment are reviewed and eliminated unless the enrollment increases. A required minimal size may be applied by level; thus classes at the junior and senior levels en-

rolling 5 or fewer students and classes at the freshman and sophomore levels enrolling 10 or fewer students may be dropped. Once
such principles are established, their application should be well-
nigh automatic unless adequate justification to the contrary is presented by the department concerned.

Another factor worth examining is the number of times the
course is offered. Faculty members may try to schedule their specialty every quarter, when the total enrollment scarcely justifies offering it once during the year. The loss of students from the fall
quarter to the spring also frequently results in departments repeat-
ing courses or reducing the average section size in multiple-section
courses so that every staff member can continue to have a full load
without regard to the marked decrease in student credit-hour productivity.

OVERLAP AND DUPLICATION

One result of the proliferation of courses is overlap and duplication in content within and among departments. In one university it was found that beginning statistics was taught in five
departments; that basic courses on health problems were taught in
five departments; that offerings in the area of marriage and the
family were provided in four departments; that basic design courses
were offered in four departments; and that work in elementary mechanical, electrical, and plumbing skills was provided in four different departments. Aside from the fact that the total number of
courses is increased by this duplication and that the average number
of students enrolled in courses is thereby decreased, a number of
other very serious questions are raised.

Statistics, as taught by departments other than mathematics
and statistics, is sometimes little more than a course in simple arith-
metical operations. The instructor himself may know little or no
statistical theory, and the students may have so little background in
mathematics that they are capable only of learning routine operations without any understanding. Indeed, precisely this circumstance
of student and instructional incompetency is often the basic reason
why such duplication in courses arises. However, sometimes departments which should serve the rest of the institution reject this re-

sponsibility and adopt a very unrealistic position as to student preparation and standards of achievement.

Although a review of the marriage and family offerings a few years earlier had resulted in a committee report that "even though many of the same references are used, the approaches are sufficiently distinctive to justify all of the offerings," one may still doubt whether there is sufficient substance in the area of marriage and family to justify four independent introductory offerings, without even an indication that the student taking one of them would not be permitted to receive credit for another. Courses in mechanical, electrical, and plumbing skills, of the type found in this curriculum review, have no place in a university, but the departments concerned would not accept this view.

In the review of departmental offerings, courses offered for various numbers of credits and with slight variation in content for different groups of students are common in certain disciplines. Thus, in one university, there were four different sequences offered in calculus, varying slightly in credit and content. One was aimed at majors, the others at various groups of nonmajors. Likewise, different sequences were provided in chemistry and in physics. While some adaptation to the needs of particular groups is perhaps necessary and desirable, critical review of all such practices is needed. Departments developing a new curriculum in which they include some limited number of hours from another related or contributive discipline are all too prone to expect special service rather than to utilize existing strengths of another department. Another type of duplication growing out of such pressure is found when, within a department, two or more introductory courses are offered at different levels to different groups of students. For example, a course numbered at the junior or senior level may be offered to a group of nonmajors who are really taking a beginning course that ought more honestly to be labeled as a freshman or sophomore course, but is placed at the more advanced level and numbered to suit the wishes of the department served.

CONTACT HOURS

Contact-hour requirements which greatly exceed credits demand repeated review. The science laboratory especially requires attention. Assuming a pattern in which a five-credit course shows two hours of lecture, two hours of recitation, and six hours in the laboratory, one might, according to the common pattern, equate the two hours of lecture and the two hours of recitation to four credits and argue that the six hours of laboratory constitute one credit. This pattern is based on the fairly generally accepted convention that one hour of face-to-face contact with the instructor yields one credit. On this basis, in one university the number of hours in laboratory for one credit varied from one to over seven hours. In a few cases, the number of credits given to a course were actually less than the number of scheduled lecture sessions, a phenomenon resulting from historical accident in that a demand by other departments for reduction in credit was acceded to, but with the proviso that all of the existing contact hours must be continued in order to provide for adequate coverage of material. Despite the general awareness of scientists of the problem of developing a laboratory which is a really significant educational experience, students commonly protest that much of the laboratory time is wasted. Laboratory space and equipment are tremendously expensive and, if the space is not effectively used, it is an unjustified drain on the resources of an institution. It is only reasonable to ask how many laboratory hours are really necessary in beginning science courses, especially for students who are taking a very limited amount of science. A number of science departments have found demonstrations adequate for these students. Three major questions can be raised about science laboratory requirements: Despite the lack of clarity in the meaning of a credit, is it fair to the student to demand many hours in the laboratory for limited or no credit? On what basis can the great variation among departments and courses be defended? and Are the additional costs and space requirements of the additional laboratory hours justified by the additional educational benefits?

CURRICULUM AND COURSE REVIEW

Class size, needless course repetition, low-credit courses, excessive course offerings, and archaic curricula are so frequently found in departments that the departmental demand for complete autonomy on curricular matters must be regarded as highly dubious. Only by external pressure based ultimately on budgeting considerations is it possible to get some departments to review and adjust their curriculum. If curricular review and control were regularly operative in universities, these stormy confrontations could be eliminated.

Most departments would benefit from a thoroughgoing review of all courses and the assignment of each to some category as in the following group:

1. Courses whose primary justification is that they are required for students majoring in other departments, curricula, or colleges. These are often called service courses, and they are not ordinarily taken by majors.
2. Courses which primarily provide a general or liberal education and are given without prerequisites as electives for majors in other disciplines.
3. Courses for majors in a department:
   a. introductory courses for departmental majors and students from other fields;
   b. courses required of all, or nearly all, departmental majors;
   c. electives for departmental majors or for majors in closely related disciplines. Such courses are often part of a sequence developing a subarea of the discipline.
4. Highly specialized courses, originating in the special interests of a particular staff member, which serve the purposes of relatively few students (and perhaps the actual needs of none).

These categories are not mutually exclusive. Some courses will fit into more than one. In some cases actual student enrollment may indicate that a course serves a rather different clientele than intended by the department. In any case, the mere act of classification will not directly accomplish any reduction in the number of courses. Each course, whatever its classification, must be critically regarded. In general, the service-course concept has been overworked. Adaptation of a course to the special interests of a particular group tends to make of the course a vocational rather than a liberal education offering. Departments offering such courses often complain about this tendency, and professors seldom find much satisfaction in teaching them, but out of good will or because of threat, departments have made such offerings quite common. All service courses should be reviewed to determine whether students might not be better served by a course in which the essential characteristics of the discipline were not modified or sacrificed to specialized interests.

Courses in the second category—general or liberal education offerings, open to all students, with few or no prerequisites—are highly desirable, but only a limited number are necessary. It would be helpful to designate these courses in some fashion that would assist students and their advisers in defining their nature and content. Since many students who enroll in general education courses take only one or two from a department, each course should be reasonably complete in itself rather than a part of some extended sequence, no one unit of which assumes full meaning. Such courses may not be suitable for majors whose extensive background requires a challenging and sequentially organized experience.

Courses in the third category—those primarily designed for students majoring in a discipline—should be planned in some sequence, with the order and prerequisites clearly indicated. For an undergraduate major of forty to sixty semester-hours, it would not be unreasonable to specify that as many as twenty-five to thirty hours be in required courses, the remainder to be elective in that department or closely related disciplines. In some cases, departmental offerings may comprehend what are regarded as two or even three distinctive majors. A department of foreign languages offering several languages is an example. In such cases, the principle should be applied to each major. In most cases, however, an introduction to the major subfields of a discipline can be provided by a limited number of electives offered at the junior and senior levels.

This rather crude review of courses in a department may do little more than clarify the sources of the student clientele. For some small departments, the review may be useless; a broader and more penetrating approach may be required. Provision for recurrent review and revision, addition, or elimination is desirable. All proposals for new courses should be carefully studied in reference to course characteristics, costs, and probable enrollment. Departments often add courses or propose programs for which institutional resources are inadequate. The institution may not possess the necessary instructional library or laboratory facilities. The department seeks permission to add a new course or program, but demands the required resources afterward. Thus a decision is made without full awareness of its implications. Moreover, the department may actually offer the course in the hope that its presence will ultimately generate the required resources.

Most courses and new curricula are added without sufficient information and evaluation. Frequently the information provided obscures the relation of the course to existing courses or is so vague that the instructor can do anything he wants. Objectives are rarely defined, no selection of content and materials is made, and no text or bibliography is provided. Departments and colleges demand approval of additional courses and curricula as an act of faith, and, unfortunately, usually succeed. College and university curriculum committees, if they exist at all, tend to give only cursory attention to new proposals, and almost never engage in review of existing programs.

The department or individual professor should not be the final authority on the content and mode of instruction in undergraduate courses. Any institution will have individuals outside of a department whose training, interests, and objectivity make them at least as well equipped to react to what is appropriate in a given department as those whose vision is limited by departmental myopia. The original decision of the university to adopt a particular program was not made by the faculty, because there was no faculty. Likewise, the decision to abandon a particular offering will not be made by the faculty involved. These extreme cases demonstrate that individuals outside the departments must be involved in major curricular decisions concerning departments. Every departmental decision or recommendation for course and curricular additions requires the allocation of institutional resources. Departmental autonomy on curricular matters is unrealistic, though it remains the major argument against central review and control of the curriculum.

Most colleges offer certain courses or curricula which reflect administrative or public pressure rather than faculty inclination, which suggests the necessity of cooperation between the administration and faculty on curricular decisions rather than complete control by either group.

Another argument against review and control of the curriculum is that too much time is lost between the presentation of a proposal for change and the effective date of that change. Departments and individuals usually want immediate authorization of new courses and curricula, whereas systematic review of proposals for curriculum change requires the collection of extensive data, the involvement of many persons, and a period of deliberation. However, delay is fully justified if the full implications of course and curricular additions are realized. Many hastily adopted, regrettable additions would have faded quietly away in the several months required for study.

Outline for Course Analysis. Our outline for course analysis includes most of the points involved in review and analysis of curricular innovations and modifiations. The outline is based on four principles. First, the department or instructor must define the course coverage and the instructional patterns to be used, and must review the adequacy of available resources. Second, the proposed course must be compared with all related courses in the university, not only by those proposing the course, but also by those involved in related courses. Third, the clientele to be served by the course must be identified and the probable enrollment estimated. Finally, the financial implications of the change or addition must be analyzed. The outline demands collection of data and deliberation, and permits intelligent administrative and committee review.

Ideally, the institution should conduct a thorough review of all existing courses, and then insist that this analysis be applied to all future additions or proposals for change. The principles which determined this outline for course review are equally relevant to curricular review and analysis.

Comments on the Outline. The outline is divided into

three sections.[1] Section 1, entitled *Identifying and Descriptive Information,* is divided into two parts. The first part indicates information which should be included in the catalog course description. Some catalogs do not include a description of the hours and types of instruction in a course. Students who are planning their future program find it helpful to have some indication of the pattern of instruction. For example 5(*2-1-4*) could be used to indicate a course offering five credits, of which there are two hours in lecture, one hour in recitation or discussion, and four hours in laboratory work. Catalog course descriptions should also indicate for what kind of students the course is designed.

The information in the second part of this section is too detailed to be included in a catalog course description. However, this information should be available to advisers or students on request. It constitutes a contract by which the department assures each student enrolling in the course that he will have an experience as indicated by the outline or syllabus. It also assures that a new course will not be just a random thought that the department should offer some previously ignored aspect of the discipline.

Section 2, entitled *Analytical Information,* requires detailed information on the type of instruction, class size, required number of staff, and scheduled hours per week. The breakdown of total credits into various types of learning experiences may carry the course-credit pattern to the point of becoming ridiculous, but if credits are to be used, there should be some relation between work expected and credits granted. This breakdown forces a department to consider whether the number of hours required by the course is appropriate to the number of credits assigned to it. Science courses, as previously noted, frequently require too much laboratory work for the number of credits received. In the social sciences, field work requirements are excessive. This information may also help institutions to assess total course costs by computing the cost of the different types of instruction. This section also demands an estimate of special or additional resources and personnel required. The depart-

[1] For curriculum study and review, an additional section specifying the purpose of the program and providing justification both for its need and for adding it in the institution would be required.

ment is asked to submit in advance a statement of the inadequacies of existing resources and of the required additional resources. Information is also required on the relation of the course to other courses offered in the department or in other departments, both in terms of prerequisites and in terms of duplication of content. When new curricula or degree programs are proposed, data should be provided on the presence of these programs in other institutions, and the justification for duplicating them should be provided—especially for expensive vocational programs such as nursing or engineering. Finally, this section requests estimates on the size and source of enrollment in the course and on the additional cost of the course.

Section 3, entitled *Historical Information,* pertains only to existing courses currently under review. The enrollment in each offering, the sources of enrollment, the section size, the number and type of staff, and the cost per credit hour may already be recorded in institutions with Offices of Institutional Research. In other cases, the information should not be difficult to obtain. Departments which carry a large service load should have a breakdown of the sources of their students. This information is particularly helpful when curriculum changes are being considered which will modify the number of hours or courses which a given group of students take in other departments. By increasing electives or requirements outside the field of specialization, the staff responsible for a particular curriculum can unload a good portion of their work on other departments without the knowledge or consent of the faculty members involved.

Outline for Course Analysis

1. Identifying and Descriptive Information
    1.1 Catalog course description including
        1.11 Departmental or generic title and number
        1.12 Descriptive title
        1.13 Prerequisites
        1.14 Terms offered
        1.15 Credits so presented as to identify hours and type of instruction provided (lecture, discussion, laboratory, independent study)
        1.16 Statement of objectives, content coverage, and students to whom directed

1.2 Outline or syllabus including
  1.21 Detailed statement of objectives
  1.22 Text and other materials to be used
  1.23 Day-by-day or week-by-week indication of topics covered, types and amounts of work expected of students, standards to be met, and methods of evaluation to be used
  1.24 Bibliography

2. Analytical Information

  2.1 Instructional model: credits, hours, and types of instruction

Type of Session	Preferred Class Size	Staff Required*	No. of Hours Per Week	No. of Credits
Lecture				
Recitation or discussion				
Laboratory				
Field work				
Independent study				

  * Indicate separately the number of senior staff (instructor or above) and junior staff (graduate assistants, assistant instructors) required.

  2.2 Special or additional resources and personnel required
    **2.21 Special facilities (classrooms, auditoriums, laboratories, and so on)
    **2.22 Library and other learning resources required (books, films, slides, prints, and so on). List with indication of whether the items are here available, can be ordered, or must be made.
    2.23 Special staff competencies required
      2.231 Number of persons now on staff qualified to teach course
      2.232 New staff requirements and individual competencies needed (project for at least two years)
  2.3 Relation to other courses
    2.31 Offered by the department
      2.311 Course or courses replaced by this course

** New courses especially

2.312 Prerequisite courses

2.313 Courses for which this course is a prerequisite

2.314 Courses covering some of the same content

    2.3141 Safeguards against acquiring of duplicate credits by the student

2.32 Offered by other departments

    2.321 Courses in which enrollment may be reduced by the selection of this course

    2.322 Prerequisite courses

    2.323 Courses for which this course is a prerequisite

    2.324 Courses covering some of the same content

        2.3241 Extent and nature of relationships

        2.3242 Distinctive factors justifying existence of this course

        2.3243 Safeguards against acquiring of duplicate credits by the student

2.33 Offered by other colleges or universities

    2.331 In the immediate community

    2.332 In the state

2.4 Size and source of enrollment

    2.41 Departmental majors (indicate whether required or elective, number involved)

        2.411 Submajor within department

    2.42 Majors in other departments, curricula, or colleges (indicate for each whether required or elective, number of students involved)

    **2.43 Anticipated enrollment in first and second year of offering, in summer, fall, winter, and spring quarters

2.5 Details of instructional planning

Objectives	Experiences Especially Related to Objective	Means of Evaluation of Student Achievement
1.		
2.		
3.		
4.		
5.		
6.		
7.		

** New Courses

**2.6 Estimated new funds required by addition of this course:
Salaries
Supplies and services
Equipment
Remodeling

3. Historical Information (for courses under review)

3.1 Enrollment during the previous two years
19............   19............
Summer
Fall
Winter
Spring

3.2 Sources of enrollment previous year

	Fr.	*Soph.*	*Jr.*	*Sr.*	*M.*	*GP*	*Ph.D.*
Majors (departmental)							
Students from Department or College A							
Students from Department or College B, and so on							

3.3 Section size for the past year

	Smallest Section	*Mean*	*Largest Section*
Lecture			
Recitation or discussion			
Laboratory			

3.4 Number (head count) of senior staff involved in past
year .... full-time equivalent ....
Number (head count) of junior staff involved in past
year .... full-time equivalent ....

3.5 Instructional salary cost per student credit hour

Procedures for Review and Analysis. Although the desirability of curriculum review is generally accepted, the means of accomplishing it is uncertain. Even under the urgency of fiscal con-

** New Courses

siderations, it is doubtful that individual departments would be sufficiently stringent in review. Furthermore, the duplication of offerings in related departments would be ignored by this approach. On the other hand, no university-wide committee can command either the competence or the time needed for comprehensive review of all courses. Also, curriculum committees made up of busy professors do not have the time for rigorous review. Load reductions for professors in such committee service and use of the services of an Office of Institutional Research would improve the situation. There are at least two other approaches: (1) Organize a number of university-wide committees, each being assigned a group of departments for review. Each committee would be made up largely but not solely of faculty members from the departments to come under review by the committee. After each department had presented its analysis of its own courses, the committee's task would be to review it and recommend acceptance or further modification. Each committee should operate within a framework of clearly defined principles or policies, rather than consider each individual proposal in isolation. Such policies may include: limitations on small classes and automatic discontinuance of courses which fail to meet enrollment requirements; restriction of study of a particular discipline to a single department; limitations on duplication or overlapping content materials; reasonable relationships between time and credit requirements; and limitations on overall departmental, college, and university offerings in relation to the number of students served. The outline above implies certain rules and principles upon which the curriculum committee can base its decisions. (2) Bring in one to three scholars of national reputation in each of several selected disciplines, with the assignment that the individual or the committee carefully review the courses in a department and present recommendations for revision that would establish the minimal set of offerings. Provided the review is rigorous, and that it leads to the combination of some courses and the elimination of others, the precedent established would increase the likelihood of similar action in other departments.

The rigorous approach involved in these procedures or in use of any detailed information request is very likely to reduce the number of proposals for change. If an individual or department must provide such detailed information, it may be decided that the proposal is neither important nor justified. Moreover, department chairmen and deans, who commonly screen such requests, are likely to be more careful in their examination when they realize that approval is not automatic. No one likes to be a party to a proposal which is denied. On major curriculum decisions, the vice-president for academic affairs or the president should have a veto privilege based on budgetary restrictions. Overexpansion results in mediocrity and, if faculty members recognize that they obtain their courses at the expense of excellence, they may limit their requests. Decisions do have implications; curriculum review and control are essential to insure that those implications will be anticipated and beneficial.

10

Management and Planning

The attainment of resources and autonomy through exercise of influence, and the achievement of confidence are not always beneficial to the university nor to higher education; and, in the face of limited resources, the results are inevitably not satisfactory to all involved. Some departments—at least in the eyes of some other departments—acquire a disproportionate amount of the resources. Even though deans and vice-presidents often share this conviction, they find serious limitations on their attempts to reallocate. Budget formulation in many institutions (especially the publicly supported ones receiving annual appropriations) has become a year-round operation, and scarcely allows time for the long view. Apparent inequities are thus ignored because commitments, such as faculty tenure and the necessity of significant annual increases in salary, on the one hand, bar any readjustment within one year and, on the other hand, account for most of the new dollars in the budget. Thus an increment to the budget base of the prior year becomes the established pattern from which an administrator or even a faculty budget committee finds it virtually impossible to deviate. So units of decreasing importance or enrollment retain a hold on the budget disproportionate to their role in the university, whereas rapidly growing units find that resources lag far behind their increasing load. Aside from the fact that the pressure of immediate operations and preparation of next year's budget neither encourage nor leave adequate time for planning, the lack of adequate and incontrovertible evidence makes it difficult to justify any marked departure from the incremented pattern. One has only to raise the question as to what professors in a given department actually do, to learn that in most departments and most universities only the professor can provide an answer. One department chairman in an excellent private university, when asked about the typical load of professors, responded with apparent irritation that each determined his own activities, although they had a gentleman's agreement that every professor offer a course or seminar sometime during the year. In a state university, a newly appointed professor with whom we sought an interview was found to be on a sabbatical leave during his first year of appointment. Such practices may be appropriate to a well-endowed private university, but something more formal in the way of planning and management is desirable in most institutions. Such circumstances have given rise to demand for application of management science to education.

MANAGEMENT SCIENCE IN HIGHER EDUCATION

Despite the attention given to application of management science in business and in government in recent years, relatively small movement in this direction is apparent in higher education. Perhaps as a result, the terminology and methodology used savors more of business operations than of educational institutions. Accordingly, a brief review of some of the concepts is a necessary prelude to considering their applicability to higher education.

Program Budgeting. In program budgeting, the first step is a definition of programs by specification of the goals or needs to be met. Next, the goals must be developed into more specific objectives, preferably in quantitative terms, such as the number and type of units to be produced. The resources necessary to carry out each program are then to be specified in detail by relating them to the various elements of the program. Consideration should be given to program priorities and to alternative ways in which a program may be carried out. If funds are not available for all programs, then choices can be made by those providing the funds. If alternative ways of achieving program goals differ significantly in costs, then examination of the relative effectiveness or of the ensuing benefits of the alternatives provides a basis for choice among them. In this approach to budgeting, each program, whether new or old, must be justified every year. The relation between resources allocated and results attained is clarified. The statement of priorities and alternatives permits more intelligent allocation of funds among agencies or program units. Planning, programing, budgeting, evaluation, and replanning form a continuing cycle so that the effectiveness and the need for every program are always under review.

Input-Output Analysis. In this approach, the various inputs into a program or process are specified in detail. This includes personnel, equipment, materials, and facilities which are preferably quantified in terms of dollars. Output, of course, is defined by the final product, although there may be various preliminary outputs at various stages of a process. Alternatively, the input may be regarded as the raw material upon which the process utilizing personnel and equipment acts to produce the final product. In the first interpretation, the ratio of output to input is essentially equivalent to a cost benefit or cost effectiveness analysis. In the second, the efficiency of the process can be judged by the relation of its costs to the value added as determined by the difference between the value of raw materials and the value of the product.

Management Information Systems. A management information system involves personnel, methods, and equipment organized to collect, store, process, and disseminate information used in management (operation, control, evaluation, and planning) of an enterprise. The management information system draws its data from the operating systems and processes these data so as to support the budgeting, administrative, and control systems. Since the effectiveness of the information system depends upon the operating systems, the development of an effective management information system may require revisions in the operating systems. In turn, the effectiveness of administration, planning, budgeting, and control depends upon the management information system.

Budgeting Systems. Although the prior-year-budget-base-plus continues to be used in many institutions and perhaps is even more extensively used in deciding on state appropriations than is generally admitted, this pattern of budgeting is no longer considered desirable. The program budget system is reportedly in operation in a number of states, but the difficulties in agreeing upon what constitutes a program in higher education and the great facility displayed by universities in exhibiting their requests in whatever pattern is requested without in the least affecting their operations raise doubts about the significance of such claims.

Formula budgeting is practiced in a number of states, including Florida and Texas. Estimates of enrollments for the next year provide the basis for predicting college, department, and course enrollments. Instructional staffing needs for each department can then be calculated by a formula applied to each course level. Research, service, administration, clerical and personnel needs, and operating budgets for departments can be determined separately or as a percentage increment to the instructional staff requirements. Administrative, library, physical plant operation, and space needs can also be developed on the basis of a formula. The formulas used may differ for various types of institutions, and they often vary with the level of courses and the instructional patterns used by the major groups of disciplines. The formulas used should, in some way, be based on costs, but, since complete adherence to this practice would provide no leverage for change, formulas tend to be developed for a few major groups of fields, levels of study, and types of institutions. Many sources of variation are thereby ignored, and it is not surprising that institutions which develop tentative budgets on the basis of formulas ignore these same formulas when finally allocating funds to colleges and departments. Thus the formula approach, which, when applied over an entire institution or major segments of it, could provide the basis for raising questions about departmental variations in loads and costs, actually has been ineffective at that level.

A simplified approach to formula budgeting provides a specified dollar allotment for students by level; for example: $400 per student in lower division, $800 per student in upper division, $1,600 per student at master's level, and $3,200 per student at doctoral level. Presumably, these figures bear some relation to average costs, but some undergraduate science programs may be more expensive than some doctoral programs. Doctorates in education are much less expensive than those in physics. Thus formulas at this gross level certainly do not accommodate departmental differences and may even be unfair in their funding of universities of different types. They also tend to encourage institutions to introduce doctoral programs to capture the higher rate of support.

Another approach to budgeting in higher education is through cost studies. Although some overtures in this direction have attempted to assign all expenditures to instruction, a more realistic approach requires delineation of the major programs or functions carried on by the university and the assignment by budgetary record and judgment (in the case of library, central administration, and so on) of expenditures to each function. Cost studies of less than all functions and all funds have limited value. Even if costs for all functions and funds are worked out in detail, they still constitute only a historical record. Continuance of the same programs will usually require more funds because of salary increases and inflationary trends. Enrollment expansion constitutes an additional cost which should be, but seldom has been, calculated on a marginal cost basis. New programs and alleviation of accumulated deficiencies (catch-ups) provide other items not included in past costs.

In some respects, the cost study approach to budgetary determination is analogous to program budgeting. Perhaps the major difference is that the cost study is always backward-oriented, whereas program budgeting places emphasis on the forward look. Cost studies indicate the cost for programs as they existed and were operated at a point in time. They suggest little in the way of alternatives, whereas program budgeting is greatly concerned with specifying the options available. If cost studies are used to raise questions about existing programs and to develop plans for expansion and for additions, they then become part of the program budgeting approach or something close to it. But those who believe that educational costs are unrealistically high because of an ineffective and inefficient operation are more likely to repose confidence in a rational analysis of funds required to perform certain programs under given assumptions. Thus program budgets and formulas are currently more attractive than cost studies.

LACK OF MANAGEMENT AND PLANNING

As indicated in the preceding discussions, departments have proved almost invulnerable to any attempt to introduce scientific management into the university. The departmental expectations of present support plus a "fair" share of new dollars continue to be roughly fulfilled, although there are quibbles about "fair." To allot new dollars for raises as a percentage of the existing salary dollars in a department is fair only if it is reasonable to assert that all departments are of the same quality and improving at the same rate. The science department with many dollars from outside sources nevertheless expects its present support plus its fair share, and, if our observations and limited data are correct, it gets it plus interest generated by the outside support. Some grants generate activity which the university agrees to take over after a period of time; others generate activity which brings more students and new programs that require added funds; still others move a department into the national scene and require increased salaries and support to keep the faculty. And some grants generate activity which the university must take over and complete when the funds prove inadequate. Humanities departments reasonably doubt that this is fair.

The restricted nature of outside funds impresses faculty members far less than it does administrators. Outside grants buy equipment, pay for travel, hire technicians and graduate assistants, and most researchers assume some limited instructional role. Thus, to the faculty member, outside funds purchase the same items and services as institutional funds. Yet administrators, caught up in their commitment to the sanctity of restricted funds and their legal obligation to maintain it, are unable to develop budgetary patterns which allow for this departmental freedom. Departments and their chairmen glory in the lack of central control. The chairman of one department stated forthrightly that his department, operating under three deans and having considerable government support, went its own way with no allegiance to any dean or college. Another stated, "So long as we get the job done, it's no one's business who does what or how funds are used." And so a graduate assistant may be hired on a research grant for a few paltry dollars to teach some courses and compensate the university for the departmental assignment of a high-salaried full professor to research. Such manipulations suggest that management is very much present in departments, but that it is dedicated to departmental and personal rather than to university goals. Furthermore, the ultimate implications are usually obscured if not actually concealed in a mass of forms. Data are neither collected nor processed in such a manner as to permit review and control based upon a carefully developed policy.

The lack of management and planning within departments or in respect to departmental operations and roles at the university level results from the interaction of many factors. There is a lack of adequate data on departments. Even such obvious matters as number of faculty members, number of majors, number of student credit-hours produced, dollars available and expended from various sources are not readily and uniformly available in some universities. Hence, long-term trends are not apparent, and appropriate interdepartmental comparisons are impossible. There are frequently no definite standards or limits on either upper or lower class size. Actually, class size is often adjusted in reference to other contingencies

—increased if it is desired to relieve someone of teaching or if enrollments are increasing beyond staff addition; or decreased, if necessary, to have more sections to keep everyone with a reasonable teaching assignment. Instructional load requirements have markedly decreased over the years; reductions in load at some point for some individuals engaged in research or graduate instruction shortly become a norm for all. Laboratory-hour requirements have little rationale and can be adjusted upward or downward at the whim of individual professors or as the availability of space and resources dictates. Laboratory size, too, is an uncertain variable, sometimes determined more by the size of the laboratory than by any educational consideration; but departments may have imposed the size limitation in their plans for a building. All of these matters, according to the departments, come under the heading of professional judgments, whichc therefore are not to be questioned by administrators. One might repose more confidence in this view if there were not recurring evidence that professional judgments are neither uniform nor consistent over time in various contexts. Yet, in the absence of concrete data, neither departments nor administrators have the evidence in hand for rational and consistent examination and modification of such practices by reference to sound educationally based policies.

MANAGEMENT NEEDS

When, under any of several different types of pressure, departments are required to submit evidence on faculty loads, the tendency is first to settle for a listing of the instructional assignments. If limited teaching loads become a subject of concern, the next step is a reporting by faculty members of their activities, which is done on a retrospective basis, with emphasis on a demonstration that everyone is very busy. On an hourly basis, such reporting shows faculty members working anywhere from 35 hours to 100 hours per week. Such reports vary greatly in what is included. Some faculty members seem to believe that everything they do is in the service of the uniiversity, whereas others limit themselves to specifically assigned duties, such as classes or advising. On the questionable side is the inclusion of such items as one hour each day reading the

New York Times; one hour three days a week chauffeuring the
wife to and from class; twenty minutes in seeking a parking place;
several hours per month spent in speaking to service clubs; or watch-
ing television news and documentaries. Occasionally a professor has
demonstrated his disgust with such reports by listing more earthy
items. But the basic fallacy of reporting after the fact resides in the
apparent sanctioning of the professor's conception of his responsibilities rather than a clear delineation of university expectations.
One research-minded professor reported—perhaps accurately—only
5 per cent of his time occupied by a graduate course, but this is a
ridiculous figure to be applied to his salary in computing the costs
of graduate education.

  When faculty members are paid from various fund sources,
some difficulty arises in relating activities to the several sources. In
addition, a faculty member may have a split appointment placing
him in two, three, or more departments. Individuals are loaned to
teach courses in other departments. The time of faculty members
on partial research appointments is occasionally borrowed for increased instructional load in one term, with adjustments made in a
later term by eliminating all instruction. Transfers after the fact of
salary charges from one fund to another increase the burden in
the accounting office while further complicating attempts to relate
funds and functions. Contingency funds in the dean's or provost's
office are used to pay for departmental operations. Thus the task of
accurately relating all functions performed at the departmental level
to all the funds used is complicated beyond resolution except by a
sophisticated computer-based management information system. Even
then, an effective system may require some modification or codifica-
tion of these practices.

  The acceptance of the previous year's base as the start of
the next year's budgeting is, in part, justified by the continuing departmental commitments to staff, but strict application of this policy
makes it impossible to recoup positions when faculty members leave
or retire. Only by establishing central control of vacancies and even
by anticipating them can a degree of flexibility be achieved in real-
locating resources.

  The need for management and for an information system

which makes this possible seems obvious, although many academicians are obdurate in insisting that moves in this direction will destroy the university. However, as financial support of the universities (private and public) increasingly includes funds from various sources, more detailed reporting and justification of requests and expenditures are inevitable. If the system for so doing can be developed by universities in full cognizance of their unique character, they should be able to moderate possible injury and achieve ultimate benefits in improved operation and in renewed confidence in the university.

A Minimum Complete Faculty. The decision to provide a program, whether of instruction, research, or service, involves a decision about human and material resource allocation that may not be entirely predicated upon load or productivity. If the decision is made to provide an undergraduate major in chemistry, certain space and equipment needs must be met. One professor cannot reasonably, either in terms of load or competency, teach all the courses required. Thus, some minimum complete faculty must be defined. Professional programs in nursing, engineering, and home economics similarly require staffing and other resources, even though only two or three students are enrolled. Doctoral programs in any field require a basic staff covering the essential specialties or subdivisions of the discipline, even though it is not intended that full programs of courses and research be available in all specialties.

Accordingly, in undertaking a new program or reviewing departmental staffing problems for existing programs, the following steps may be required: (1) List and define the several areas or specialties which comprise the disciplines covered by the department. Areas or specialties not now covered in the department should be included. (2) For each specialty indicate whether courses are now provided, or whether any should be added. It may also be desirable to indicate whether the specialty is unique among departments of universities in the state or immediate area. (3) Indicate priorities for specialties to be added. (4) For each specialty determine the number of faculty required to provide an adequate and balanced program. Numbers of students are irrelevant at this point. The matter at issue is to decide, in reference to usual patterns of specialization of faculty members, how many would be required. (5) Since faculty members may be competent in more than one specialty and since only part of an individual's time may be required to cover a single specialty, it is necessary to indicate the full time equivalent for each specialty. Thus, only half or less of the time of a specialist in Canadian history may be required to offer the one, two, or three courses considered necessary in that specialty. It is also possible that a faculty member with a special competency may not be fully employable in terms of his specialty, and he may not have other useful competencies. For example, the decision to offer a year's work in study of Arabic will require an Arabic scholar who may not be qualified to teach any other subject. The minimum complete faculty has to be examined in regard to both head count and full-time equivalent faculty requirements. If the right combination can be found, the full-time equivalent total represents the minimal faculty requirements. (6) Presently employed faculty, both in respect to head count and full-time equivalent requirements can then be lined up against the minimum complete faculty to determine where deficiencies or excesses exist. (7) Instructional patterns and curricular requirements must be considered before an appropriate relation can be finally established between students and faculty. Some courses may be offered totally or partially in lecture form, whereas others may require seminars, discussions, or clinical experience in groups of ten or fewer students. Hence, with a given number of students, say sixty, one section may suffice in one specialty while six or more are required in another. Two or three full-time faculty members may be required in one specialty while the one in another specialty is underemployed. Either combinations of specialties or increases in the numbers of students must be sought if an optimum relationship is to be attained in staffing and costs. In some professional programs this relationship may be sufficiently clear that student enrollments must be controlled within one or two students by the admissions process. If increases are planned, the faculty and student increases must be carefully plotted to avoid sudden and unjustified increase in costs or erosion of the instructional patterns and curricular requirements.

This minimum complete faculty approach to planning should

be used with caution. It is essential in certain highly structured professional programs. It is less appropriate to departments in the arts and sciences and, if used, might unrealistically increase the faculty relative to the students enrolled. Yet even in these departments such an approach can be useful in achieving balance, and it is essential in adding graduate programs. A recurring complaint in the departments in our study was that certain subspecialties of the department were highly favored in new appointments or replacements, with no apparent concern for balance. Fortunately, in large-enrollment departments there are basic and advanced undergraduate courses which can usually be used to fill out the loads of the specialist, provided he will accept such an assignment. In smaller departments, this minimum complete faculty approach is also necessary, but the specialties must be limited and carefully selected in relation to program requirements rather than to unrealistic departmental aspirations.

Defining Programs. The first essential in the injection of management within departments involves clarification of the functions or programs carried on in departments. One attempt in this direction developed in cooperation with a number of department chairmen representative of various disciplines and colleges resulted in definition of the following five programs:

1. *Instruction and Related Activities*—includes all effort dedicated to the teaching of students, whether the teaching situation is formal or informal. The students taught must be in one of the following categories: (a) registered for degree credit; (b) receiving instruction at college or university level in a program sponsored by the university; or (c) engaged in completing degree requirements. Lectures to civic groups or laymen who are not students or practitioners in the subject field are excluded here and placed under "service Programs." Reading related to a research project or general reading in one's professional field not specifically related to courses taught is subsumed under "Research and Scholarly Activities" or possibly "Professional Development."

   a. Preparation of lectures, laboratory materials, outlines, examinations
   b. Reading student papers and examinations

    c. Conferences with students

    d. Reading course-related materials in preparation for instruction

    e. Course revision

    f. Course coordination, including supervision and conferences

    g. Planning of new courses

    h. Writing of textbooks and production of course materials

    i. Academic advising and program planning:

        (1) Undergraduate—lower division, majors

        (2) Graduate—master's candidates advised and active theses directed, doctoral candidates, committee memberships, committee chairman, active dissertations directed

        (3) Postdoctoral fellows

2. *Research and Scholarly Activities*—includes all effort dedicated *primarily* to the discovery and application of new knowledge. Excluded are any activities for which the *major* purpose is the training of students or the improving of instruction, both of which should be accounted for under "Instruction." Consulting or other activity for which individuals receive more than token payment from an outside source is also excluded.

    a. Proposal development

    b. Separately budgeted research projects

        (1) university-supported

        (2) outside-sponsored

    c. Departmental research projects not separately budgeted

    d. Coordination and direction of activities in b. and c. above

    e. Artistic composition and creation

    f. Preparation of research articles and monographs

    g. Participation in research seminars and conferences

3. *Service Programs*—includes all effort dedicated to professional help rendered to one or more of the following groups: (a) parties external to the university who pay no or only token remuneration (public service); (b) parties internal to the university who make no direct payment or only token payment for the service; and (c) parties internal or external to the university who contract with and reimburse the university, not the individual, for a specific service rendered (includes auxiliary services but excludes private consulting).

    a. Noncredit courses (except those judged to be college level, therefore worthy of credit and included under "Instruction")

    b. Preparation of informational bulletins

    c. Clinical services
    d. Speeches, conference planning and participation
    e. Consultation to business, industry, government, and other educational institutions
    f. State and national committee membership
    g. Officer in professional societies
    h. Editor of professional publications

4. *Administrative*—includes all effort devoted to managerial and supervisory tasks (except course supervision) performed for the department, college, or university as a whole, but supported by the department.
    a. Service on committees (mainly applicable when faculty involvement is necessary for decision making)
    b. Scheduling of space and personnel
    c. Supervision of internal department services
    d. Planning of buildings
    e. Review of curricula
    f. Formulation of new departmental or college programs
    g. Faculty and senate meetings, commencement, and so on—generally ignored as representing a low-level common faculty time commitment
    h. Correspondence, phone calls, travel—generally ignored as representing a low-level common faculty time commitment. Should usually be subsumed without special notice among the first three programs.

Where effort devoted to administrative duties can be specifically assigned to an instructional, research, or service program, it should be included under that program heading.

5. *Professional Development* (keeping up with the field)—includes general professional reading, leaves, and other activity designed to maintain and improve one's general professional competence rather than one's performance of current instructional, research, or service responsibilities.

If all of one's effort can be specifically assigned to instruction, research, service, and administration, none need be recorded under this heading. For example, a leave granted solely for the purpose of research should be recorded in the research category.

In these definitions, instruction includes much more than assignments to structured courses. Many of these items, such as student conferences, academic advising, and graduate committee memberships, are ignored in determining faculty loads. Their inclusion would materially aid in achieving recognition of the importance of these activities and of their significance in faculty load. Research and scholarly activities vary in nature and in sources of support. The essential nature of research, scholarly and creative activity, and the differentiation of this from instruction and service activity certainly must be left to the department. Even so, some difficulties arise. How shall the direction of dramatic plays which involve students and which are attended by a diverse audience of students, faculty, and townspeople be regarded? Is this instruction, creativity, or service, or a combination of all three? Any decision is arbitrary, and the necessity of making one is both dubious and distasteful to those involved. Perhaps no standard form can incorporate all departmental activities, yet undue extension of categories militates against effective usage. Service programs, too, exhibit variations and raise some issues concerning their relations to other categories. Some persons would prefer to regard a journal editorship as a creative activity, and so it may be. We included it under service. The categories of administrative efforts and of professional development are auxiliary rather than directly productive (as are the other three, which represent the time-honored obligations of the university), and they are of such nature as not to be readily attributable to the initial three, but they account for significant portions of total departmental resources.

In actual practice, a form such as that in Figure 1 should be filled out by the department chairman in consultation with individual staff or departmental committees. A procedure in which each faculty member fills out his own form, whether before or after the fact, fails to establish agreed-upon expectations for responsibilities and ultimately for evaluation and reward. Furthermore, it is essential that only those commitments which are departmental or university responsibilities be weighed in completing the form. Thus an editorship or an office in a national professional organization should not be included if they have been accepted by a faculty member as an additional commitment beyond what the chairman considers a full departmental assignment.

Several immediate and desirable results emerge from an a priori commitment: (1) The full range of responsibilities of faculty

Figure 1   FACULTY RESPONSIBILITIES

Name ....   % Employed in Dept. (E) ....

Soc. Sec. No. ....   Salary ....

Rank ....   Department ....

Appt. Basis (10 or 12 Mo.) ....

Instruction	Course development: Lower undergraduate .... Upper undergraduate .... Master .... Doctoral .... Academic advising: Lower undergraduate .... Upper undergraduate .... Master .... Doctoral .... Thesis direction: Master .... Doctoral .... Instruction-related committees: Department .... College .... University .... Instruction: Lower undergraduate .... Upper undergraduate .... Master .... Doctoral .... % Instr. (I) ....
Research	Contract research: Separately budgeted .... University-supported .... Outside sponsor .... Departmental research, not separately budgeted .... Artistic composition and creation .... Research seminars and conferences .... Research proposal development .... % Research (R) ....
Service	Professional services: Internal to the university (without reimbursement to the university) .... External to the university .... Reimbursement to the university .... % Service (S) ....
Administration	Administrative-related committees, or management: Department .... College .... University .... % Admn. (A) ....
Prof. Dev.	Maintenance of general professional competence rather than current responsibilities .... % Prof. Dev. (P) ....

Note: E = I+R+S+A+P

is made explicit, and an obligation is assumed to reward an individual for performance of what he was asked *and* agreed to do. (2) A distinction is made between university-assigned responsibilities within a forty- to forty-five hour week and activities in which individuals engage because of their own interests or ambitions. To the extent that these latter activities make faculty members more valuable, more rapid promotions and salary increases may be expected for them than for those who perform only the duties assigned. (3) The extent to which human resources are utilized in various functions or programs is made explicit and can be reviewed and adjusted.

Some illustrative results for a number of departments in which this procedure was carried out are exhibited in Table 11. Differential departmental characteristics are readily apparent. Department A (in a professional school) is relatively more involved in service, commits a possibly exorbitant amount of faculty time to administration, and shows no formal commitment of time to professional development. Department B (one of the humanities) has a relatively heavy commitment to teaching, very little to service, and a modest allocation of staff time to administration. Department C (with over 85 per cent of its expenditures from other than general funds) has major commitments to research and graduate instruction, with significant time allocations to service, administration, and professional development. Department D (a physical science), although regarded as a research-oriented department, displays strong commitment to instruction. This department tends to the view that no research activity should be undertaken unless it contributes to the instructional program. A knowledgeable and competent observer of the department's operation might infer that the research function has been reported as using a smaller proportion of resources than is actually the case. No reporting or assignment form can entirely avoid the effect of personal and departmental values and philosophy. Perhaps the greatest revelation to several departments making these analyses was in learning the extent of resource commitment to administration in the department. One department with a very elaborate committee structure concluded, after deliberation on this evidence, that some reduction in committees and time in-

Table 11.

PERCENTAGE OF FACULTY TIME ASSIGNED TO VARIOUS FUNCTIONS

	Rank	(N)	Instruction	Research	Service	Administration	Professional Development
Department A	Professors	(3)	44	2	31	23	0
	Assoc. Professors	(5)	46	23	16	15	0
	Asst. Professors	(2)	75	0	7	18	0
	Instructors	(4)	39	23	15	23	0
	Total		48	15	19	19	0
Department B	Professors	(3)	63	27	2	6	2
	Assoc. Professors	(3)	66	30	0	4	0
	Asst. Professors	(3)	60	26	0	9	4
	Instructors	(1)	84	16	0	0	0
	Total		65	27	1	6	1
Department C	Professors	(4)	22	44	13	14	7
	Assoc. Professors	(4)	37	31	9	10	14
	Asst. Professors	(3)	20	35	19	23	2
	Total		27	37	13	15	8
Department D	Professors	(5)	43	18	13	18	8
	Assoc. Professors	(2)	55	30	3	8	5
	Asst. Professors	(1)	55	29	7	7	2
	Total		48	23	9	14	6

volvement might be appropriate. The benefits of an elaborate committee system may not be in proportion to the resources involved.

The Department of Electrical Engineering and Systems Science at Michigan State University has developed a rather more elaborate analysis. Figure 2 shows the form used for summarizing the human resources in full-time equivalents allocated to each of the various outputs. Notice that this form includes graduate assistants, technicians, and secretarial and other personnel. At the left the number of each type of personnel would be entered, and the horizontal cell entries computed on percentages of individual time used in each activity must total the initial number. Column totals indicate the total full-time equivalent allotted to each function. In the columnar headings, quantitative indications of output may be entered. For example, the number of doctoral candidates involved in dissertations may be 25, and the number of graduate students counseled, 135. Although these are not ultimate outputs, they are significant elements in the process, and an indication of the time commitment and costs can be used to raise questions about the effectiveness of the operation. Outputs in the categories of research and service could be designated in terms of research studies completed, publications, or number of persons or agencies to which service has been provided; from this the unit costs of each output can be approximated. This department found that thesis direction cost the department $461 per student per quarter, and undergraduate advising about $15 per student per quarter. Total dollar expenditures per quarter for several functions were found to be (approximately):

Specific Instructional Items

Thesis direction	$ 7,000
Graduate advising	2,500
Undergraduate advising	5,000
Graduate instruction	65,000
Undergraduate instruction	51,000
Course development	5,000

FIGURE 2   INPUT-OUTPUT ANALYSIS OF FACULTY RESOURCES[a]

Output / Input	Instruction						Research			Services		Management		
	Thesis Direction	Graduate Counseling	Undergrad. Counseling	900 Level Instruction	800 Level Instruction	300 and 400 Level	Contract Research	Dept. Spon. Research	Proposal Prep.	Consultation and Reviews	Lectures and Seminars	Department Management	University Management	Professional Development
Professor														
Assoc. Prof.														
Asst. Prof.														
Inst.														
Grad. Asst.														
Undergrad. Asst.														
Technicians														
Secretary														
Hourly Labor														
Other														

[a] Adapted from Figure 2 in "A Systems Model for Management, Planning and Resource Allocation in Institutions of Higher Education," a paper prepared by Herman E. Koenig, Department of Electrical Engineering and Systems Science, Michigan State University, for the WICHE-ACE Higher Education Management, Information Systems Seminar held in Washington, D.C., April 24–26, 1969.

Major Functions

Instruction	$88,000
Research	46,000
Service	6,500
Management	10,500
Professional development	3,000

These figures are based on salaries only. Since salaries account usually for 70 per cent or more of departmental expenditures and represent that aspect of expenditures which is most immediately subject to modification, emphasis on personnel time and salary expenditures is the key to management. Space and equipment can be similarly analyzed, and their total contribution to cost is significant. It is somewhat disconcerting (and amusing) that in many institutions much effort is expended in monitoring expenditures for supplies, services, and travel which, in fact, constitute a relatively insignificant portion of the total. The expenditures for equipment and materials used in large-enrollment courses in the sciences are an exception.

Space and equipment usage and expenditures on a departmental basis are virtually unknown quantities at most universities. Data on use of teaching laboratories may be available as part of a space utilization study, but the use of research laboratories and equipment is a matter known only by those directly involved. Obviously, the number of hours of use of a laboratory or of a piece of equipment is not an indication of its value, but when visits to departments reveal space and equipment which have obviously not been used in weeks, the need for some recurrent review is suggested. Space and equipment expenditures have been greatly augmented in recent years by federal grants and contracts. In fact, many science departments report that it would not have been possible to have adequate facilities otherwise. Although these bonanzas have created additional costs reflected usually in the increase of the departmental general fund budget, university budgeting practices are usually limited to the general fund and do not, therefore, keep in view total departmental operations and needs. If, as now seems probable, the federal government moves in the direction of cutting salaries, equipment, and facilities out of project research grants and of allocating these directly to the institutions in lump sums, the result may be chaotic. These dollars should be incorporated into the total budgeting process, but that process is not presently adequate to the task. For one thing, those involved in it simply do not know how federal grants have been expended in departments. Furthermore, in state institutions, major unrestricted federal institutional grants may lead immediately to decreases in state support unless the relationships between various resource inputs, processes, and outputs can be presented so as to justify budget requests both in respect to need and to results.

USE OF MANAGEMENT DATA

Obviously, data are used to provide effective control of program priorities, programs operations, and quality. There are uses at a number of different levels and times. Thus, if data are available on a department showing allocations to the several programs or functions, the department itself may raise questions. Are the time and money involved in committee and other administrative activity really worthwhile? Is enough time or too much time being assigned to research? Since no absolutes exist, departments may become quickly interested in obtaining the same type of data on similar departments. A dean or vice-president will surely wish to review the data, make some comparisons, and raise some questions. If the English department shows only 40 per cent of its staff time assigned to instruction while the history department shows 70 per cent, does this indicate inequities in budgeting, the effect of external funds, the sacrifice of instruction to research, or simply a confusion or distinction in the interpretation of what constitutes research and instruction? It is also conceivable that the history department has primarily an undergraduate program, whereas the English department is heavily committed to graduate education. Much of this examination can be conducted without introducing dollars. The data do not directly indicate courses of action, but they do permit the raising of questions which are of as much concern to departments as to deans and central administration. Most universities have inequities in loads and in staff allocations which are artifacts of history and personality and which the present lack of data either conceals entirely or fails to delineate sufficiently clearly for action.

At a second level, input can be related to output to provide a more refined basis for study of departmental efficiency or for comparisons among departments. For example, the student credit-hours produced at various levels may be related to the full-time equivalent faculty. To delineate this relationship it is necessary to have first allocated the faculty to the several functions. When the sch/ftef varies greatly from year to year or from department to department, reasons should be sought, and, when no logical explanation is available in terms of unique departmental instructional programs, budgetary adjustments should follow. If dollar costs are computed, differences in the proportion of faculty at the several ranks will often explain marked cost variations, but careful examination of the reasons for these differences in distributions by rank and possible long-term correction may be appropriate. If heavy commitment of resources to research is not accompanied by evidence of publication and recognittion, either the size of the allocation or the quality of the faculty may require adjustment. Thus departmental costs, productivity, and evidence of excellence provide the basis for modification of the budget or of overhaul of the department. Correspondence between departmental and university priorities become subject to examination and planned modification.

At a third level, the university is able to bring together and summarize its total commitment to various programs and to indicate the results and costs. It may also be desirable to consider outputs in terms of degrees or some other unit which transcends the department. Thus the university can better interpret its activities and justify the resources required to conduct them. To attain this state requires several years. Early steps in the development of a management information system require education of people and modification in procedures. Collection must be followed by dissemination so that a self-correcting procedure becomes operative and confidence in the accuracy and meaning of the data is established. Data on students, faculty, instructional patterns, and expenditures must be developed into a unitary system so that these can be interrelated in a number of distinctive ways. As the data and reporting systems are developed, they will raise many questions at all levels. Wide dissemination should be encouraged, although there are always those who would prefer to collect and maintain their own data so that they retain power and avoid review and questioning of policies and operations. Ultimately, the data collection, processing, and reporting process has to be coordinated with immediate (next year's) budget allocations, the following year's proposed budget, the annual report of departments, and the long-term plans of the department and the university.

A complete cycle in collection and use of departmental management information involves several stages within each year, each stage based upon plans covering three to five years in advance. These stages are outlined below in points 1 through 7; the years are, of course, only exemplary:

1. Preparation of budget request for academic year 1970–1971 (September 1969)

Input	*Process*	*Anticipated Output**
Planned allocation of personnel to several programs.	Organization into classes, research commitments	Projections of: student credit-hours, course or curriculum planning to be completed, books or articles to be completed, public services to be provided.
Other resources required and their sources.	Committees, curriculum development, and so on.	

* Based on explicit statements regarding expansion of or reduction in old programs and introduction of new ones.

2. Complete analysis of expenditures and unit costs of prior year, 1968–1969 (December 1969)

3. Review of departmental requests in process of institutional budget preparation (October–December 1969; May 1970).

4. Determination of total institutional budget for 1970–1971 (April or May 1970).

5. Assignment of college and departmental allocations for 1970–1971 (May, June 1970). Consideration of any alterations in September requests based on institutional budget, altered circumstances, and complete analysis of past year's operations (see 2).

6. Submission of annual reports by departments and colleges, July 1970.

   Section 1. Statement of 1969–1970 accomplishments, credit-hours, research, service, curriculum developments, and so on.

   Section 2. Special problems faced by department.

   Section 3. Reconsideration and modification of three-to-five-year plan, including extension for one additional calendar year. Include projected financial requirements.

7. Annual review and approval or modification of long-term plans. Specification of plans for gradual reallocation of resources through recovery of positions, elimination of programs, staff replacements at lower ranks and salaries, and so on.

These steps call for much more elaborate procedures than are now found in universities. Listed in this fashion, they may appear unreasonably detailed. Yet, in some sense, these steps are always present. Departmental budget requests are usually formulated in the late summer or early fall. Possibly these can be incorporated into stage 6 the previous spring, but in large public institutions major changes in fall enrollments may dictate fall formulation of next year's request. Certainly the earlier formulation would permit more careful review (stage 3). Financial statements for the prior year are completed in the fall, and it is not until the basic data for these are available that accurate departmental expenditures and costs can be determined (stage 2). The final estimate of next year's income cannot usually be made until the spring and, in state institutions, sometimes as late as June or July (stage 4). College and departmental allocations are not made until reliable total income estimates are available (stage 5). Annual reports are usually prepared in July, but frequently serve no purpose other than to provide tidbits for the president's annual report. These reports should be more elaborate— reporting accomplishments and reconsidering further projection of plans (stage 6). Consideration of these plans and approval or rejection then set the stage for repetition of the cycle. In embryonic form these stages are present in most universities. However, they are not based on accurate data; thus they become perfunctory, and do not really affect departmental programs and plans or provide needed evidence in support of the universities' search for funds. Once the pattern becomes established, the cycle should be but little more demanding in time than is needed in meeting the present requirements at each stage. This procedure requires that a management information system be operative so that it contributes to the decisions at each stage and is further augmented by the new data demanded or generated at each stage.

11

Future of Departments

In this final chapter, we take the risk of generalizing from our study—our work with, and observations of, departments and universities—to describe problems of departmental operation and to prescribe some possible solutions thereto. The formal research encompassed a wide range of data, extending from the highly subjective reports of interviews conducted on the campuses through the still subjective but more systematic responses of faculty members to a questionnaire, to presumably objective (although sometimes unavailable) data on faculty size, faculty turnover, enrollments, and funds expended. Less extensive data were collected on institutes, because of their less formal structure and relatively recent appearance. The discussions of curriculum review, departmental self-study, and management are based much more on a single institution, and may be described as resulting from institutional research. Yet our wider observations and study confirm their applicability to other universities.

In Chapters Two and Three, subjective impressions of our consultants and of individual faculty members of some of the problems and priorities of departments were presented. Although differences in points of view between observers with administrative experience and faculty members are to be expected, it is apparent that some faculty members see some of the same problems and express some of the same doubts as do the consultants.

Chapters Four and Five reported significant relationships among department variables. Our attempts to categorize and characterize departments were complicated by blurred patterns caused by some nonconforming or even contradicting relationships. These difficulties did not surprise us. Our sample of universities was limited and included neither the most prestigious nor the weakest in the nation. Disciplines sampled included only a few in the university, and our faculty responses were rather less extensive and less representative than desired.

We had expected that the discipline might play a more significant role than our data indicated in determining the character of departments. In fact, the university structures (by policies, patterns of operation, and goals) much of what happens in most departments, and hence there appears to be more commonality across departments on a campus than among departments in the same discipline across campuses. In addition, the stature of the university goes far to determine the caliber of faculty attracted to it. Add to this the impact of unpredictable personality patterns of deans and chairmen and the equally unpredictable impact of vacant administrative posts filled by acting paper shufflers, and it becomes apparent that each situation contains some distinctive elements which defy generalization. Despite these idiosyncratic elements, we believe meaningful generalizations and recommendations are possible. We present them on an impressionistic basis rather than a statistical one, and thereby avoid or deliberately ignore some of the confusing relational discrepancies noted in previous chapters.

Chapter Six, on institutes, suggested that the development of these units is, in itself, an indication of the inadequacy of departments. Furthermore, the administrative confusion and the dilution of resources caused by these institutes is of concern to departments, and institutes frequently find their original concerns about applied research and service negated by departmental control of appointments.

Chapter Seven presented what some may regard as a cynical view of exchanges and negotiations between departments and deans or vice-presidents, but pointed out that departments have been apt observers and imitators of the university in their dealings with the clientele. The chapter raised the basic question as to whether the demands for auntonomy may not have become unrealistic.

Chapters Eight, Nine, and Ten presented several approaches to study and analysis of departmental problems and operations. All three chapters emphasized the lack of careful planning and the lack of adequate data for departmental decisions, whether made internally or externally. Practically all decisions regarding departmental operations have budgetary implications.

UNIVERSITY IN TRANSITION

One pervasive element found in all of the institutions included in our study was a sense of change. The transition was from a simple day-to-day locally oriented operation to a more complex pattern, with a gradual and continuing adjustment to a mutual commitment to competition in the national and international scene. Sometimes we were confused, like many students, as we tried to locate the headwaters of leadership and authority. In some cases, a state system made it unclear as to just how much decision making was vested in a campus and how much was reserved to an office concerned with several campuses. The point was effectively made in the initial stage of our study as we attempted to make contact directly with one campus of a state system. We were advised that all such requests must originally be addressed to the chief executive of the total system. Within institutions there were also indications of great variation in extent of centralization and decentralization. Some presidents responded immediately, indicating that the institution would be pleased to participate in the study. Others referred our request to the academic vice-president, still others to the deans of the various colleges, and, in some cases, answers were forthcoming only when departments had an opportunity to vote upon participation. Yet later experience indicated that these levels of centralization or decentralization had little to do with departmental autonomy or faculty involvement in the institution. In one institution, the vice-president simply notified departments that they would be involved in the study. The reception was excellent, with faculty generally indicating that they had confidence in the vice-president's judgment and saw no need to waste their time discussing or voting on minor issues. In other institutions, systematic buck-passing of minor issues was noted, apparently as a device to keep deans and departments busy while the chief administrative officer handled major issues. Whatever procedure was followed, it was clear on each campus that faculty members and organizations were playing a vital role in decisions. Administrators were generally quite sensitive to the reaction of faculty committees and departments to policy matters, even on such minor matters as commitment to participation in a research project.

In addition, size and increasing variety in the programs offered in a university have made it impossible for deans and higher-level administrators to keep track of all operations. The expansion of graduate study and of research supported by federal funds has developed new lines of academic administration and new obligations in business offices which, in many cases, bypass the college dean and academic vice-president. Individuals and departments successful in acquiring extensive funds from nonuniversity sources chafe at the imposition by the university of any limitations on the departmental search for external funds or the expenditure thereof. Administrators are the first to applaud the departmental initiative, while simultaneously recognizing erosion of their own authority and the inability to plan for the future of the university.

The development of new fields of study is reflected in the proliferation of institutes, new departments, schools, and colleges. Faculty members involved in international projects have encouraged interdisciplinary study and non-Western courses. Demand for such offerings is such that, in most of the universities, a new course or program proposed by a prestigious individual or group of individuals is quickly accepted. Seldom is there any demand for critical examination of budgetary consideration or exploration of the number or kind of students who may profit from the new development. Seldom, too, is there any suggestion that existing offerings be screened and refurbished before rushing to add new ones.

Administrators seemed generally favorable to service and applied research programs because these place the university in a favorable position in the public eye. Since faculty have traditionally been somewhat less interested in these matters, continuing education and other outwardly oriented programs have been set up quite independent of academic departments and their faculties. Thus the organization of the university becomes ever more complicated and its operation ever more diffuse. Administrative leadership seems to be most highly regarded, both on and off the campus, when its presence is documented by *new* buildings, *new* programs, *new* levels of graduate-professional education, and increased faculty and students. Leadership in critical review of *existing* operations and in their improvement is much more difficult. It is highly unpopular with the faculty, and is unlikely to result in many bouquets for harassed administrators who pursue this thorny path. In some respects, one of the best things that can happen to a university is a period without significant budgetary increase or even an actual cutback. Under these circumstances, administrators are forced to turn their attention from giving approval and publicity to new programs to the necessity of reviewing and cutting back on old ones. Also at this point, the faculty, recognizing the financial strictures, do, though reluctantly, face up to the necessity of reassessment. Unfortunately, neither the reputation of administrators nor of faculty is made by measures and policies designed to improve effectiveness and efficiency. The reward system, likewise, provides no incentive for such activity.

DEPARTMENT IN TRANSITION

If the university is in transition, it is almost self-evident that departments must also be. There is some question, however, as to whether it is the changing nature of the university which forces changes in the departments or whether it is the changing character of departments which forces changes in the university. The history of higher education and our own observations suggest that the original decision to move a university into the national scene as a recognized graduate and research center has been, in the past, largely an administrative one. Departments and faculty fall in line, reluctantly or enthusiastically, depending upon personal interests and probable impacts of the change on their own educational views and aspirations. In recent years the phenomenon of federal support has, on occasion, provided the basis for an individual or a department to force the institution to admit a new program or recognize a different order of priorities. The faculty member who succeeds in bringing a sizable grant or contract to an institution automatically attains the right to be heard and very likely heeded. Yet, in the main, departmental autonomy and extensive faculty participation in decision making appear to come only after the course of the institution has already been well established.

Chapters Four and Five already pointed toward a number of different departmental types in terms of priorities, reference groups, and internal organization. At this point, we suggest that there are three major types of departments, and we shall identify them primarily in terms of whether the department is oriented to the university, to its own operations and problems, or to the discipline which it represents. Departmental priorities and even internal organization are, to a considerable extent, determined by this orientation.

University Orientation. In a university of moderate size, with a strongly undergraduate emphasis, departments tend to be dependent on general funds. Activities of the department are likely to be limited and closely adjusted to university priorities. If graduate programs exist, they are just beginning or are small and limited in nature. Both funds and lines of authority stem from central administration, and departmental faculties look to heads and forceful deans for indications of how their efforts should be channeled to meet university concerns. In this pattern, the department is a convenient organization to get work done. It brings together a reasonably small group of people having certain common interests who, through these interests, serve the university by providing instruction for nonmajors and programs for majors. Advising plays an important role, and is seen as a university responsibility. Prestige within a department depends heavily on rank and seniority. On the whole, the department is a pleasant place to work because the expectations are clear and the future secure.

Departmental Orientation. As the university becomes larger or more complex, develops more specialization within the department, and fosters a concern with research and graduate programs and a national reputation therein, its character and orientation change. Although the decision to move the department to this level is usually a university decision and the major financial support for the move is from an addition of university funds, once the move is made, the development of the department in its own right becomes a major concern. The presence of senior faculty with a university orientation and the department's awareness of the critical importance of university support result in continuing awareness of an obligation to the university and to undergraduate education. However, there are now more choices of emphasis in a department. An individual who does research and publishes attains recognition, promotion, and salary increases in a shorter period of time than was usually required when the primary activity of everyone was undergraduate instruction. Thus the prestige of the chairman and the seniority of older men are challenged by the stature of younger men based upon a new set of priorities. The chairman may have been picked, as a scholar of rank, to exert leadership on the forward movement of the department. If he wishes to continue to be influential, he must operate his department in a more democratic way, for he finds himself presiding over a divided department, with older faculty unhappy because of lost stature and because they sense that, in the eyes of many of the younger faculty, they have become nonproductive charity cases. At this stage of development, the department has become a means of fulfillment and advancement. It may have one or two widely known scholars, but, on the whole, it seeks for younger men, makes much of their efforts, and moves them ahead far more rapidly in rank and salary than would be true in a department in one of the top-ranking universities.

Disciplinary Orientation. As the research character of a department becomes established, publication, the search for outside funds, and the development of a national reputation for individuals and the department result in increasing lack of concern with university affairs and with undergraduate education. A chairmanship, once a position of prestige, attained in part by outstanding scholarship, now becomes a threat to that scholarship. In any case, the chairman finds himself in a berth of no great significance in a situation with very different measures for prestige. Individualism becomes rampant as professors, by virtue of their reputations and funds obtained through their own efforts, develop sections and fiefdoms within their department which are virtually immune to any intervention by chairman, dean, or other administrative levels. Where the disciplinary orientation holds sway and research productivity and publication establish a ready means of transfer from one institution to the other, a department for many of the professors becomes only a convenient, perhaps necessary, but very likely a temporary attachment. Undergraduate instruction, even the service instruction to nonmajors, may continue to be prized in such a department as long as it is a necessary vehicle for the employment of graduate assistants, assistant instructors, and teaching fellows to relieve the professors of undergraduate instruction and to assist them in research activity as well as to increase graduate school enrollment. If fellowship and research support becomes adequate to provide the assistance required, the faculty have no compunction about turning the teaching of undergraduates over to graduate assistants admitted on a marginal basis or even under a waiver of usual graduate admission requirements. A still further step desired by some faculty with disciplinary orientation would be the elimination of all responsibilities for undergraduate education, except possibly for a few very carefully selected honors undergraduates who are able to move into graduate education and research at an accelerated pace. In the department with a disciplinary orientation, a few faculty members may still be found with a departmental or even a university orientation. Some of these individuals may have attained tenure twenty-five or even thirty years ago; their lot is not a happy one, and yet they may play a significant role in undergraduate advising, coordinating of graduate teaching assistants, and the like. Within such a department there may also be a few individuals whose promise as researchers five or ten years earlier brought them tenure, but whose more recent lack of productivity is explained or excused by heavy involvement in committee work, AAUP, or letters to the editor.

PROBLEMS OF DEPARTMENTS

The transition of departments from university to disciplinary orientation is, in one sense, a success story, both for the department and for the university. It is, at the same time, a source of internal frustration and of external criticism. Internally, administrators who in one breath criticize the department for its lack of concern about undergraduates, in the next breath praise the department for its outstanding record of doctoral production and research output and for its attainment of recognition in the Cartter report. Departments, having been supported into the development of a disciplinary orientation, are irked by and ignore complaints of deans and other administrators about their lack of attention to undergraduate education and their disinterest in university problems. Ultimately, the discipline-oriented department achieves its reputation from the reputations of scholars associated with it, and it is an altogether reasonable conclusion on the part of the scholar that the university exists for the sake of the faculty because it is the faculty that makes the university reputation.

The student who seeks a university in part because of a reputation established on entirely different bases than his immediate concerns require complains bitterly, and occasionally takes overt action to try to force administrative intervention into a pattern which administrators may indeed have initiated, but which they no longer control. Outside the university, legislators and the public generally are both irked and awed by the financial demands of institutions originally initiated to serve society, but which now demand rapidly expanding support to serve their own ends. In fact, the supporting clientele of higher education tends to look at the university in much the same way as university administrators look at the department. And the university acts toward its supporting clientele in much the same way as the department acts toward the administration. The tendency is to resent any intervention or any demand for detailed information, and yet to expect ever-continuing support. Evasion, half-truths, and even dishonesty are equally justified by department and universities in their search for support on the grounds that the cause is just, and that the facts would only confuse individuals incapable of understanding higher education. University operations tend to be characterized by opportunism, by temporizing in the face of external criticism rather than frankly meeting it, and by expediency rather than by long-term planning. Despite pious commitments to the search for truth, the public stance of the university too often exemplifies the view that the ends justify the means. Departments have simply emulated all too faithfully the example set by the university.

Deans and presidents are inconsistent in their dealings with departments, and not only in rewarding graduate education and research while criticizing lack of interest in undergraduates. They also criticize departments for failure to provide adequate and firm data to justify budget requests, but often are unwilling to share data compiled in central administrative offices. They are impatient with the aspirations of some departments, but indirectly encourage them by not forthrightly denying them.

Autonomy of a department and the authority of its chairman are inadequately spelled out in many institutions. Both vary from one college to another, and, in some cases, they vary markedly from one department to another under the same dean. For example, in one institution no money for equipment or for travel was budgeted for a department. The extent to which a department achieved either new items of equipment or extensive travel depended entirely upon the determination of the chairman as he approached what he considered the appropriate authority. Those who approached the dean got no results. Those who approached the academic vice-president or business manager apparently found little difficulty in getting whatever they requested. Practices with regard to salary recommendations and promotion recommendations also revealed marked variation. One dean might give a chairman a total dollar figure for the department to divide as deemed appropriate. Another would suggest that recommendations be made for raises without regard to any total amount, with the dean or someone else making necessary adjustments in terms of actual sums available. In some institutions departments are apparently encouraged to recommend for promotion all faculty that they believe to be qualified, with gradual reduction in the number on some kind of competitive basis as consideration moves closer to the top and someone arbitrarily imposes a quota, based either on an unstated tenure percentage for the faculty, or on the budgetary implications of promotions. Other institutions impose at some point or other a statement of requirements for various ranks, with departments interpreting these and justifying recommendations as best they can.

In some institutions the rules of the game are varied almost every year in an attempt to eliminate inequalities or simply to prevent an institutionalization of certain patterns which individuals and departments can then attempt to manipulate to their own ends. In this kind of competitive situation, the department which consciously adjusts its requests to actual needs or to university difficulties is all too likely to find its modest request taken as an indication of weakness or, alternatively, to find that all requests are cut back on essentially the same basis without any attempt to reduce overinflation in some of them. The success of a department chairman lies in his attaining not just the full share of the institutional resources due his department, but in attaining something more, if at all possible, to provide that department with an edge not only within the institution but in the national competition implied by the disciplinary orientation.

The Institute. The rapid development of the institute type of organization is one indication of departmental deficiencies. In a pattern of department or disciplinary orientation, interdisciplinary research or instruction is not highly prized, and individuals engaging in it are likely to become lost in the struggle for rewards. The obvious solution for the enterprising individual with such interests is to seek for an organization of his own. If his interests represent a subdivision of a discipline, he may attain a new department, but institutes and centers are much more readily approved. Administrators, too, easily become enchanted with ideas that are not easily sold to the departments, and often they have their own man in mind to develop an activity. The readiness with which institutes are set up and the ease with which they become permanent items in the university budget are a serious source of concern to departments which are constantly pressed for an expansion of their own programs, but continually find difficulty in obtaining the resources to support them. Thus, as with other problems which we have discussed, the institute represents an extension of university activities without adequate awareness of the ultimate costs involved or of the increasing complication of the university organization brought about by adding units almost at random.

Corrective Measures. The problems of the department vis-à-vis the university involve both questions of organization and questions of management. If one is to assume, as is done at many universities, that the department is the heart of the university, and that any academic appointment with faculty status and under tenure rules must be made in the department, then attention must be focused upon the improvement of management procedures. If, on the other hand, one accepts the view that undergraduate instruction, graduate instruction, basic research, service, and applied research are distinctive and perhaps mutually incompatible functions, then doubts may be raised about the appropriateness of the department as a basic unit for accomplishing all of these functions. Both management and organization are being looked at in universities. The phrases *program budgeting, cost effectiveness,* or *cost benefit analysis* reflect attempts to develop a management procedure in which the various types of input would be rationally related to the output so that it would be possible to improve the allocation of resources and to audit the effectiveness of their use. At present, most departmental functions ride on instruction. Increased attention to research, service, or other missions or functions is made visible only by reduction in teaching loads.

Neal Gross[1] has effectively pointed out the critical difference

[1] Neal Gross, "Organizational Lag in American Universities," *Harvard Educational Review,* 1963, *33,* 65.

between industrial and military organizations and higher education: "Although the university is organized on a departmental basis and one can speak of a departmental product, the producing unit in universities is essentially individual academic man. The most highly rewarded activities, scholarship and research publications, are not departmental products, but the products of individual faculty members. . . . The frame of reference of academic man is his own specialized area of competency, his courses, his students, his research publications, his consulting activities; and the reward system of the university in the disciplines is based on individual, not group productivity." Because of the apparent incompatibility of the several functions in the department and the high degree of individualization which seemingly almost defies any careful analysis, some universities have turned to the possibility of organizational change to reinstate some control. Continuing education centers and institutes represent ventures in which individuals can be employed with fewer restrictions as to academic qualifications and with more specificity in regard to the assignment. We also found examples of departments and of colleges in which the assignment of faculty members' time to research was reflected by a formal action attaching him to a research bureau for that portion of this time.

IMPROVING MANAGEMENT PROCEDURES

None of the departments contacted in our study maintained any records which would make it possible to indicate exactly how either human or material resources were assigned to the various missions or functions of the department. Many of them had difficulty putting together figures on course enrollments or student credit-hours produced. It is obvious that, in these circumstances, any attempt to relate resource allocations to productivity is impossible.

Typically, department-determined manpower needs were based upon new faculty positions required to meet increased enrollments, expanding knowledge, or demands for services. Seldom were there provisions for the elimination of positions opened by departure or death, and the usual pattern seemed to be that of filling a vacancy at the rank and at the same or higher salary than the previous incumbent had. Rarely was there an effective system of position control based upon the task to be done. Generally, department chairmen do not plan ahead for departmental growth but, rather, seek new positions as particular crises provide justification for so doing and the availability of funds makes it possible.

Departments could make more realistic estimates of manpower requirements. A first step is for the university to draw definite plans with regard to size and programs to be offered and to provide the department with some indication of the anticipated load. Central university offices could also do much more than is presently done in analyzing the effects of curricular changes and in advising given departments as to whether these changes are likely to increase or decrease their load. Unless such information is furnished by the university, it may be expected that departments will continue to scramble as they try to take care of unanticipated emergencies.

A graduate-research-oriented department has to take some steps independent of enrollment. It needs to define specialties which must be represented within the department before it can legitimately offer a complete program; for example, in psychology, regardless of enrollment, some faculty members are needed in clinical, experimental, industrial, and psychometric specialties. Most departments would argue that, even if one or two of these are offered as Ph.D. specialties, some general work must be offered. The department may feel that one man is sufficient to represent each specialty. In certain cases, the specialty may require initially only a half-time commitment of the faculty member, but this arrangement may be impossible to make. Some such approach should yield an indication of a minimum complete faculty so that necessary full-time faculty equivalents can be assigned on a base line growing out of disciplinary requirements. Undoubtedly, departmental representations on these matters need some review by higher administrative officials, for departments naturally seek to offer graduate specialization in all of the subdivisions of the discipline, and it would be a rare case in which the basic needs of the department would be underestimated.

Assuming the presence of university information as to enrollment prospects and a definition of a minimum complete faculty, the second step is to determine what courses are required and how faculty resources will be distributed across the course offerings. Section size, physical facilities, and equipment may be factors in these deliberations. For really effective management, all of these factors must be consulted simultaneously. An example was found of a department which had successfully sold the officials involved in planning a new building on the idea that no classroom or laboratory should accommodate more than twenty-five students. Having accomplished this, the department then was able to insist that no sections of more than twenty-five could be permitted because facilities would not accommodate them. Actually, patterns of instruction are flexible and class size is a matter of personal prejudice rather than demonstrated effectiveness. Some resolution must be achieved between departmental desires and the total resources available.

Beyond faculty requirements for coverage of the discipline and meeting classes, there are additional requirements for the functions of advising, research, service, faculty improvement programs, and the like. The resources assigned to each of these should be made specific, although the determination of faculty load is a most elusive and frustrating job. Faculty members consider themselves to be professionals and are not responsive to any conception of load assignments or hours per week worked at various functions. Some departments, to avoid judgments of research productivity and service activities, agree that every person will have a standard teaching load of so many courses or credits. In others, attempts are made to adjust load in regard to the total activities of the individual, but questions arise as to which are university-related activities and which are taken on because of personal interests. A faculty member tends to interpret all of his reading, contacts with students, and attendance at meetings as a part of his work load and expects that they should be so accepted by the institution. Yet department chairmen frequently indicated that certain activities were not regarded as university-related. Our contacts with chairmen indicated that many of them would welcome a pattern which would require chairmen or departmental executive committees to negotiate with each faculty member as to the proportion of his effort to be devoted to various activities within a specified future period of time. Such an approach would permit some planning of resources for the year ahead and would set a pattern whereby expenditures and results might be matched. Also, it might make it more apparent how much of faculty effort is involved in often unproductive administrative and committee activities.

The department chairmen found it difficult to relate numbers of degrees, numbers of publications, and requests for service to the resources provided them in salaries, supplies, equipment, and labor budget. Typically, if they kept any records in the department, they were in terms of what is known technically as "object codes," which cover funds spent for salary for various classes of personnel and for categories such as telephone, postage, travel, student labor, and equipment. Departments usually kept some records on federal grants and other nonuniversity funds, for the university may maintain only such controls as are necessitated by the conditions of the grant and by regularly deducting indirect costs. Since budgetary allocations by the university do not generally take into account other funds available to the department, a department may be able to purchase equipment, pay for travel, buy supplies, or even cover some teaching costs from such funds. Thereby it achieves a flexibility and a level of support for its various functions that are not at all recognized in the university budgeting and accounting procedures.

In many respects, this practice is analogous to that of state universities in their dealings with the state budget office and the legislature. They resist or even refuse to provide data on the amount of money from sources other than legislative appropriation and student fees, and argue that appropriations should be based on numbers of students, degrees produced, or credit-hours without regard to other funds available to the institution. As long as the public university maintains this stance with respect to its sources of support, it is difficult to invoke a management pattern for the departmental operation. Until such time as the department is required to plan in advance how its resources are to be utilized and to provide after the fact evidence as to the results obtained, the present pattern of departments trying to maximize and utilize resources for departmentally defined programs will continue. Thus, evasions, minor dishonesties, and deliberate misinterpretations of rules and policies will continue.

A high degree of departmental autonomy is not unreasonable. It is probably necessary for effective operation. It must, however, be developed along with departmental responsibility and effectiveness. Increasing autonomy without accountability generates inequities in budgetary allocations and in loads, and ultimately creates many of the problems which elicit student complaints and public criticism. It will be difficult for any one university to impose such a management system, although we believe that responsible deans and department chairmen will generally welcome it. We also believe that departments which feel that they have had inequitable treatment will welcome an approach which permits reasonable comparison among closely related disciplines and provides for correction of inequities. On the other hand, those departments which have been benefited by past patterns and know it—those which have been recipients of extensive funds from nonuniversity sources, those which contain highly individualistic faculty members—will strongly resist. The resistance can take either of two forms: departure to another institution, or evasion in carrying out the responsibilities assigned. Our interviews lead us to suspect, however, that it may not be the really outstanding scholars in departments who most strongly resist the management approach but, rather, those who have profited from a laissez-faire pattern which permitted them to hide behind a facade that more careful examination would destroy.

REORGANIZATION

Our recommendations for management may be impossible in the present university structure. Departmental organization based upon disciplines is perhaps altogether too simplistic a concept for university organization. In fact, departments are not always based upon a disciplinary organization of knowledge. A number of departments may operate generally within the same discipline, some may be based upon some aspect of business or industry drawing upon several disciplines, while still others may rely upon accumulated experience without any structure, theory, or unifying concepts. The range of services and functions in the modern university bears little relation to departmental organization. Most departments in arts and sciences are not interested in service or in applied research. Numerous examples indicate that the effectiveness of the institute pattern may be destroyed by the insistence that the institute staff must first be appointed in departments. As a result, the institute can be perverted to disciplinary theorizing rather than the practical approach which originally justified its introduction.

Many universities have already recognized the need for some type of organization apart from the departmental one. Continuing education programs serving short-term conference and longer-term training programs have found it necessary to enlarge their own professional faculty to carry on these activities. Early attempts to involve departmental staff were found to be difficult because the continuing education activities did not usually fit the quarter or semester system upon which the department operated. Furthermore, the academic man usually had a full schedule of teaching and research. He either disdained involvement in continuing education or demanded additional recompense for it. Continuing education centers in some cases have had sad experiences with supporting positions in departments in return for departmental contribution to continuing education. In the course of time, the departmental positions, while still budgeted by continuing education, have been gobbled up into departmental operations, and departments report no one available to staff continuing education functions.

In land-grant institutions, cooperative extension programs and experiment stations represent long-time commitments to the service and research areas. Many of the employees in cooperative extension have been outside the academic faculty, largely because their work and qualifications would not compare favorably with the standards departments expect. Experiment station funds are often used for part-time appointments housed in academic departments, so that research projects are clearly assigned to individuals rather than accepted as departmental responsibility. Our study did not involve departments in agriculture, home economics, or sciences related to experiment station activities. Other sources of information suggested, however, that similar problems have arisen here. Thus some departments would prefer to regard experiment station funds as an assignment to the department to be used as it wishes so long as the department makes an appropriate contribution in terms of research activity, although dual appointments with functions related to salary sources provide much clearer and readier accountability.

Research units of traditional types have long existed. These units are found in colleges of education, colleges of business, and even in departments. For example, departments of sociology have frequently included as a part of their organization a research or survey institute. Beyond these traditional patterns, recent years have seen the development of large research foundations associated with universities, although often separately incorporated. Nevertheless, the presence of university officers on the board of the research foundation and perhaps the existence of what amounts to dual appointments between university and foundation have permitted research and services which could not have been readily accommodated within the university structure. The precedent and even the need for an alternative structure to departments and colleges thus does seem to be documented by experience to date.

The discipline-oriented department is best adapted to effective performance in two related areas: graduate study and pure research. Although our experience with departments indicated that those strongest in graduate education and basic research had effectively abandoned the master's program, this issue may not be serious because students seeking terminal master's degrees are tending to do so in a professional or vocational sense. The department is also the appropriate vehicle for the education of advanced undergraduates who are definitely committed to the discipline.

Graduate professional study (which is typically not departmentalized to the same extent as the arts and sciences) is now provided reasonably effectively in separate schools or colleges. Undergraduate professional education now provided in some of these colleges may gradually be displaced, as more and more emphasis is placed upon graduate study as a basis for a career. Graduate schools in business, engineering, and other fields may well become the preferred vehicle for professional study.

At the graduate level, there will undoubtedly also be a need

for institutes or centers of interdisciplinary nature to bring together
faculty from a number of departments for research and to provide
for interdisciplinary graduate study. Institutes focusing on service
or applied research should be set up separate from the departmental
structure and permitted to hire their own staff in terms of the particular problem that they undertake. Many institutes might be set
up on a temporary basis, dependent upon the continuance of outside support, which would mean that tenure in the usual sense
could not be provided, but job security equivalent to that provided
in business and industry would be possible. With the ability to select
the staff in terms of particular interests and experiences appropriate
to the job, the institute should be able to play a more vital role in
dealing with social issues and in solving social problems than is
presently true in many of the institutes which are delimited by the
pressure of departmental thumbs. The programs of some institutes
might ultimately be assimilated into other aspects of the university's
operation, but seldom should they become permanent fixtures.

To provide broad liberal education, the university may need
to introduce one or more undergraduate colleges of nondepartmental structure with faculties of their own. These could include such
units as a university college providing a broad-gauge four-year general education for large numbers of students. It could involve a
number of residence-type nondepartmentalized colleges within the
framework of the university, each operating as a liberal arts college
with its own faculty, or providing some particular emphasis with a
problem or interdisciplinary orientation. In such undergraduate
units, faculty members would be employed and rewarded for their
contribution to undergraduate education. Individuals from the departments who indicated a special interest in undergraduate education might be given dual appointments in an undergraduate college
with full understanding that, as long as they remain in a department, their career would be largely dependent on their performance there. Assuming the existence of a number of colleges at the
undergraduate level, the need for special units to exploit interdisciplinary study at the undergraduate level would be eliminated.
Rather, such programs of study might provide the theme for a col-

lege curriculum or for interdisciplinary courses which could readily be developed in a college that is structured without departments.

A university organized in this fashion would probably have under the president a vice-president concerned with coordination of undergraduate instruction, a vice-president concerned with graduate education and research, and a vice-president concerned with applied research and service. Faculty members would not be prohibited—might indeed be encouraged—to use their talents in more than one major division of the university, but, once this decision were made, the appointment and salary division would correspond to the assignment, and full accountability would be established for the various functions carried out by the individual. In a department where major emphasis would be on a type of research intimately related to graduate study, no distinction would need to be made between instruction and research. It would simply be understood that, in this segment of the university, a particular kind of instruction was being carried on which involved the production of researchers and, therefore, the heavy involvement of the faculty in research. Individuals spending full time in a department would not be expected to contribute to undergraduate education (other than on an advanced level) or to service activities, except in an incidental way. In this pattern, an individual carrying out several distinctive functions would have a corresponding division of his salary and would report to two or more deans or directors, each of whom would be, in turn, accountable for the resources allotted to that division of the university. At this point, management procedures, such as we have already discussed in relationship to the department, could be much more readily applied, because they would be imbedded in the organization. In our judgment, some such reorganization of the university is essential if its various functions are to be effectively and efficiently discharged. Internal unit organization, communication, patterns of influence, and other matters examined here would not be automatically resolved by such reorganization, but the alleviation or elimination of tensions and of maneuvering arising from disagreements over priorities and over allocation of resources to various functions would greatly simplify these problems.

CONCLUSION

The universities and the departments within them are out of control. Administrators and faculties too readily interpret their own aspirations as meeting or transcending the educational needs of the clientele which they serve. In seeking support to fulfill these aspirations, they engage in half-truths and reluctantly acquiesce to requests for data which are so selected, manipulated, and presented as to support their case. In the defense of administrators, it must be said that they are caught between the insatiable demands of departments and faculties more concerned with self-advancement than with service and a supporting clientele which often does not understand the university and therefore is capable, wittingly or unwittingly, of using the truth to impede or destroy its effectiveness. In most cases, too, presidents and vice-presidents do not know just what is going on in the colleges and departments, for these units also engage in half-truths and misrepresentations shrewdly calculated to attain their own ends. Yet there is a surprising accord between the aspirations and ends sought by the faculty and those sought by the administrators, for the reputation of a university and of its faculty and administrators is based largely on research and on the range of programs offered, rather than on education of students and service to society. Hence the university, confident of its own superior wisdom, does not hesitate to demand or beguile the public into increasing support used to forward its own ends. Administrators are more aware of this dilemma than faculties, and they are victims of it, as recent departures of many educators evidence.

Departments and other units within the university must be brought under control so that their resources are allocated and used in accord with priorities set for the university by the university in cooperation with those who support it. This can be done only if more detailed information—a management information system— is developed and used to assure allocation of resources based on careful consideration of the requirements for those programs agreed upon as appropriate to the university. In all likelihood, some reorganization of the present confused university structure will also be required. It is to be expected that departments and faculties will strongly resist any reorganization or any system which permits review and control of their activities, and administrators will be powerless to effect such alterations until public pressure makes continuing support contingent upon full revelation and upon adherence to priorities on which that support is predicated.

Despite its dissatisfaction with the university, the public, too, is confused. Large segments of it have come to accept the faculty and university view that excellence is measured by size, range of programs, and the research output of faculty. In evidence of this, one can point to the large number of young people encouraged to seek their undergraduate education at universities whose reputations and emphases are primarily in research and graduate education, and who charge professional prices for graduate assistant instruction. Also, each developing university has among its clientele many who support its ambitions. Individual state legislators, while resisting increase in appropriations for higher education, nevertheless demand them for the institution in their bailiwick. The universities are out of control because there is no agreement as to whether or what control should be applied—especially when the focus is on a particular institution. There are also those within and without the university who would have the faculty take over the operation of the university and even organize for adversary bargaining to advance their own ends, which, unfortunately, do not accord with societal needs.

From some viewpoints, the university has been an outstanding success. It has accommodated a vastly increasing enrollment and offered an amazingly varied range of programs. It has made major contributions to knowledge and to technology. The discipline-based department has been the key unit in these developments. However, in its success, the department or the dominant personalities in it have become arrogant and lost the vision of service, which must be a central characteristic of any profession. Reform and realignment of priorities are needed. In this volume we have indicated some essential elements in this process. One heartening factor is that within most universities (if our sample is indicative) there are faculty members, chairmen, deans, and others who recognize the need.

And there are indications that student concerns are increasingly focusing on the inadequacies of the curriculum and instructional deficiencies of the department. Certainly there are pressures from without. Assuming that these concerns and pressures can be coalesced and concentrated on the main issue—the reordering of priorities and better allocation of resources to achieve them—rather than on peripheral changes of minor significance, reform may be closer than it appears.

The issues raised in this volume, and especially in this final chapter on the university department, may be surprising to some, irritating to others, and irrelevant to still others. To show that we are not alone in these concerns, we close with a quotation:[2]

> By and large, higher education has been slow to innovate, slow to discard the obsolete. By and large, it is woefully sloppy on matters of rudimentary management. All too many faculties are "dog-in-the-mangerish" about academic housekeeping. The consequence is utilized and unutilized facilities that would have bankrupted profit-oriented institutions decades ago. Our personnel systems tend to be shoddy. We resist systematic evaluation by peers, students, alumni, or administrators and thereby are thrown into a jungle of unsystematic evaluations by the very same groups. The red herring of academic freedom is drawn across the path of systematic evaluation of performance. Basically the motivation is not defense of academic freedom at all, but fear of the insecure that their shortcomings might be verified or their sloth exposed.
>
> We are reluctant to plan for fear of closing options or clarifying wasteful jurisdictional overlaps.
>
> Disciplinary pride at its best is the glory of academic excellence, but at its worst, it reinforces quite unproven prejudices about class size and optimum teaching loads, and fetters the curiosity of majors and graduate students.

[2] Stephen K. Bailey, "Public Money and the Integrity of the Higher Academy," *Educational Record,* 1969, *50* (2), 153.

Appendix

Plan and Procedures
of the Study

The study did not begin with a set of well-specified hypotheses constructed with operationalized variables. The nature of the university and of organization theory did not permit such a strategy. As our review of empirical research on university departments indicates, few studies provide guidelines for investigation; many of the studies are concerned with but a few variables and are not linked together in any manner to permit the formulation of specific hypotheses. The current state of organization theory—and this statement ap-

plies to sociology, psychology, business administration, and other fields
concerned with the problem—have produced a plethora of speculative theories and typologies based primarily on research conducted
in industrial concerns with primarily blue-collar workers as respondents. However, a modern American university is by far the most
complicated type of organization yet devised by man. To limit one-
self at the outset to one particular existing theory would be to close
one's purview prematurely and make it easy to overlook many important phenomena.

   The authors of this volume have diverse backgrounds, and
the first few months of our study were devoted to discussions and
working papers that sought common grounds for initiating the research. Our basic problem was to explore the operation and function of departments in the large university: what role do they play
in the achievement of university goals? The discussions finally focused upon a few variables which appear in writings about higher
education as well as in some of the organization theories: goals or
missions, influence, communication, faculty orientations, resource
allocation, quality, conflict, and competition. We realized that different echelons in the hierarchy would probably have different
perspectives of these variables, and we wanted data from faculty,
chairmen, deans, and a few key upper administrators. Early in the
research we realized that time did not permit gathering data from
students at any level, although this certainly would have been desirable.

   Our first step in the research was to select universities. We
decided to study the same large departments in universities that
varied by region, public and private sponsorship, Cartter report
ratings, and religious affiliation. Of the thirty universities initially
contacted, ten reported that it would be impossible to cooperate.
The very pattern of rejections almost became a variable of interest:
in some cases, the upper-echelon administrator rejected our offer,
whereas in others, the departments indicated they did not want to
participate. One amusing case was a prestigious eastern university
whose president had given a well-publicized speech calling for more
research on universities and their operations. When we wrote to him
a week later indicating we were about to do exactly what he had

wanted, he quickly responded that his university could not be included in the study because of new developments being initiated which would bias the research. As with all the rejectors, he offered his moral support.

Of the twenty affirmative replies, we selected ten for the study. Five of the remaining were sufficiently enthusiastic about the study that we decided to include them with a limited involvement. One purpose for their inclusion was to detect some of the bias in the selection of the basic ten: we could compare faculty questionnaire responses and basic departmental data to see what effect our visits made. If there was none, then the time-consuming and expensive visits might be eliminated in further research.

Our study progressed with a three-pronged attack on the data. We first sent the basic data forms to each university and had them filled out by the appropriate person for each department. In some cases, the central administration had all the data we requested; in others, departments completed the forms. In a few cases, the data we required were simply not available from any source. We were to find that data over time were extremely difficult to obtain, and some departments simply do not keep records very accurately or carefully. Some items were virtually impossible to calculate because of the great variety of record-keeping. For example, student load is calculated in some universities in terms of credit-hours, in others, by head count. We finally could not use this variable because of the wide diversity.

The second prong of the research strategy was to hold a meeting of the consultants and discuss the study with them. The design of the research was presented and the outline of their interviews and reports discussed. Basing our conclusions upon these expert opinions, we revised and modified the format. All consultants were presented with copies of the basic data forms of the universities which they were to visit; in this way they became cognizant of the overall parameters of the departmental structures which they were to investigate. Although consultants were urged to follow the outlines we presented them, it was made clear that they were to conduct flexible interviews and utilize their insights and expertise in order to maximize the depth of the study.

Campus visits usually required four or five days. A member of the study staff was present for the first two days and conducted interviews with institute or center directors in addition to meeting a few deans and department chairmen. The schedule of interviews was arranged in advance by a representative of each university. Reports were then written on each university by the study staff member and the consultant. Some of the data in these reports were then quantified and used in this book. Other data and insights were utilized to complete the picture we had of each department from the questionnaire and the basic data. Ten universities were visited in this manner; five other universities were visited by a member of the study staff, and interviews were conducted primarily with deans, chairmen, and directors in addition to some members of the upper administrative echelon. Reports were also filed on these campus visits, which usually required two days.

Camapus visitors left copies of the faculty questionnaire in each department for distribution to all full, associate, and assistant professors; a self-addressed envelope was included for the completed instrument. (Returns from instructors or others who mistakenly received the questionnaire were discarded.) These data provided us with the third level, or prong, of our investigation. Considering the number of persons involved in the research—consultants, co-ordinators in each university, faculty, and administrators—we must conclude that cooperation was excellent and the project ran very smoothly.

Fifty-one per cent of the faculty sampled responded to our questionnaire. Disciplines varied somewhat from a low of 35 per cent for mathematics to a high of 68 per cent for management. Future investigators may wish to know what biases are contained in the questionnaire response rates. In our discussion we have tried to weed out as much of this bias as possible by analyzing and, in some cases, controlling for variations in response rate. For example, we expected there would be a very great difference between the universities which were visited by consultants and staff members and those where we made a very brief contact and then distributed our questionnaires. Here there was absolutely no linear consistency whatsoever: the universities which were not visited tended to fall at the extremes of response rates. These universities had either high or low response rates, whereas those which we visited tended to fall in the middle.

The response rates did vary by whether or not the department was mentioned favorably in the Cartter report: those rated favorably in the report tended to have lower response rates in our study. Similarly, we found that universities which were privately supported had a higher response rate than those which were public-supported. In terms of the individuals responding, we found no difference by either rank or length of time within the department. The reference group of the respondents did vary, however. Departments where the faculty were oriented primarily to the university had a relatively high response rate, whereas those oriented to the department had a medium response rate, and those oriented to the discipline had a low response rate.

In general, it appeared to us that departments where chairmen exercised more constraint over the faculty had higher response rates. For example, on the question asking how decisions about a number of different departmental concerns are executed, almost all of these items had high response rates coming from departments where the chairman operated with relatively little pressure from faculty. However, the question which asked directly about the influence the chairman had over departmental matters showed no variation in terms of response rates. In fact, with the exception of the influence of the dean and the influence of special departmental committees, there was no difference in response rates and influence. (Both of these mentioned positions came from high-response-rate departments.)

The communication question showed no variability by response rate; nor did such items that inquired about autonomy of the department, or how one goes about receiving special consideration for a variety of concerns.

In terms of departmental missions, we found that high-response-rate departments stressed undergraduate and graduate instruction, whereas the low-response-rate departments stressed basic research. None of the other missions, however, were related in any way to departmental response rates. It should also be added that the question inquiring about what *should* be emphasized within departments was also related to response rates. That is, departments where it was felt that basic research should be emphasized had a low response rate, whereas those suggesting that undergraduate instruction and graduate instruction should have great emphasis came from high-response-rate departments.

Some readers may feel that these variations in response rates severely limit the use of the data contained in this report. However, as mentioned above, we have tried whenever possible to take into account these variations in response rates when discussing our findings and their implications.

Appendix

Empirical Research on Departments

Most research concerning university departments and their role in the larger university has been conducted by observation and reflection. Retiring or practicing administrators have discussed their views of tenure, the role of chairmen, small cliques which control curriculum, promotions and rewards, and the resistance to administrative suggestion. (WICHE Conference[1] is a prototype; Barzun[2]

[1] Terry F. Lunsford (ed.), *The Study of Academic Administration.* Papers Presented at the Fifth Annual Institute on College Self-Study, Uni-

241

is a recent example.) Undoubtedly, such statements provide educators with insights into university administration which no other source could provide, but it is difficult to generalize the observations of one administrator based on intimate knowledge of one institutional setting. Unfortunately, the settings are seldom specified, and the relationships described (among faculty and administrators or faculty and students, and so on) can neither be validated nor generalize fruitfully. The views expressed are very likely biased by observations from an administrative position.

Faculty members seldom write about university operations, and when they do, it is often to attack the administration for conservative or constraining practices. See, for example, Harris's attack on Columbia officials and faculty for their behavior in 1968.[3] Faculty organization has been left largely to the novelists for comment and satire. One notable exception is Maranell,[4] who writes about the assistant professors' subculture, identifying it as a "culture of travail" defined by three major characteristics: marginality and indifference, anxiety and uncertainty, and inequality. He concludes that it is the inequality which leads to the other characteristics and brings about problems of identity for the persons involved and problems of communication to the department as a whole.

The role and power of the departmental chairman (or head) has received some systematic investigation. Perhaps the most extensive work was done by Doyle[5] in thirty-three small private colleges. Corson's comments on the role of the academic department are based largely on Doyle's study.[6] Doyle concludes that depart-

---

versity of California at Berkeley, July 22–26, 1963 (Boulder, Col.: Western Interstate Commission for Higher Education, 1963).

[2] Jacques Barzun, *The American University: How It Runs, Where It Is Going* (New York: Harper and Row, 1968).

[3] Marvin Harris, "Big Bust on Morningside Heights," *The Nation,* 1968, *206,* 757–763.

[4] Gary M. Maranell, "An Assistant Professor's View of Academia," *Kansas Journal and Sociological Review,* 1964, *1,* 4–11.

[5] Edward A. Doyle, S.J. *The Status and Functions of the Departmental Chairman* (Washington, D.C.: Catholic University of America Press, 1953).

[6] John J. Corson, *Governance of Colleges and Universities* (New York: McGraw-Hill, 1960).

mental chairmen are selected on the basis of three criteria: previous teaching experience, teaching ability, and administrative talent. Only two of the thirty-three colleges had rotating chairmen; only four specified the term of office. These chairmen spent most of their time teaching and no administrative details. Least time was spent in supervising new professors in the department, although about half of the chairmen felt the need to do some supervision.

The department chairmen of large universities, both private and state, have yet to be investigated empirically. Corson believed that the influence of the chairman decreases with the professionalization of the faculty members and that university chairmen spend much more of their time in meetings and in social contact with administrators from other departments. Corson compares the department chairman to the foreman in industry: a man in the middle whose subordinates frequently possess skills which the supervisor cannot evaluate because of their specialization. Obviously, the greater specialization is dependent upon the size of the staff, and indirectly, the size of the student body to be educated and trained. In order to facilitate administration, especially in the large departments, certain practices and routines have to be delegated to committees. But the formation of committees may decrease the ability of the chairman to coordinate activities, as overlapping functions become evident and rivalry emerges. It is no surprise, then, that certain practices for personnel will tend to become formalized in larger departments. Haas and Collen[7] have suggested that hiring and evaluation practices are the first to be formalized in the large departments.

Attempts to measure the power of the chairman as perceived by faculty were made by Hill and French.[8] They found that chairmen are perceived to have less power collectively than any other administrative or faculty group. However, faculty respondents also reported great variability for individual chairmen. One interesting

[7] Eugene Haas and Linda Collen, "Administrative Practices in University Departments," *Administrative Science Quarterly*, 1963, 8, 44–60.

[8] Winston W. Hill and Wendell L. French, "Perceptions of Power of Department Chairmen by Professors," *Administrative Science Quarterly*, 1967, *11*, 548–574.

finding of the Hill and French study was that in departments where the faculty reported relatively greater power for the chairman, the faculty satisfaction and productivity was also relatively higher.

Hemphill[9] attempted to examine the validity of using the reputation of a department for being well administered as a criterion for determining the quality of administration in college departments. Larger departments tended to have better administrative reputations than smaller departments, indicating perhaps that more care was exercised in selecting chairmen of large departments. Hemphill concluded that reputation may provide a criterion of excellence of administration.

If there is some confusion about the role of the department chairman, there is even greater confusion about the faculty. It is often assumed that most faculty members are autonomous persons engaged in research and teaching. Except for the novelists, few observers of faculty have paid departmental politics and interactions any attention. The individual is seen as being guided by higher aims of his discipline, possessing little attachment to his university, ready to leave when offered greater freedom and resources. Were it not for the secretaries, graduate students, and other persons concerned with departmental affairs, nothing would ever get done. The work of Ellis and Keedy tends to support this view.[10] After interviewing graduate students, they found that professors were not accorded esteem for effective teaching, and the typical faculty member was not evaluated impartially. Many personal factors affected the ranking he received.

Gouldner's work at a small Midwestern college differentiates between two types of faculty, cosmopolitans and locals.[11] The former were discipline-oriented and opportunistically mobile. The lo-

[9] John K. Hemphill, "Leadership Behavior Associated with the Administrative Reputation of College Departments," *The Journal of Educational Psychology*, 1955, *46*, 385–401.

[10] Robert A. Ellis and Thomas C. Keedy, Jr., "Three Dimensions of Status: A Study of Academic Prestige," *Political Sociological Review*, 1960, *3*, 23–28.

[11] Alvin W. Gouldner, "Cosmopolitans and Locals: Toward an Analysis of Latent Social Roles," *Administrative Science Quarterly*, 1957, *1*, 281–306; and 1958, *2*, 444–480.

cals were engrossed in the immediate situation, had many local contacts, and were concerned with university rules and regulations. They were also less dissatisfied with pay than the cosmopolitans and less eager to publish and attend professional meetings.

This distinction between locals and cosmopolitans focuses directly upon splits within the mythical homogeneous faculty. Hamblin and Smith[12] were able to show that local stature increased with teaching ability and professional demeanor of the person, but professional status increased with the merit of publications, merit of teaching, and negative cordiality (maintaining social distance). Length of service was also positively related to professional status. Although the Gouldner and Hamblin-Smith papers are not completely comparable, it is clear that two sets of orientations are discernible by both the faculty themselves (Gouldner) and by the graduate students who view their behavior (Hamblin and Smith).

In an examination of the emerging large-scale research institutes and centers, Rossi[13] pointed out that two hierarchies are now operating on many campuses. Faculty often move back and forth between them, and evaluation of performance from one to the other becomes increasingly difficult. He suggested we establish two standards for distributing rewards, one based on excellence in teaching, and another based on research productivity. Worcester[14] applied economic analysis and indifference curves to the problem of incentives for faculty. He suggested that applying different rewards to these two major specialties, research and teaching, would encourage greater division of labor and permit greater utilization of economic resources. In a more speculative vein, Gross[15] discussed problems of organization lag in universities and concluded that the university does not recognize the contribution of research and must be willing to provide additional resources for it. It is interesting to

[12] Robert L. Hamblin and Carole R. Smith, "Values, Status and Professors," *Sociometry*, 1966, *80*, 183–196.

[13] Peter H. Rossi, "Researchers, Scholars and Policy Makers: The Politics of Large Scale Research," *Daedalus*, 1964, *93*, 1142–1161.

[14] Dean A. Worcester, Jr., "Standards of Faculty Tenure and Promotion: A Pure Theology," *Administrative Science Quarterly*, 1957, *2*, 216–234.

[15] Neal Gross, "Organizational Lag in American Universities," *Harvard Educational Review*, 1963, *33*, 58–78.

note that all three of these writers suggesting alternative reward structures were nonprofessional educators, and one would look in vain for administrators to offer similar alternatives. Perhaps the professional administrator and the departmental faculties, too, see the addition of alternative reward structures as admitting too great a diversity and complexity under existing departmental authority lines. The advent of the institute on many campuses is one mechanism for handling this diversity.

Many administrators have discussed the department structures in terms of clique structures. Although there is little systematic research on this important issue, Williams[16] reported that careful analysis of the departmental meetings which he attended showed a small group of senior professors controlling the proceedings. He also reported that competition among the cliques provided recognized status for individuals. Unfortunately, Williams provides no clue as to whether or not such cliques were based on splits within the staff over teaching and research or primarily on graduate or undergraduate education. The basis for the cliques is of utmost importance because of their ability to influence the rewards offered to members in the department.

Mercer and Pearson[17] reported that factors influencing academic ascendancy for sociologists lay outside of the department. This would imply that irrespective of who controlled rewards inside the department, ascendancy would be unaffected. However—and this is an important point on which we have no data—control of resources in the department may affect the ability to gain visibility and maintain contact with some of the outside influences. Mercer and Pearson, in a follow-up article[18] reported that sociologists do not approve of behavior that is status-striving within the department, but that 55 per cent of respondents admitted to have engaged

[16] Lloyd P. Williams, "Democracy and Hierarchy: A Profile of Faculty Meetings in Department," *Journal of Educational Sociology*, 1956, *30*, 168–172.

[17] Blaine E. Mercer and Judson B. Pearson, "Personal and Institutional Characteristics of Academic Sociologists," *Sociology and Social Research*, 1962, *46*, 259–270.

[18] Blaine E. Mercer and Judson B. Pearson, "The Ethics of Academic Status-Striving," *Sociology and Social Research*, 1962, *47*, 51–56.

in such behavior. Perhaps this finding helps explain why there is greater satisfaction reported among faculty when they have a relatively powerful chairman: clique structures are decreased in importance, and faculty can devote more time to their own interests outside of the departments which lead to rewards. A weak chairman creates a power vacuum which others attempt to fill.

The influence of the dean is seldom investigated, and almost all education administrators will say their university likes to have strong deans. Bachman,[19] in a study of 658 faculty members in twelve small Midwestern colleges, tried to measure the bases of power employed by deans. He reports that expert power ranked first, followed by legitimate and referent power, with reward power being utilized somewhat to a lesser degree. Coercive power was used only to a slight degree. Interestingly, these rankings of the bases of power were very similar to other rankings for insurance agencies, utility company work groups, and so on. In short, from these data there is little reason to assume that deans use a different form of power than other supervisory positions in American society.

Bachman also reports that satisfaction measures correlated significantly and positively with the use of expert power and referent power; but there were strong negative relationships between reward power and coercive power. (There was no statistically significant relationship between legitimate power and faculty satisfaction.) One might recall that faculty satisfaction was also related to the department chairman's power in the study of Hill and French. What is needed now is a study to examine bases of power for the chairmen and the amount of power for the deans. Unfortunately, we do not have the information to tie our knowledge together in this important area. What seems to be important, however, is that faculty satisfaction does not decrease under conditions of power if this power is based upon actions which are considered appropriate by those who must provide compliance. The implications of these two studies are that satisfactions are not based on pure autonomy and lack of structure. An assumption frequently found in the litera-

[19] Gerald Bachman, David Bowers, and Philip M. Marcus, "Bases of Supervisory Power," in A. Tannenbaum (ed.), *Control in Organizations* (New York: Mc-Graw-Hill, 1968).

ture is that faculty resent hierarchic influence over their actions. Research thus far does not confirm this assumption.

The picture we have drawn of the department and its structure was based primarily upon the little empirical research available. In the literature, the extent of the discussion of this topic greatly exceeds the facts and generalizations based on systematically gathered evidence. Perhaps the day is near when academics will study themselves as expertly as they study industrial workers, teachers, and members of other occupations. Certainly, the problems which confront those interested in higher education can no longer be solved by speculation or reflection. Systematic evidence and careful analysis are required.

ADDITIONAL REFERENCES

Nicholas J. Demareth, Richard W. Stephens, and R. Robb Taylor, *Power, Presidents, and Professors* (New York: Basic Books, 1967).

Robert Dubin and Fredric Beisse, "The Assistant: Academic Subaltern," *Administrative Science Quarterly,* 1967, *11,* 521–547.

R. W. Gerard, "Problems in the Institutionalization of Higher Education: An Analysis Based on Historical Materials," *Behavioral Science,* 1957, *2,* 134–146.

Edward Gross and Paul V. Grambsch, *University Goals and Academic Power* (Washington, D.C.: American Council on Education, 1968).

Paul F. Lazarsfeld and Wagner Thielens, Jr., *The Academic Mind: Social Scientists in a Time of Crisis* (Glencoe, Ill.: Free Press, 1958).

Appendix C

Schedules and Forms

SCHEDULE OF TOPICS AND QUESTIONS FOR STUDY OF DEPARTMENTS

1. *Departmental Organization*

   1.1 What is the title of the chief administrative officer of the unit? Is there a formal statement of his duties and responsibilities? (If so, get two copies if possible.)

   1.2 What is the mode of selection and term of office?

   1.3 What are the titles and specific responsibilities of auxiliary administrators (assistant heads, committee chairmen, administrative assistants)?

   1.4 What is the mode of appointment and term of office of each?

1.5 What committees exist in the department? What are their charges? How are they selected? How do they operate? What types of decisions do they make (specific, general practices, policies)?

2. *Communication and Decision-Making Process*

2.1 What means of staff communication are regularly used (bulletin board, weekly or intermittent news sheet, regular staff meetings, word of mouth, secretary or members of the staff)? How effective are these?

2.2 How frequently are staff meetings held? Who is expected to attend? What constitutes a typical agenda? How is the session conducted?

2.3 What persons are involved and what processes are used in making decisions (or departmental recommendations) on each of the following points? To what extent are these decisions subject to review and denial at other levels?
   a. Recruitment and selection of new faculty
   b. Promotions and tenure
   c. Salary increases
   d. Leaves of absence
   e. Authorization of expenditures for travel
   f. Authorization of expenditures for supplies and equipment
   g. Course assignments
   h. Teaching load
   i. Assignment of office and research space
   j. Award of assistantships, fellowships, scholarships
   k. Adding new courses
   l. Requirements for majors and graduate students
   m. New equipment

2.4 Is the department a closely knit, cohesive unit, or is it divided? What is the basis for the division?

2.5 Which of the following is most descriptive of the operation of this department?
   a. Autocratic—dominated by chairman, with high regard for his prerogatives and decision-making authority
   b. Paternalistic—dominated by chairman who has evident concern for the welfare of each and every individual

    c. Oligarchic—run by a few influential members of the department

    d. Bureaucratic—well-(perhaps over-)organized with assignment of specific tasks and responsibilities to individuals and committees and with elaborate procedural policies

    e. Democratic—all members of department involved in discussion and formulation of policies and recommendations

    f. Laissez-faire—little organization, maximal freedom of individual to determine his own role and carry it out as he wishes

3. *Records*

    3.1 What types of records on students are kept in the departmental office? Range of data included? Who is responsible for maintenance of these? (Get two copies of forms if possible.)

    3.2 What types of departmental records are kept on the faculty? Range of data included? Who is responsible for maintenance? (Get two copies of forms if possible.)

    3.3 What types of records are kept on finance? Range of data included? Who is responsible for maintenance? (Get two copies of forms if possible.)

    3.4 Is there a manual for students and/or faculty? (If so, get two copies if possible.)

4. *Concern for Students*

    4.1 What special provisions does the department make for the advising and instruction of its own undergraduate majors?

    4.2 What special courses (if any) does the department provide for majors in other departments? How are these courses coordinated and planned to meet the needs of these students?

    4.3 Does the department encourage its students (graduate and undergraduate) to take courses in other departments? What is the rationale for its position?

5. *The Department and the University*

    5.1 Is the department isolated and self-sufficient, or is it influential as a unit or as individuals in the councils of the university? What is the evidence for this?

5.2 How is the department regarded by other units in the university? In what respects is it regarded as excellent, good, mediocre, poor? Evidence?

5.3 What special problems, concerns, or complaints has this department regarding:
a. Internal policies and practices,
b. College or university policies and practices?

5.4 What special problems, concerns, or complaints do deans and other higher-echelon administrators have regarding this department?

6. *Departmental Priorities*

Fill out for the department one of the Checklists of Departmental Priorities (Item 5 of Departmental Study Inventory). Then comment upon and summarize the evidence to which you had recourse in filling out the checklist.

INTERVIEW SCHEDULE FOR INSTITUTES,
CENTERS, AND SIMILAR UNITS

1. *Origin of the Unit*

1.1 What circumstances led to setting up this unit?

1.2 What were its original purposes and functions?

1.3 When was it started?

1.4 What changes in purposes and functions have taken place since then?

1.5 Are there special university policies which specify procedure, purposes, functions, or names of such units?

1.6 What future developments are anticipated for this unit?

2. *Organization and Administration*

2.1 How are staff members selected and appointed to the unit? (Full-time or part-time?)

2.2 How is the director (specify title) selected?

2.3 Are staff members housed together?

2.4 What part does this unit play in personnel decisions on its own members?

2.5 Where is the unit placed in the administrative pattern?

2.6 In what ways is this unit similar to or different from a department?

3. *Role of This Unit in the University*

3.1 What are its relationships to other units, institutes, departments, colleges?

3.2 What special problems or concerns does this unit have regarding colleges or university policies and practices?

3.3 What special problems, concerns, or complaints do deans and other administrators have regarding this unit?

3.4 What special contribution does this unit have to offer the university, its members, or other departments which could not be provided by an existing department?

BASIC DATA ON DEPARTMENTS

I. *Academic Staff*

1. *In Fall 1967,* what was the total number of persons at each rank affiliated with this department? (write in number on each line)

Group A	*Group B*
a. .... Professors	d. .... Instructors
b. .... Associate Professors	e. .... Lecturers
	f. .... Teaching Fellows or Assistants
c. .... Assistant Professors	g. .... Research Fellows or Assistants

2. *In Fall 1957,* what was the total number of persons at each rank affiliated with this department? (write in number on each line)

a. .... Professors	d. .... Instructors
b. .... Associate Professors	e. .... Lecturers
	f. .... Teaching Fellows or Assistants
c. .... Assistant Professors	g. .... Research Fellows or Assistants

3. *In Fall 1967,* what was the total number of persons in Group A above holding joint appointments?

(write in number) .... persons

3a. In which other university departments or units were these joint appointments held? Please list and write in number and rank of persons from your department holding joint appointments.

	Number and rank of persons holding joint appointments		
Joint appointments are held in these departments or units:	Profs.	Assoc. Profs.	Asst. Profs.
....	....	....	....
....	....	....	....
....	....	....	....
....	....	....	....
....	....	....	....
....	....	....	....
....	....	....	....
....	....	....	....
....	....	....	....
....	....	....	....

4. *In Fall 1957,* what was the total number of persons at the rank of assistant, associate, and full professor who held joint appointments? (write in number) .... persons

4a. In which other university departments or units were these joint appointments held? Please list and write in number and rank of persons from your department holding joint appointments.

	Number and rank of persons holding joint appointments		
Joint appointments are held in these departments or units:	Profs.	Assoc. Profs.	Asst. Profs.
....	....	....	....
....	....	....	....
....	....	....	....
....	....	....	....
....	....	....	....

....
....
....
....
....

5. *In Fall 1967,* what was the total number of persons holding primarily research appointments (75 per cent or more regardless of fund source) ? (write in number)

   In Group A above: .... persons

   In Group B above: .... persons

6. *In Fall 1957,* what was the total number of persons holding primarily research appointments? (write in number)

   In Group A above: .... persons

   In Group B above: .... persons

7. *In Fall 1967,* what was the total number of persons holding "courtesy" appointments (responsibilities mainly administrative or in another department) ?

   (write in number) .... persons

8. What was the total number of new appointments at each rank from *January 1, 1966, to December 31, 1967?* (write in number on each line)

   a. .... Professors   d. .... Instructors

   b. .... Associate   e. .... Lecturers
       Professors

   c. .... Assistant
       Professors

9. What was the total number of resignations at each rank from *January 1, 1966, to December 31, 1967?* (write in number on each line)

   a. .... Professors   d. .... Instructors

   b. .... Associate   e. .... Lecturers
       Professors

   c. .... Assistant
       Professors

II. *Staff Activities*

For the following questions, the term *members of this department* refers to those persons at the ranks of assistant, associate, and full professor whose salaries and tenure are determined *primarily* by this department.

10. What is the modal schedule class-hour assignment per week for *members of this department?* (write in number in each line)

a. Professors .... hours

b. Associate Professors .... hours

c. Assistant Professors .... hours

d. Instructors .... hours

11. How many *members of this department* are currently serving on *college committees?*

(write in number) .... members

11a. How many of these committees are major (highly influential) ones? (write in number) ....

12. To what extent are *members of this department* involved in national professional activities? That is, how many *members of this department:*

a. served as officers of national professional organizations over the past three years? .... members

b. served as journal editors over the past three years?
.... members

c. served as governmental agency consultants over the past three years? .... members

d. served as industry or private agency consultants over the past three years? .... members

13. How many *different members of this department* have published how many scholarly works in the past three years? (write in numbers on each line)

a. .... textbooks were published by .... members

b. .... monographs were published by .... members

c. .... advanced research treatises or research articles were published by .... members.

III. *Offices and Facilities*

    14. What are the office assignments of the *members of this department?* (write number on each line)

	Number having private offices	*Number sharing with one other*	*Number sharing with two or more*
a. Professors	....	....	....
b. Associate Professors	....	....	....
c. Assistant Professors	....	....	....

    15. How many Group A (question 1) *members of this department* are housed in another building or at some distance from the main office?

        (write in number) .... members

        15a. How many persons listed in Group B (question 1) are housed in another building or at some distance from the main office? (write in number .... persons

IV. *Clerical and Technical Staff*

    16. How many persons were employed by this department in *Fall 1967* at each level listed below? (write in number)

	Total number[1]	*Number paid from grant or contract funds*
a. Clerks, typists, secretaries	....	....
b. Administrative or professional personnel (no academic rank)	....	....
c. Technicians (laboratory, equipment operation, maintenance, and so on)	....	....
d. Other	....	....

[1] Full-time equivalent. Include student help on the basis of forty hours a week equal to one full-time worker in appropriate category.

V. *Students*

17. How many degrees were granted with majors in this department? (write in number)

	1957	1965	1966	1967
a. Baccalaureate	....	....	....	....
b. Master's	....	....	....	....
c. Doctorate	....	....	....	....

18. What is the instructional load in this department (majors and service, in credit hours or course enrollments for current term)? (indicate unit used)

	Majors in department		From other departments	
	1957	1967	1957	1967
a. Undergraduate	....	....	....	....
b. Graduate	....	....	....	....

VI. *Expenditures*

19. What was the total amount of money expended for each of the following: (write in numbers)

	Educational and general funds		Grants and contract research funds	
Personnel	1956–57	1966–67	1956–57	1966–67
a. Academic staff	$..........	$..........	$..........	$..........
b. Clerical and technical staff	....	....	....	....
c. Fellowships, graduate assistants	....	....	....	....
d. Number of federal traineeships	....	....	....	....
Operating Funds				
a. Supplies, services, materials	....	....	....	....
b. New equipment	....	....	....	....
Total	$..........	$..........	$..........	$..........

Departmental Study Inventory

1. WHAT IS YOUR PRESENT RANK? MARK ONE.

PROFESSOR :::: ASSOCIATE PROFESSOR ::::

ASSISTANT PROFESSOR :::: INSTRUCTOR ::::

LECTURER :::: OTHER ::::

2. HOW LONG HAVE YOU BEEN IN THIS DEPARTMENT? MARK ONE.

0-3 YEARS :::: 4-8 YEARS :::: 9-15 YEARS :::: OVER 15 YEARS ::::

3. DO YOU HOLD A JOINT APPOINTMENT? MARK ONE.

YES :::: NO ::::

4. HOW ARE DECISIONS REACHED IN YOUR DEPARTMENT FOR EACH OF THE FOLLOWING? MARK ONE ON EACH LINE WHICH MOST NEARLY APPROXIMATES YOUR UNDERSTANDING OF HOW DECISIONS ARE MADE.

	DEPARTMENT CHAIRMAN ACTING WITHIN ESTABLISHED POLICY	DEPARTMENT CHAIRMAN IN CONSULTATION WITH AN ADVISORY GROUP	VOTE OF TENURED FACULTY	VOTE OF ALL MEMBERS OF DEPARTMENTAL STAFF
a RECRUITMENT AND SELECTION OF NEW FACULTY	::::	::::	::::	::::
b PROMOTIONS AND TENURE	::::	::::	::::	::::
c SALARY INCREASES	::::	::::	::::	::::
d LEAVES OF ABSENCE	::::	::::	::::	::::
e TRAVEL AUTHORIZATION	::::	::::	::::	::::
f BUDGET ITEMS FOR SUPPLIES AND EQUIPMENT	::::	::::	::::	::::
g TEACHING ASSIGNMENTS	::::	::::	::::	::::
h OFFICE AND RESEARCH SPACE	::::	::::	::::	::::
i AWARD OF ASSISTANTSHIPS, FELLOWSHIPS AND SCHOLARSHIPS	::::	::::	::::	::::
j REQUIREMENTS FOR MAJORS AND GRADUATE STUDENTS	::::	::::	::::	::::

5. WITHIN YOUR DEPARTMENT, HOW MUCH EMPHASIS IS PLACED ON EACH OF THE FOLLOWING? MARK ONE ON EACH LINE.

	A VERY GREAT AMOUNT	A GREAT AMOUNT	SOME	A SLIGHT AMOUNT	NONE AT ALL
a UNDERGRADUATE INSTRUCTION	::::	::::	::::	::::	::::
b ADVISING OF UNDERGRADUATE MAJORS	::::	::::	::::	::::	::::
c INSTRUCTION OF UNDERGRADUATE NON-MAJORS	::::	::::	::::	::::	::::

Departmental Study Inventory

d INSTRUCTION OF GRADUATE STUDENTS

e CAREER DEVELOPMENT OF JUNIOR STAFF

f BASIC RESEARCH

g APPLIED RESEARCH

h EXPRESSING DEPARTMENTAL VIEWS AND INTERESTS IN THE COLLEGE AND THE UNIVERSITY

i ADVANCING THE DISCIPLINE AND THE PROFESSION NATIONALLY

j SERVICE TO BUSINESS AND INDUSTRY

6. FROM THE LIST IN QUESTION 5 SELECT THE THREE ITEMS YOU FEEL SHOULD RECEIVE THE GREATEST AMOUNT OF EMPHASIS. MARK THE LETTER FOR EACH OF THE THREE YOU SELECT

	a	b	c	d	e	f	g	h	i	j
GREATEST AMOUNT OF EMPHASIS	:::	:::	:::	:::	:::	:::	:::	:::	:::	:::
SECOND MOST EMPHASIS	:::	:::	:::	:::	:::	:::	:::	:::	:::	:::
THIRD MOST EMPHASIS	:::	:::	:::	:::	:::	:::	:::	:::	:::	:::

7. IF ONE OF YOUR COLLEAGUES NEEDED SPECIAL CONSIDERATION TO SOLVE THE FOLLOWING PROBLEMS, TO WHOM WOULD YOU RECOMMEND HE GO FOR ASSISTANCE? MARK ONE ON EACH LINE.

	YOUR DEAN	YOUR DEPARTMENT CHAIRMAN	CERTAIN FACULTY IN YOUR DEPARTMENT	A UNIVERSITY ADMINISTRATOR (PRES. VICE-PRES.)	FACULTY IN ANOTHER DEPARTMENT OR INSTITUTE	A CHAIRMAN OF ANOTHER DEPARTMENT OR INSTITUTE	OTHER
a A PROMOTION OR TENURE ACTION	:::	:::	:::	:::	:::	:::	:::
b A LARGER SALARY INCREASE	:::	:::	:::	:::	:::	:::	:::
c A LEAVE OF ABSENCE	:::	:::	:::	:::	:::	:::	:::
d TRAVEL EXPENSES	:::	:::	:::	:::	:::	:::	:::
e A CHANGE IN TEACHING ASSIGNMENT	:::	:::	:::	:::	:::	:::	:::
f A CHANGE IN OFFICE OR RESEARCH SPACE	:::	:::	:::	:::	:::	:::	:::
g INTRODUCTION OF A NEW COURSE	:::	:::	:::	:::	:::	:::	:::
h MONEY FOR RESEARCH AND SCHOLARLY PURSUITS	:::	:::	:::	:::	:::	:::	:::
i ADDITIONAL GRADUATE STUDENTS AS ASSISTANTS	:::	:::	:::	:::	:::	:::	:::

8. WHICH OF THE FOLLOWING IS MOST CRITICAL IN DETERMINING THE EXTENT OF DEPARTMENTAL AUTONOMY IN YOUR UNIVERSITY? MARK ONE.

UNIVERSITY POLICY ::::	ABILITY AND/OR PRESTIGE OF THE CHAIRMAN ::::
COLLEGE POLICY ::::	DEPARTMENTAL SIZE ::::
DEPARTMENTAL PRESTIGE IN THE SCHOLARLY COMMUNITY ::::	DEPARTMENTAL ENTERPRISE IN OBTAINING OUTSIDE FUNDING ::::

9. IN GENERAL, HOW MUCH SAY OR INFLUENCE DO EACH OF THE FOLLOWING HAVE OVER WHAT GOES ON IN YOUR DEPARTMENT? MARK ONE ON EACH LINE.

	VERY GREAT INFLUENCE	GREAT INFLUENCE	SOME INFLUENCE	SLIGHT INFLUENCE	OF NO INFLUENCE AT ALL
a THE DEPARTMENT FACULTY AS A WHOLE	::::	::::	::::	::::	::::
b THE DEAN OF THIS SCHOOL	::::	::::	::::	::::	::::
c THE DEPARTMENT HEAD OR CHAIRMAN	::::	::::	::::	::::	::::
d THE SPECIAL DEPARTMENT COMMITTEES	::::	::::	::::	::::	::::
e THE GRADUATE STUDENTS	::::	::::	::::	::::	::::
f THE UNIVERSITY ADMINISTRATION (PRES., VICE-PRES., ETC.)	::::	::::	::::	::::	::::
g YOU, PERSONALLY	::::	::::	::::	::::	::::
h ALL UNIVERSITY COMMITTEES	::::	::::	::::	::::	::::

10. TO WHAT EXTENT DO YOU DISCUSS YOUR OPINIONS AND IDEAS ABOUT THE DEPARTMENT WITH EACH OF THE FOLLOWING? MARK ONE ON EACH LINE.

	TO A VERY GREAT EXTENT	TO A GREAT EXTENT	TO SOME EXTENT	TO A SLIGHT EXTENT	TO NO EXTENT AT ALL
a THE CHAIRMAN OF YOUR DEPARTMENT	::::	::::	::::	::::	::::
b FACULTY IN YOUR DEPARTMENT	::::	::::	::::	::::	::::

Departmental Study Inventory

c CHAIRMAN OF SPECIAL DEPARTMENT COMMITTEES   :::: :::: ::::

d THE DEAN OF YOUR SCHOOL OR COLLEGE   :::: :::: ::::

e GRADUATE STUDENTS   :::: :::: ::::

f CHAIRMEN OF OTHER DEPARTMENTS OR INSTITUTES   :::: :::: ::::

g FACULTY IN OTHER DEPARTMENTS OR INSTITUTES   :::: :::: ::::

h UNIVERSITY ADMINISTRATORS (E.G., PRES. OR VICE-PRES., ETC.)   :::: :::: ::::

11a. ARE THERE GROUPS OF PERSONS IN YOUR DEPARTMENT WHO ARE HELD TOGETHER BY A SIMILARITY OF INTERESTS? MARK ONE.   YES ::::   NO ::::

11b. IF YES: TO WHAT EXTENT IS THERE DISAGREEMENT BETWEEN OR AMONG THESE GROUPS? MARK ONE.
TO A VERY GREAT EXTENT ::::   TO A GREAT EXTENT ::::   TO SOME EXTENT ::::   TO A SLIGHT EXTENT ::::   TO NO EXTENT AT ALL ::::

12. WHEN CONSIDERING A NEW POSITION WHICH ONE OF THE FOLLOWING WOULD BE MOST ATTRACTIVE TO YOU? MARK ONE.

a MAKING MORE MONEY.   ::::

b JOINING A FACULTY WITH HIGHER PRESTIGE.   ::::

c GOING TO A MORE DESIRABLE CLIMATE TO LIVE.   ::::

d JOINING A FACULTY WITH MORE AFFABLE PEOPLE.   ::::

e BECOMING A CHAIRMAN, DEAN, OR OTHER ADMINISTRATOR.   ::::

f HAVING MORE TIME TO PURSUE MY OWN INTERESTS.   ::::

13. IN GENERAL, DO YOU USUALLY THINK OF YOURSELF PRIMARILY AS A MEMBER OF YOUR: MARK ONE.

a UNIVERSITY   ::::

b DEPARTMENT   ::::

c DISCIPLINE   ::::

Index

A

Activities of deans and central administration, 6

Administration: development of, 198, 213, 220; central, 6; confidence of, 140; defense of, 232; departmental, 41, 42, 152, 158; influence of, 93–106; informal organization of, 36; of institutes, etc., 123–124; least, 23; new, 12; overhead monies of, 30; quality of, 244

Advising: undergraduate majors, 71, 79; undergraduates, 39

Alumni, 158

Analysis: of course and curriculum, 37, 180–184; of data, 111–115; detailed, 162–163

ANDERSEN, K. J., 3

Appointments: in institutes, 126; joint, 98–101, 103, 193; new, 74, 79; research, 125–126

Autonomy, 145; controls on, 134; existence and desirability of, 108–110; as license, 97–106, 108, 111–119, 145–146, 220, 227; major forces for, 5; as overused, abused term, 132; as source of difficulty, 11

AXELROD, J., 125